AF784989

Presidential Defiance of "Unconstitutional" Laws

Recent Titles in
Contributions in Legal Studies

Between Civil and Religious Law: The Plight of the *Agunah* in American Society
Irving A. Breitowitz

The Death Penalty and Racial Bias: Overturning Supreme Court Assumptions
Gregory D. Russell

The Rehnquist Court: In Pursuit of Judicial Conservatism
Stanley H. Friedelbaum

Parallel Importation in U.S. Trademark Law
Timothy H. Hiebert

John Marshall's Law: Interpretation, Ideology, and Interest
Thomas C. Shevory

Group Defamation and Freedom of Speech: The Relationship Between Language and Violence
Monroe H. Freedman and Eric M. Freedman, editors

Innovation, Reaction, and Atrophy: The Impact of Judicial-Selection Method on Policy in State Supreme Courts
Daniel R. Pinello

Controversy, Courts, and Community: The Rhetoric of Judge Miles Weldon Lord
Verna C. Corgan

Constitutional Politics in the States: Contemporary Controversies and Historical Patterns
G. Alan Tarr, editor

Law and the Great Plains: Essays on the Legal History of the Heartland
John R. Wunder, editor

Judicial Entrepreneurship: The Role of the Judge in the Marketplace of Ideas
Wayne V. McIntosh and Cynthia L. Cates

Solving the Puzzle of Interest Group Litigation
Andrew Jay Koshner

Presidential Defiance of "Unconstitutional" Laws

Reviving the Royal Prerogative

Christopher N. May

Contributions in Legal Studies, Number 86
Paul L. Murphy, Series Editor

GREENWOOD PRESS
Westport, Connecticut • London

Library of Congress Cataloging-in-Publication Data

May, Christopher N.
Presidential defiance of "unconstitutional" laws : reviving the royal prerogative / Christopher N. May.
p. cm. — (Contributions in legal studies, ISSN 0147–1074 : no. 86
Includes bibliographical references and index.
ISBN 0–313–30064–X (alk. paper)
1. Executive power—United States. 2. Law enforcement—United States. 3. Constitutional law—United States. I. Title. II. Series.
KF5065.M39 1998
342.73'06—dc21 98–11095

British Library Cataloguing in Publication Data is available.

Copyright © 1998 by Christopher N. May

All rights reserved. No portion of this book may be reproduced, by any process or technique, without the express written consent of the publisher.

Library of Congress Catalog Card Number: 98–11095
ISBN: 0–313–30064–X
ISSN: 0147–1074

First published in 1998

Greenwood Press, 88 Post Road West, Westport, CT 06881
An imprint of Greenwood Publishing Group, Inc.

Printed in the United States of America

The paper used in this book complies with the Permanent Paper Standard issued by the National Information Standards Organization (Z39.48–1984).

P

In order to keep this title in print and available to the academic community, this edition was produced using digital reprint technology in a relatively short print run. This would not have been attainable using traditional methods. Although the cover has been changed from its original appearance, the text remains the same and all materials and methods used still conform to the highest book-making standards.

For Barbara

Contents

Tables ix

Preface xi

Introduction xiii

PART I. THE ORIGINAL UNDERSTANDING

1. The Royal Suspending and Dispensing Powers 3

2. The Founders' Understanding 9

PART II. PRESIDENTIAL PRACTICE, 1789–1981

3. Presidential Practice: Introduction 45

4. Laws Enacted over a Constitutionally Based Veto 53

5. Signing Statements: Introduction 71

6. Signing Statements: Acquiescence, Avoidance, and Compliance 81

7. Signing Statements: Noncompliance 101

8. Laws Enacted During a Prior Administration 119

9. Presidential Practice: A Summary of the Historical Record 127

10. Limiting Presidential Defiance 141

Notes 155

Selected Bibliography 199

Index 205

Tables

4.1 Statutes Enacted over President's Constitutionally Based Veto (1789–1981) 54

5.1 Presidential Signing Statements (1945–1997) 74

5.2 Statutes Objected to in Signing Statements: Grounds for Objection and Nature of President's Response (1789–1981) 77

7.1 Presidential Noncompliance with Laws to Which President Had Constitutionally Objected in a Signing Statement (1789–1981) 102

8.1 Presidential Noncompliance with Laws Enacted During a Prior Administration (1789–1981) 120

9.1 Incidents Where Presidents Defied an Allegedly Unconstitutional Law (1789–1981) 128

Preface

During the 1980s, I was examining the federal government's continued reliance on its war powers after the 1918 armistice. I was surprised by President Woodrow Wilson's response to one of these laws. Though he believed that the measure was unconstitutional because the war emergency had ended, Wilson insisted that he had no choice but to enforce the statute until Congress chose to repeal it. My reaction at the time was that a president was free to disregard a law if, in good conscience, he believed it to be unconstitutional. Yet, as I began to inquire further into the matter, I realized that my initial reaction, however intuitively appealing, was indeed wrong. This book is a product of that inquiry.

Many people have assisted me in this endeavor. I am especially grateful to two close friends, Allan Ides and Lary Lawrence, for their insight and support. I am indebted to my colleagues David Leonard, Larry Solum, and Laurie Levenson for their comments on a preliminary version of this study that appeared in 21 *Hastings Constitutional Law Quarterly* 865–1011 (1994) (© 1994 by University of California, Hastings College of the Law. Reprinted from *Hastings Constitutional Law Quarterly*). A number of former students—Clark Peterson, Lilly Kim, Lauren Raskin, and Eric Enson—provided valuable research and editorial assistance. As usual, my secretary, Ruth Busch, helped me out of many a jam. Throughout the nearly ten years this study was under way, I received generous financial support from the James P. Bradley Chair at Loyola Law School. This book is dedicated to my wife, Barbara.

Introduction

Since the mid-1970s, American presidents have with growing frequency claimed that they have the power simply to ignore any law that, in their view, is unconstitutional. In 1989, the Justice Department, seeking to defend Ronald Reagan's refusal to comply with the Competition in Contracting Act, told a federal court that the "President has the authority to decline, in the absence of a judicial resolution in the matter, to implement a statute that is patently unconstitutional or that he reasonably believes undermines his powers under the Constitution."[1] In 1994, the Justice Department advised the Clinton White House that a president is not "limited to choosing between vetoing [an] Act and executing an unconstitutional provision in it. In our view, the President has the authority to sign legislation containing desirable elements while refusing to execute a constitutionally defective provision."[2] From 1974 through 1996, a period of barely twenty years, Presidents Ford, Carter, Reagan, Bush, and Clinton signed but objected to the constitutionality of approximately 250 laws.[3]

The assertion that the White House may refuse to honor any provision of law that the executive deems unconstitutional has become another "staple of presidential advocacy."[4] It forms part of a pattern of rhetoric through which late-twentieth-century presidents and their advisers have sought to expand the scope of executive authority in areas such as the war powers, impoundment, executive privilege, the line item veto, and now the disregard of statutory provisions that are said to be unconstitutional.[5]

To the extent that presidents follow through on their stated objections by declining to execute the law in question, they, in effect, exercise an absolute item veto—"absolute" because Congress has no opportunity to override the president's action and an "item veto" because it operates surgically against only those parts of a law that the White House finds objectionable.[6] This is a far more powerful weapon than the statutory line-item veto that Congress gave to the president on a temporary basis in 1996, for the latter—even if found to be constitutional—may be employed only with respect to taxing and spending provisions, may be overridden by a two-thirds vote of the House and the Senate, and may be repealed at any time.[7] The claimed authority to defy allegedly invalid laws threatens to further enhance the already "imperial" trappings of the American presidency.[8] That this asserted power is limited to statutes that are thought to be unconstitutional does little to narrow its scope, for as Judge Frank Easterbrook has noted, "constitutional 'questions' are everywhere—it is easy to pose questions and occasionally is possible to characterize a mistaken view of the law or the facts as 'arbitrary,' and 'abuse of power,' hence unconstitutional."[9]

This book examines the claimed presidential power to ignore allegedly unconstitutional laws from two perspectives. In Part I, we explore the understanding of those who drafted and ratified the Constitution to determine whether the asserted power squares with their vision of the presidency. The evidence on this score convincingly demonstrates that the Founders did not wish the executive to possess a power to suspend the laws, even when the president believes that a particular law is unconstitutional.

Part II explores the historical record from George Washington through Jimmy Carter—with occasional references to Ronald Reagan, George Bush, and Bill Clinton—to ascertain the extent to which presidents have actually defied the laws on constitutional grounds. The evidence shows that while chief executives have from time to time refused to execute statutes that were thought to be unconstitutional, this has occurred with relative infrequency. If there is now an emerging practice of presidential defiance of allegedly unconstitutional laws, it is one that dates from the 1970s—too late in the day to upset the framework created by the Founders under which the president is bound to "take Care that the Laws be faithfully executed."[10]

PART I

The Original Understanding

1

The Royal Suspending and Dispensing Powers

When the president refuses to honor a law on the ground that it is unconstitutional, he exercises a power indistinguishable from the royal suspending and dispensing powers—two of the most formidable prerogative powers once wielded by the British Crown. From the Middle Ages through the late seventeenth century, the kings and queens of England routinely suspended or dispensed with laws, often on the ground that a law was unconstitutional. After centuries of struggle between the Crown and Parliament, the suspending and dispensing powers were forever stripped from the English Crown by the Bill of Rights of 1689. In the United States, however, as the twentieth century draws to a close, presidents have increasingly claimed that they now possess the virtually identical power to ignore allegedly unconstitutional laws.

The constitutional history of England is in large measure the story of Parliament's efforts to limit the scope of the royal prerogative. Though the term "royal prerogative" has been said to be "undefinable,"[1] Locke, writing in the late seventeenth century, described it as the king's "power to act according to discretion, for the publick good, without the prescription of the Law, and sometimes even against it."[2] In the view of Crown lawyers, "if the King was of opinion that the public interest required a particular exercise of his discretionary power, his opinion was conclusive. It was also an essential part of the royal doctrine of the Prerogative that the King's discretionary powers could not be taken away by statute."[3] At one time, the Crown claimed that the royal prerogative included both the power to make laws and the power to set them aside.[4]

In fourteenth-century England the lawmaking authority rested exclusively with the Crown. It acted as legislator in response to grievances submitted to it by petition, usually from Parliament. If the Crown chose to redress a grievance, it could do so by issuing either an ordinance or a statute. The Crown preferred ordinances to statutes, for ordinances, unlike statutes, could be withdrawn at any time. The royal prerogative had once included a power to revoke statutes as well, but by the late thirteenth century, this was no longer deemed proper[5]—even where the Crown claimed that a statute was unconstitutional. Thus, when Edward III revoked an act of Parliament in 1341 on the ground that it unconstitutionally impaired his royal prerogative, he insisted that Parliament repeal the act, acknowledging that his unilateral revocation was ineffectual.[6]

Although the Crown favored issuing ordinances to statutes, Parliament began conditioning grants of revenue sought by the Crown on its agreement to redress Parliament's grievances by statute. This parliamentary tactic neutralized the Crown prerogative of vetoing the petition as well as its prerogative of granting the petition by ordinance, for if the Crown chose either of those routes, it would not receive the funds it sought from Parliament.[7]

However, English monarchs strenuously resisted these efforts by Parliament to limit the Crown's lawmaking prerogative. From the fourteenth century until the end of the seventeenth century, relations between the Crown and Parliament were characterized by the Crown's resort to a host of stratagems designed to obtain funds from Parliament without satisfying the conditions on which a grant of revenue was made. An early tactic was for the Crown to agree to the petition of Parliament but to then draft the statute so that it differed from what it had agreed to, or so that it included a clause that gave it the discretion not to fulfill its promises. Parliament later foreclosed these devices by presenting the Crown with a proposed statute or bill, rather than leaving it up to the Crown to draft the statute, and by carefully monitoring the bill until it became law to ensure that its language was not changed. On other occasions, the Crown would fail to issue the promised statute in hopes that the matter would eventually be forgotten by Parliament. Another ploy was for the Crown to issue a statute but then arrange for someone to submit a petition which the Crown would grant by an ordinance that amended or nullified the earlier statute. Alternatively, the Crown might simply ignore a statute, thereby forcing Parliament to petition that it honor the law.[8] "The constant complaints, recorded in the petitions on the Rolls of Parliament, show that resort was had to each of these means of evading the fulfillment of the royal promises even when the grants of money were made conditional upon their performances."[9]

One of the most effective means by which the Crown reneged on its promises to Parliament was by exercising the royal prerogatives of either suspending or dispensing with the laws. In these cases, the Crown would issue the statute sought by Parliament. After receiving the revenue for which the statute had been a precondition, the Crown would either suspend the measure entirely, or dispense with its application as to certain named individuals.[10] The suspending power abrogated a statute across the board, whereas the dispensing power nullified it only as to those specifically granted exemptions.[11] The dispensing power was also known as the *non obstante*, that is, the grant of permission to act notwithstanding the terms of a law.[12] The sole difference between the suspending and dispensing powers "consists rather in the extent to which the law is abrogated than in the quality of the prerogative exercised. In both cases the law is put out of action."[13] In contrast to a pardon, which relieved a person of the legal consequences of having violated a law, the effect of suspending or dispensing with a statute was to legalize the conduct in question.[14] While the suspending and dispensing powers were most often employed with respect to penal statutes, this was not always the case. For example, the dispensing power was used to nullify statutory provisions that limited sheriffs to a term of one year, and to exempt specific individuals or towns from having to pay taxes.[15]

The suspending and dispensing powers were uncontroversial when employed for their original purposes of meeting emergencies or preventing the hardship that may result from a rigid adherence to the law.[16] Elizabeth I freely granted dispensations to many of the obsolete laws that, in Sir Edward Coke's words, "did vex and intangle the Subject."[17] Charles II, in order to cope with necessities created by war or bad harvests, suspended clauses in a number of statutes regulating trade. He also suspended a law prescribing wheels of a certain size for carriages after it appeared that due to a lack of carriages to which the wheels could be fitted, the law would have decimated England's internal trade.[18]

What provoked opposition was the Crown's use of the suspending and dispensing powers to abrogate laws that the Crown opposed or to confer special privileges on royal favorites and those able to purchase dispensations.[19] When employed in these ways, the suspending and dispensing powers placed the Crown above the law, for they enabled it to set a law aside as to everyone or to benefit a favored few. Moreover, these prerogatives could be used to nullify an entire statute or just certain sections and clauses.[20] The Crown sometimes justified resort to the suspending and dispensing powers by claming that a law was unconstitutional because it was inconsistent with the "theory of sovereign right" or "contrary to his prerogative right."[21]

By the late fifteenth century, while Parliament's legislative supremacy was acknowledged in theory, that supremacy was compromised by "the undoubted power which the Crown possessed of dispensing from or suspending the operation of statutes."[22] In response to these practices, Parliament sought to restrict the Crown's use of the prerogative in a variety of ways. It was only after these efforts had failed that the suspending and dispensing powers were finally abolished by the Bill of Rights of 1689.

One of the unsuccessful means by which Parliament sought to curtail the dispensing power was by providing in a statute that the Crown could not dispense with its provisions. For example, a fifteenth-century law limiting sheriffs to a term of one year in office stated that any royal dispensation from the provision would be "void, and of no Value . . . any Clause or Word of Non Obstante . . . notwithstanding."[23] After Henry VII nonetheless dispensed with this provision and granted the Earl of Northumberland a patent to serve as sheriff for life, the Court of Exchequer Chamber in the *Case of Non Obstante* (1487) held that Parliament's attempt to limit the royal prerogative was invalid. According to Sir Edward Coke, the case established the principle that "No Act can bind the King from any prerogative which is sole and inseparable to his person, but that he may dispense with it by a *non obstante*." One of these "inseparable" prerogatives was the Crown's "sovereign power to command any of his subjects to serve him for the public weal."[24] The Crown thus had a right to dispense with this law, for it unconstitutionally impaired its absolute prerogative to retain the services of sheriffs for longer than a year. It was unclear whether the court viewed the suspending and dispensing powers as themselves being inseparable and inviolable prerogatives. If they were, *any* parliamentary restriction on these powers would be invalid—whether or not it interfered with the Crown's ability to retain the services of its subjects.[25]

Having failed in its attempt to attack the dispensing power directly, Parliament tried another tack in a statute regulating the leather trade. The law provided that if the Crown granted dispensations from any of its provisions, those provisions "shalbe utterlie repealed voide and of no effect."[26] This tactic ensured that if anyone should be exempted from the law, everyone would then be, but it did so at the expense of the statute.[27]

A third parliamentary device sought to take advantage of the distinction between *malum in se* and *malum prohibitum. Malum in se* involved conduct that was inherently evil and wrongful whether or not it was prohibited by law. *Malum prohibitum*, on the other hand, was conduct that was permissible in the absence of a statutory prohibition. It had long been recognized that the Crown could suspend or dispense with *mala prohibita*, such as coining money or selling goods without a license, but not with *mala in se*, such as murder, arson, or engaging in a public nuisance.[28] In two 1662 laws that prohibited the export of certain goods, Parliament seized on this distinction and attempted to transform into *malum in se* conduct which would otherwise have been *malum prohibitum*. Each law contained a clause declaring any exports contrary to its terms "to be a common and publick Nusance."[29] Although the intended effect of these nuisance clauses was to prevent the Crown from abrogating the two statutes, Charles II nevertheless suspended both measures.[30] Parliament later employed the same device in a law barring the importation of Irish cattle; this time, however, the king made no attempt to suspend or dispense with the measure.[31]

The struggle between Parliament and the Crown over the suspending and dispensing powers came to a head in the last half of the seventeenth century. The Stuart monarchs claimed that the royal prerogative was a matter of "divine right" rather than of common law and that Parliament therefore could not regulate or restrict it in any way.[32] Parliament briefly gained the upper hand over the Stuarts when Charles II was restored to the throne in 1660. Charles wished to ease the many statutes that made it illegal for Catholic and Protestant nonconformists to practice their religion or to hold public office. Hoping to avoid a confrontation with Parliament, he asked Parliament for permission to exercise the suspending and dispensing powers but was refused.[33] Charles then decided to act on his own. In 1672, he issued a Declaration of Indulgence that suspended all of the penal laws that were aimed at religious nonconformists. He also announced that he would grant dispensations to individual Protestant congregations so that they might hold public worship. This exercise of the royal prerogative was unprecedented in scope, for Charles in one stroke had abrogated some forty laws. Parliament reacted by demanding that he renounce all use of the suspending or dispensing powers "in matters Ecclesiastical."[34] Charles was forced to back down. He revoked the Declaration of Indulgence, thereby annulling the suspensions; however, the individual dispensations he had granted remained in effect.[35]

Upon Charles's death in 1685, James II ascended the throne. James was determined to be less compromising with Parliament than his brother Charles had been. James's hand was strengthened by the decision in *Godden v. Hales* (1686) in which the King's Bench upheld the dispensing power in terms so sweeping as to suggest that none of the royal prerogatives was subject to parliamentary control. The case involved the 1673 Test Act, which prevented Roman Catholics and Protestant dissenters from holding civil or military office.[36] James granted numerous dispensations from the act in order to staff the army with Catholics. One of these dispensations was issued to Sir Edward Hales, a Catholic, who was named to the office of colonel. When Hales was sued for failing to comply with the Test Act, he asserted the dispensation in defense. Counsel urged the court to uphold the dispensation on the basis that the act had impaired the king's inseparable prerogative to command the service of his subjects, thereby violating the rule laid down 200 years earlier in the *Case of Non Obstante*.[37] Instead of adopting this narrow ground of decision, however, the Lord Chief Justice declared that because "the Kings of England were absolute Sovereigns" and "the laws were the King's laws," it followed "that the King had a power to dispense with any of the laws of Government as he saw necessity for it; that he was sole judge of that necessity; [and] that no Act of Parliament could take away that power."[38]

Emboldened by this decision, James issued a Declaration of Indulgence in 1687 proclaiming it the "royal will and pleasure that from henceforth the execution of . . . all manner of penal laws, in matters ecclesiastical . . . be immediately suspended."[39] Among the statutes abrogated by this declaration were the Corporation Act (1661), the Test Act (1673), and the Parliamentary Test Act (1678), all of which barred religious dissenters from public office or from sitting in Parliament.[40] A year later, James issued a second Declaration of Indulgence and ordered that it be read in every church in England. When the archbishop of Canterbury and six other prelates objected to doing so, they were charged with seditious libel.[41] In the *Trial of the Seven Bishops* before King's Bench, the issue became the legality of the Crown's suspending power. While some of the justices supported the Crown, Justice John Powell warned the jury that if this prerogative "be once allowed of, there will need no parliament; all the legislature will be in the king, which is a thing worth considering.''[42] The jurors agreed with Powell. Their verdict acquitting the bishops dealt the suspending and dispensing powers what proved to be a fatal blow.[43]

James's abuse of the royal prerogative led to his abdication in the Glorious Revolution of 1688. The verdict in *Trial of the Seven Bishops* was constitutionalized in the Bill of Rights of 1689, whose preamble charged the king with having subverted the laws and liberties of the kingdom ''[b]y assuming and exercising a power of dispensing with and suspending of laws and the execution of laws without the consent of Parliament.''[44] The first section of the Bill of Rights abolished the suspending power, declaring: ''That the pretended power of suspending of laws or the execution of laws by regal authority without consent of Parliament is illegal.''[45] Fifteen years earlier, when Charles II had issued his Declaration of Indulgence, Parliament objected only to the suspension of ecclesiastical laws. Now, the condemnation was complete. The suspending power, which the English Crown had employed for some 400 years to nullify the laws, was totally abolished.[46]

The Bill of Rights also put an end to the dispensing power. It declared that ''the pretended power of dispensing with the laws, or the execution of laws by royal authority, as it hath been assumed and exercised of late, is illegal.''[47] While this appeared to leave some room for the Crown to continue granting dispensations, another section of the Bill of Rights provided that ''[f]rom and after this present session of Parliament, no dispensation by *non obstante* of or to any statute, or any part thereof, shall be allowed, but that the same shall be held void and of no effect, [1] except a dispensation be allowed of in such statute, and [2] except in such cases as shall be specially provided for by one or more bill or bills to be passed during this present session of Parliament.''[48] Because that Parliament was unable to agree on such a bill, the dispensing power could no longer be employed except as to laws that expressly authorized its use. The prerogative of dispensing with the laws without the consent of Parliament was dead.[49]

In abolishing the suspending and dispensing powers, the Bill of Rights made no exception for cases where the Crown claimed that a law was unconstitutional. Until then, it had been firmly established that an act of Parliament could not impair an inseparable prerogative of the Crown and that its power to abrogate such unconstitutional laws—whether by suspension or dispensation—was absolute.[50] The Bill of Rights rejected this principle. To have allowed an exception for allegedly unconstitutional laws would have legitimized the very suspensions and dispensations that had triggered the Bill of Rights. Both Charles and James had invoked these prerogatives against laws that, by preventing religious nonconformists from holding civil or military office, encroached upon the Crown's inseparable prerogative to demand the services of its subjects. Those actions would have been fully justified if the Crown could suspend or dispense with the laws in order to protect the royal prerogative. Instead, the Bill of Rights stripped the Crown of all authority to abrogate the law without Parliament's consent—even when the Crown believed that a statute was unconstitutional.

2

The Founders' Understanding

THE ROLE OF ORIGINAL UNDERSTANDING

One of the great debates among students of the Constitution concerns the role that original intent should play in the process of interpreting the Constitution. Is the text to be read by itself, without regard to what those who drafted and ratified the document understood it to mean? Or should we construe the Constitution in such a way as to implement the understanding of those who brought it into being? If we do seek to carry out the Founders' intent, are we limited to the specific practices and rights they had in mind, or may we seek to implement the more general principles they sought to embody in the Constitution?

At one time, the participants in this debate were divided into three distinct camps. "Originalists" urged that courts should construe the Constitution in a manner that reflects the understanding of the Founders. For these purposes, the Founders include the delegates to the Federal Convention that drafted the Constitution and those who participated in the state ratification conventions.[1] "Textualists," on the other hand, argued that the Constitution's text alone is authoritative without regard to what the Founders thought it meant. Finally, "nonoriginalists" took the view that the text and original understanding are not binding and that courts may rely instead upon other sources such as political theory, moral philosophy, history, or logic. Though each of these camps contained a spectrum of viewpoints, each was characterized by a distinctive stance toward the role that the text and original understanding should play in constitutional interpretation.[2]

The debate between textualists, originalists, and nonoriginalists has now largely run its course.[3] While there are still advocates of textualism and nonoriginalism, most scholars and judges today subscribe either to a sophisticated version of originalism or a moderate form of nonoriginalism. Sophisticated originalists maintain that in construing the Constitution, courts should remain faithful to the text and to original intent if it can be ascertained. Where the Founders' understanding as to a specific governmental practice is known, it must be followed; if it is unknown, sophisticated originalism instead seeks to carry out the general principles the Founders sought to protect—even if this produces results that the framers and ratifiers did not envision.[4] For example, the Founders did not specifically intend to protect radio, television, or cable broadcasting, since these technologies were unknown in the eighteenth century. Yet these modes of communication are deserving of protection under the general principle of freedom of expression that the Founders embodied in the First Amendment. Sophisticated originalists agree, however, that courts may not invoke general principles to validate a governmental practice in the face of clear evidence that the Founders regarded that practice as unconstitutional.[5] Finally, most sophisticated originalists temper their approach by applying it only to open questions of constitutional law; if an issue has been settled by long-standing practice or Supreme Court precedent, the need to maintain stability usually outweighs the goal of preserving original intent.[6]

The willingness of sophisticated originalists to reach specific results that the framers did not envision or endorse, along with their adherence to original intent only with respect to open questions of constitutional law, makes it difficult to distinguish between a sophisticated originalist and a moderate nonoriginalist. Both typically employ original understanding as a starting point in the analysis, yet both are prepared to depart from it in certain instances.[7] While a moderate nonoriginalist is more likely to depart from the Founders' intent than is a sophisticated originalist, each starts with a presumption in favor of original understanding to the extent it can be ascertained.[8] Most contemporary scholars and judges, in other words, believe that the Founders' intentions play a critical if not a definitive role in determining whether or not a particular practice violates the Constitution.

In this chapter, we will seek to ascertain how the Founders viewed the claimed presidential power to ignore allegedly unconstitutional laws. We will examine the text of the Constitution, the records from the Federal Convention, and the debates of the state ratifying conventions—all in an effort "to identify those founding arguments that offer the most coherent interpretation of the ratified arrangements."[9] In an undertaking of this type, it is imperative that the words of the Constitution be read "holistically in light of the entire document," not as isolated fragments.[10] It is also critical to bear in mind "the background assumptions as to how the constitutional system would work in practice,"[11] as well as the "history of the era."[12] For without thus taking "context" into account, we risk giving to the Constitution a meaning far removed from that which was intended by the Founders.[13]

PRELUDE: AMERICANS AND THE GLORIOUS REVOLUTION

The Americans who created the United States Constitution were closely acquainted with English constitutional history and with the Glorious Revolution of 1688 that culminated in the Bill of Rights. Indeed, the Founders "felt themselves the heirs of the Revolution, of the glory derived from 1688. Americans of the 1770s felt they were approaching a 'centennial' of their own, reliving memories of the English Bill of Rights."[14] A critical part of that legacy was the hard-won principle that the executive does not possess the power to suspend or dispense with the law. As William Blackstone, one of the most influential constitutional commentators of the Founders' generation,[15] wrote in 1765:

> An act of parliament, thus made, is the exercise of the highest authority that this kingdom acknowledges upon earth. . . . And it cannot be altered, amended, dispensed with, suspended, or repealed, but in the same forms and by the same authority of parliament. . . . It is true it was formerly held, that the king might in many cases dispense with penal statutes: but now, by statute . . . it is declared, that the suspending or dispensing with laws by regal authority, without consent of parliament, is illegal.[16]

In contrast to the English Bill of Rights, the American Constitution does not expressly bar the executive from exercising a suspending or dispensing power. As Frederic Stimson of the Harvard Law School noted in 1908, "English constitutional history clearly establishes . . . [t]hat the king can neither make laws, nor suspend laws, nor grant pardons in advance for a crime or breach of the law, nor ever in cases of impeachment. The first and the last are expressed clearly in the Federal Constitution, and it might be wished that the other two were also."[17] Yet, though these presidential prerogatives are not expressly banned, the text of the Constitution and the debates that accompanied its adoption convincingly demonstrate that the Founders endorsed the principle, set forth in the English Bill of Rights and in *Blackstone's Commentaries*, that statutes may be suspended only by the lawmaking authority, not by the executive acting alone.

THE REJECTION OF AN ABSOLUTE VETO

The case against a presidential power to ignore allegedly unconstitutional laws is strongly supported by the fact that the Founders insisted upon giving the president a qualified rather than an absolute veto. One of the colonists' main grievances with the English Crown was the absolute veto that the king and his American governors had exercised over colonial legislation.[18] Resentment of the veto was so strong that it constituted the basis of the first article of the Declaration of Independence, which charged that the king "has refused his assent to laws most wholesome and necessary for the public good." When the colonies broke with England and created new governments of their own, most of them completely stripped the executive of a veto power. South Carolina, which gave its governor an absolute veto in 1776, abolished the veto entirely two years later. Only New York and Massachusetts allowed for an executive veto, and in both cases, it was qualified rather than absolute.[19]

The framers of the federal Constitution were equally opposed to giving the president an absolute veto. Attempts to confer such a power were overwhelmingly rejected. A motion by James Wilson proposing an absolute veto was unanimously defeated by the Committee of the Whole on June 4, 1787.[20] Two weeks later, the delegates declined to take up Alexander Hamilton's plan for an executive that would possess an absolute veto.[21] Finally, on August 7, the convention voted 9 to 1 to reject a similar motion by George Read.[22]

Even proposals for a qualified veto encountered serious opposition. Indeed, due to "the monarchial roots of [the veto] power and the resentment that its use by the king and his colonial governors had engendered in America," the term "veto" nowhere appears in the Constitution's text. During the debates, the word "veto" was rarely uttered. The delegates instead used the "terms 'negative,' 'qualified negative,' 'revisionary power,' and 'restraining power' . . . as synonyms."[23] Apprehension over the veto persisted until the very end of the convention. In one of their final acts before adjourning, the delegates voted to make it easier to override a presidential veto by reducing from three-fourths to two-thirds the majority needed for Congress to pass a law over the president's objection.[24] The change was prompted by fears that a three-fourths rule "puts too much in the power of the President."[25] The decision to relax the override requirement would have been utterly pointless if the president possessed an independent power to suspend any law that he wished.

The convention in fact rejected a proposal to give the executive a temporary suspending power in lieu of a qualified veto. On June 4, after defeating a motion to grant the president an "absolute negative," the delegates took up Pierce Butler's motion that a resolution providing for a qualified veto "be altered so as to read—'Resolved that the National Executive have a power to suspend any legislative act for the term of____.' " The only recorded debate on Butler's motion was Elbridge Gerry's objection that "a power of suspending might do all the mischief dreaded from the negative of useful laws; without answering the salutary purpose of checking unjust or unwise ones." "On the question 'for giving this suspending power' all the States . . . were—no."[26] In place of the rejected suspending power, the convention then voted to give the president a qualified veto.[27]

No one proposed giving the president a suspending power in *addition* to the qualified veto, for this would have rendered the veto utterly superfluous. As the framers well knew, the royal prerogative of suspending the laws closely resembled an absolute veto. If they had understood the executive to possess a suspending power, there would have been no point in giving a qualified veto; for if Congress passed a law over the president's veto, he would then be free to suspend the measure.

Moreover, to have given the president a suspending power would have provided him with a weapon far more versatile than the absolute veto that the framers had repeatedly rejected.[28] Unlike the veto, a suspending power could be used against previously enacted laws, could be applied merely to portions of a law, and could be invoked on a temporary basis rather than a permanent basis. It is virtually inconceivable that a convention that rejected the absolute veto in favor of a qualified veto, and that then decided to ease the override requirement, would have been so naive as to give the president the option to circumvent the qualified veto mechanism by simply suspending the law.

The case for a presidential suspending power is no stronger if such a power were confined to laws that the President believes to be unconstitutional, for these were the very laws for which the qualified veto was designed. As Elbridge Gerry explained at the convention, "The primary object of the revisionary check in the president is not to protect the general interest, but to defend his own department."[29] James Madison agreed that "the object of the revisionary power is [first] to defend the Executive Rights."[30] Thomas Jefferson likewise believed that the president's veto is "chiefly for cases" where Congress had been "misled by error, ambition, or interest" into passing laws that are "unauthorised by the Constitution."[31] Hamilton, writing of the veto power in *The Federalist Papers*, noted that "the primary inducement to conferring the power in question upon the Executive, is to enable him to defend . . . against an immediate attack upon the constitutional rights of the executive."[32] Even leading Anti-Federalists recognized that one of the main reasons for giving the president a veto power was "to prevent the legislature from encroaching upon the executive or judiciary."[33] To have augmented the veto with a power to suspend laws that the president believes unconstitutional would have rendered the veto redundant in the very class of cases where it was expected to play a role.

By giving the president a qualified rather than an absolute veto, the Founders necessarily envisioned that there might be occasions when a president's constitutional objections would be overridden by Congress. James Wilson urged the convention that for this very reason, "[t]he Executive ought to have an absolute negative." He added that "without such a Self-defence the Legislature can at any moment sink it into non-existence."[34] Yet Wilson's proposal for an absolute veto was unanimously rejected.[35] The framers were simply unwilling to give the president anything more than a qualified veto, despite the express recognition that this might allow the legislature to enact unconstitutional laws. In the event that such laws were passed over the president's veto, the courts—rather than the president—would have the responsibility for declaring the measure unconstitutional.

Hamilton was one of those who had supported Wilson's motion to give the president an absolute veto.[36] He did so believing that the veto's principal purpose was to protect the executive against unconstitutional laws.[37] Once the convention rejected the absolute veto, however, Hamilton acknowledged that if such a measure became law, the judiciary was the only branch that could decline to enforce it on constitutional grounds. Writing in *The Federalist*, Hamilton explained that

> the complete independence of the courts of justice is peculiarly essential in a limited Constitution. By a limited Constitution, I understand one which contains certain specified exceptions to the legislative authority; such, for instance, as that it shall pass no bills of attainder, no *ex post facto* laws, and the like. Limitations of this kind can be preserved in practice *no other way than through the medium of courts of justice*, whose duty it must be to declare all acts contrary to the manifest tenor of the Constitution void. Without this, all the reservations of particular rights or privileges would amount to nothing.[38]

Conspicuously absent was any suggestion that the president might refuse to honor such laws, even though all of Hamilton's examples involved criminal statutes uniquely suited to executive inaction.

Madison, too, shared Wilson's view that the president ought to have an absolute veto over unconstitutional laws. At the time the Constitution was framed, Madison "denied the right of the courts to overrule another department's interpretation of the extent of its constitutional powers."[39] Though he later accepted the principle of judicial review,[40] in 1787 Madison believed that each branch of government should possess the final authority to resolve those constitutional issues that concerned its own sphere of action, as long as rights of the states or individuals were not impaired.[41] Under this scheme, the president would have enjoyed an absolute veto over laws that he felt encroached on the executive domain. Yet despite these theoretical views, Madison voted against Wilson's proposal for an absolute veto, noting that "to give such a prerogative would certainly be obnoxious to the temper of this country; its present temper at least."[42] As a political realist, Madison apparently feared that to grant the President authority to suspend allegedly unconstitutional laws might doom the prospects for ratifying the proposed Constitution.

Interestingly, Madison did not suggest a compromise that would have given constitutionally based vetoes greater protection than those resting solely on policy grounds. A year after the convention adjourned, he outlined such a plan to Jefferson as part of a constitution for Kentucky. Madison proposed giving both the executive and the judiciary a qualified veto over bills passed by the assembly. If either branch rested its veto on constitutional grounds, however, the law would be suspended until a new election for the assembly had occurred; only then could the assembly seek to override the veto.[43] Max Farrand asserted that this proposal was "identical with the one [Madison] made in the Federal Convention, on August 15, which was voted down."[44] In fact, Madison's August 15th motion did not provide that only a newly elected Congress could override a presidential veto, nor did it treat constitutionally based vetoes any differently than those resting on policy grounds.[45] A federal provision comparable to the Kentucky proposal would have allowed the president to suspend, for as long as two years, bills that he found constitutionally objectionable. Madison's failure to offer such a proposal at the convention may have reflected his sense that just as the country would not accept an absolute veto, neither would it countenance giving the president a temporary version of the royal suspending power.

The Founders thus chose not to give any special protection to constitutionally based vetoes. Instead, if Congress passes a measure that the president believes is unconstitutional, he may veto the bill and hope that Congress will sustain him. But if that veto is overridden, the executive has a constitutional duty to enforce the law. As Professor Westel W. Willoughby wrote in 1929:

> That there is danger that Congress may by a chance majority, or through the influence of sudden great passion, legislate unwisely or unconstitutionally, was foreseen by those who framed our form of government, and the provision was drawn that the President might at his discretion use a veto, but this was the entire extent to which he was allowed to go in the exercise of a check upon the legislation. It was expressly provided that if, after his veto, two-thirds of the legislature should again demand that the measure become a law, it should thus be, notwithstanding the objection of the Chief Executive. Surely there is here left no further constitutional right on the part of the President to hinder the operation of a law.[46]

THE POWER TO SUSPEND THE WRIT OF HABEAS CORPUS

The only mention of the suspending power in the Constitution is with respect to suspending the writ of habeas corpus. Article I, section 9, clause 2 declares that "[t]he Privilege of the Writ of Habeas Corpus shall not be suspended, unless when in Cases of Rebellion or Invasion the public Safety may require it." When this clause was first introduced in the convention, it specified that the power to suspend the writ was to be vested in "the Legislature."[47] As finally adopted, the clause was less specific, but nothing in the debates suggests that the revision was meant to abandon the English Bill of Rights' principle that reserved the suspending power exclusively to the legislature.[48]

The placement of the clause within Article I, section 9 reinforces this conclusion. While there are two clauses in section 9 that restrict the president's powers rather than those of Congress, these presidential limitations appear at the end of the section, as clauses 7 and 8. Clauses 1 and 3 through 6 all clearly pertain to Congress, indicating that clause 2—dealing with suspension of the writ of habeas corpus—was so intended as well. If the Founders had intended the president to possess a general suspending power but wished to qualify its use with respect to habeas corpus, the restriction on suspending the writ would presumably have appeared at the end of section 9, or in Article II where other restrictions are placed on the president's powers.[49]

Contemporaries and early commentators on the Constitution thus read Article I, section 9, clause 2 as giving the suspending power to Congress, not to the president. In the Massachusetts ratifying convention, those who discussed the clause treated the suspending power as belonging to Congress.[50] In his 1803 American edition of *Blackstone's Commentaries*, St. George Tucker explained that "[i]n England," where the right was protected by the Habeas Corpus Act,[51] "the benefit of this important writ can only be suspended by authority of parliament. . . . In the United States, it can be suspended, only, by the authority of congress."[52] Four years later, in *Ex parte Bollman*,[53] Chief Justice John Marshall expressed the same view that the power to suspend the laws is legislative rather than executive in nature. Noting that the first Congress had specifically authorized the federal courts to issue writs of habeas corpus, Marshall surmised that Congress had done so to ensure that Article I, section 9 was not violated. For without such an act of Congress, the courts could not have issued the writ, and "the privilege itself would be lost, *although no law for its suspension should be enacted.*"[54] In his 1833 *Commentaries on the Constitution*, Joseph Story agreed that "the power is given to congress to suspend the writ of habeas corpus."[55] Finally, when President Abraham Lincoln suspended the privilege on his own initiative during the Civil War, Chief Justice Roger B. Taney ruled the action unconstitutional;[56] Lincoln later obtained authorization to suspend the writ from Congress.[57] Like the suspending power in general, the power to suspend the writ of habeas corpus was universally understood as resting with the legislative branch rather than with the president.

THE TAKE CARE CLAUSE

Article II, section 3 of the Constitution declares that the president "shall take Care that the Laws be faithfully executed." Today, these words may have a self-evident if superfluous quality to them. However, they take on a deeper meaning when viewed against the background of England's 400-year struggle to limit the king's prerogative and thereby achieve a government by law rather than by royal fiat. That struggle, with which the Founders were closely familiar, culminated in the Bill of Rights of 1689 that made it illegal for the Crown to suspend or dispense with the laws or refuse their execution, without the consent of Parliament. The effect of the Bill of Rights was to transfer both the suspending and the dispensing power from the Crown to Parliament.

Read in the light of this history and of the framers' repeated rejection of an absolute veto, the requirement that the president "take Care that the Laws be *faithfully executed*" is a succinct and all-inclusive command through which the Founders sought to prevent the executive from resorting to any of the panoply of devices employed by English kings to evade the will of Parliament. The duty to execute the laws "faithfully" means that American presidents may not—whether by revocation, suspension, dispensation, inaction, or otherwise—refuse to honor and enforce statutes that were enacted with their consent or over their veto. Many scholars have agreed that the Take Care Clause was meant to deny the president a suspending or dispensing power.[58]

The history of the clause in the Constitutional Convention reinforces the conclusion that it was designed to serve as a limitation on executive power. As initially contained in the Virginia Plan, in the New Jersey Plan, and in both Madison's and Hamilton's proposals to the convention, the clause would have given the president the "power" or "authority" to execute the laws. The Committee on Detail, however, transformed the clause from one that conferred power to one that imposed a duty. As amended by the committee and approved by the convention, the clause read: "He shall take care that the Laws *of the United States be duly* and faithfully executed." After the Committee on Style shortened the clause by deleting the italicized language, it was approved by the convention in its present form.[59]

Some have argued that the duty faithfully to execute the law was not intended to apply if the president believes that a law is unconstitutional. According to this view, the Take Care Clause is qualified by Article VI's Supremacy Clause, which states that only those "Laws of the United States . . . made in Pursuance of" the Constitution are "the supreme Law of the Land." Statutes that conflict with the Constitution, it is said, are not "laws" within the meaning of the Take Care Clause, and the president is therefore not required to enforce them. Indeed, if the president were to honor such a law, he would allegedly violate his oath under Article II, section 1 to "preserve, protect and defend the Constitution of the United States."[60]

There are a number of difficulties with the claim that the president's obligation to execute the laws is qualified by the Supremacy and Oath Clauses.[61] First, the clause is addressed specifically to the "Judges in Every State," not to the president or to any other federal official. The clause was debated exclusively in the context of ensuring the supremacy of federal over state law with no "discussion of the relationship between the Constitution and national legislation."[62] By addressing the Supremacy Clause solely to state judges, the framers were careful not to give the executive a pretext for evading its duty to honor and enforce the laws. Second, had the Founders intended to qualify the president's duty faithfully to execute "the laws," one would expect them to have tracked the language of the Supremacy Clause, which carefully distinguishes between the "laws of the United States" and those laws made "in pursuance of" the Constitution. The Take Care Clause draws no such distinction. It commands the president to execute "the laws"—not just those that he believes to be "in pursuance of" the Constitution.

This reading of the Take Care Clause does not force a president to violate his oath to uphold the Constitution. The Oath Clause, which is phrased in broad and general terms, does not purport to excuse the president from performing other specific duties placed upon him by the Constitution. "It is perfectly plausible to say that the Constitution sometimes requires the president to enforce a law that he considers, on balance, to be unconstitutional. If that is what the Constitution requires, then the oath requires the president to enforce the law—not to defy the law in pursuit of his own interpretation of the Constitution."[63]

As Edward Corwin wrote, "The fact that the President takes an oath 'to preserve and protect' the Constitution does not authorize him to exceed his own powers under the Constitution on the pretext of preserving and protecting it."[64] A President honors his duty to "preserve, protect and defend the Constitution" by defending the country against attack; by safeguarding the personnel, property, and instrumentalities of the federal government; and by exercising only those powers that fall within his constitutional authority—not by refusing to execute the laws.[65]

In light of the fact that some of the most controversial uses of the suspending power by English monarchs involved laws that impaired the royal prerogative, it is understandable that neither the Bill of Rights of 1689 nor the Take Care Clause of Article II contained an exception for allegedly unconstitutional laws. The critical difference between the wording of the Take Care and Supremacy Clauses reflects the Founders' deep hostility to the suspending and dispensing powers. It may also have reflected an awareness that if state judges were to evade their duty under the Supremacy Clause by ignoring federal law, review would almost certainly be available in the Supreme Court. By contrast, if the president were to disregard an allegedly unconstitutional law, he might well have the last word, for there is no assurance that a lawsuit challenging his action could be filed.

THE EXECUTIVE POWER

The Vesting Clause of Article II, section 1 provides that "the executive Power shall be vested in a President of the United States." There are two competing theories as to the source and scope of the "executive Power" conferred by Article II.[66] Yet under neither approach does the executive power embrace a presidential prerogative to suspend or ignore allegedly unconstitutional laws.

One theory of the executive power reads the Vesting Clause of Article II, section 1 as merely identifying the president as the person who shall possess the executive power. Under this view, the content and scope of the executive power are defined by Article II, sections 2 and 3, which give the president certain specific executive powers such as the power to act as commander in chief of the armed forces, the power to make treaties, and the power to appoint federal officers.[67] Since according to this theory the only powers the executive enjoys are those enumerated in Article II, the president cannot claim the unenumerated power to suspend the laws—either generally or in situations where he believes a statute is unconstitutional. Rather, the president's constitutional duty is, as spelled out in Article II, section 3, to "take Care that the Laws be faithfully executed."

The theory that the executive power is confined to those powers expressly enumerated in Article II is often qualified by a recognition that the president may act to protect the nation in time of emergency even though no such prerogative is conferred by the Constitution.[68] However, because the president's *constitutional* powers are viewed as being limited to those that are spelled out in Article II, this emergency prerogative is deemed to be extra-constitutional in nature. Consequently, a president who invokes this prerogative acts, as Jefferson put it, "at his own peril," and must "throw himself on the justice of his country and the rectitude of his own motives."[69] Even in times of crisis, a president has no *constitutionally sanctioned* power to suspend, dispense with, or otherwise act contrary to the laws.[70] Since any such power is extra-constitutional and limited to emergency situations, it cannot support the claim that presidents have a constitutional right to ignore any law they think is unconstitutional.

In contrast to the theory that the executive powers are limited to those specifically enumerated in Article II, many scholars contend that the Vesting Clause of Article II, section 1 was intended as a grant of power to the president.[71] Under this view, the specific content of the executive power is not enumerated in the Constitution. Instead, the executive power is a residuum consisting of those powers that the English Crown possessed in 1787 and that the Constitution has neither assigned to another branch nor permitted the president to exercise in only a qualified form.[72] For example, in 1787 one of the Crown's prerogatives was to declare war; this is not part of the president's executive powers, since Article I, section 8, clause 11 expressly assigns this power to Congress. Under the residuum approach to executive power, most of the provisions in Article II, sections 2 and 3, rather than being grants of power to the president, limit the president's ability to exercise powers that were held by the Crown.[73] Thus, at the time of the drafting of the Constitution, the authority to make treaties and appointments rested solely with the Crown; Article II, section 2 qualifies both of these powers by permitting the president to exercise them only with the advice and consent of the Senate.[74]

The residuum theory of executive power is consistent with the fact that the Founders created the presidency against the backdrop of the English Constitution, as it existed in 1787. In deciding what powers the American president should possess, the Founders' "constant point of reference" was a late eighteenth-century English monarch whose prerogatives had been curtailed over the centuries by Magna Charta (1215), the Petition of Right (1628), and the Bill of Rights (1689).[75] This was the same baseline that Thomas Jefferson had adopted in his 1776 draft constitution for Virginia. There, Jefferson defined the "executive powers" as a residuum, consisting of "the powers formerly held by the king save only that . . . he shall not possess" certain "prerogatives" and powers that were specifically described.[76] Under this approach, in order to deny the state's governor the authority to veto bills approved by the assembly, Jefferson had to expressly exclude that power, since the absolute veto was a prerogative still possessed by the Crown of England.[77]

The English Crown served as a model for the presidency as well, albeit largely a negative one. When the convention took up the question of the federal executive, Charles Pinkney voiced fear that the president would become "a Monarchy, of the worst kind, towit an elective one."[78] James Wilson agreed, stating that "[h]e did not consider the Prerogatives of the British Monarch as a proper guide in defining the Executive powers."[79] Because it was critical to the framers that the executive not replicate any of the undesirable features of the English Crown, they were careful to specify those respects in which the American president would differ from the English counterpart. As Justice Antonin Scalia has observed:

> The traditional English understanding of executive power, or, to be more precise, royal prerogatives, was fairly well known to the founding generation, since they appear repeatedly in the text of the Constitution in formulations very similar to those found in Blackstone. It can further be argued that when those prerogatives were to be reallocated in whole or part to other branches of government, or were to be limited in some other way, the Constitution generally did so expressly. One could reasonably infer, therefore, that what was not expressly reassigned would—at least absent patent incompatibility with republican principles—remain with the executive.[80]

In *The Federalist* No. 69, Hamilton presented "a Comparison Between the President and the King of Great Britain" in which he contrasted each of the president's powers with those of King George III. In most of Hamilton's examples, the Constitution had narrowed the president's authority vis-à-vis that of the English king. In not a single instance did the president possess greater powers than those that were retained by the Crown. It has been suggested that in *The Federalist*, Hamilton deliberately magnified the powers of the British monarch in order to make those of the president appear modest and that he and others who lost the convention battle for a stronger presidency hoped that the vaguely worded "executive power" would one day expand to royal proportions.[81] Yet even if Hamilton favored an "elective king," there is no evidence that he wanted the president's powers to be *greater* than those of George III. At most, he desired the "executive power . . . to be given to the president in much the same shape that it was enjoyed by a *constitutional* English king"—one whose powers had been curtailed by the Bill of Rights of 1689.[82]

If one subscribes to the residuum theory, the executive power thus consists of the prerogatives enjoyed by the Crown in 1787, minus those taken away or assigned elsewhere by the Constitution. Under this theory, the president lacks the authority to suspend allegedly unconstitutional laws, for the power to suspend the laws—including laws thought to be unconstitutional—had been stripped from the Crown a century before the drafting of the Constitution. The president lacks such a power even though it is not specifically denied by Article II, sections 2 and 3. Those sections merely limit powers that were still retained by the Crown in 1787 and that, unless qualified, would have been conferred by the Vesting Clause. Therefore, since the power to suspend unconstitutional laws does not fall within the Vesting Clause, the only way the president could exercise such authority is if it were expressly granted by some other clause in the Constitution—which it is not.

Leading proponents of the residuum theory of executive power acknowledge that the president may not suspend or dispense with the laws or otherwise act *contra legem.*[83] A few advocates of the residuum approach have nevertheless suggested that a president may ignore an allegedly unconstitutional law.[84] Yet this position is difficult to reconcile with a theory that denies the president any unenumerated powers greater than those that the Crown enjoyed in 1787 and that acknowledges that "the Framers . . . definitely did not wish to make the President of our federal republic even remotely as powerful as the English King."[85]

In short, whichever approach one takes to defining the executive power, that power does not embrace a presidential authority to suspend unconstitutional laws. No such power is expressly conferred by Article II, nor is such a power within the reservoir of powers possessed by the English Crown at the end of the eighteenth century. As Edward Corwin noted, "The President may veto a bill on the ground that in his opinion it violates the Constitution, but if the bill is passed over his veto, he must, by the great weight of authority, ordinarily regard it as law until it is set aside by judicial decision, since the power of interpreting the law, except as it is delegated by the law itself, is not an attribute of 'executive power.' "[86] Bernard Schwartz was likewise clearly correct when he wrote:

> The Framers of the American Constitution were familiar both with the repudiation of the Stuart claims to absolute prerogative and the more limited prerogative which was conceded in the Crown after [1689]. It must be presumed that, in their large outlines at least, the conclusions reached in the English experience were incorporated by them in the organic document. . . . Certainly, it was the furthest thing from their intentions to fashion the Executive which they were creating in accordance with the claim for which Charles I lost his life and James II his throne.[87]

THE PARDON POWER

Article II, section 2 gives the president the "Power to grant Reprieves and Pardons for Offenses against the United States, except in Cases of Impeachment." By invoking this power, the president may relieve persons of the consequences of their having violated a federal criminal statute. Pardons are usually granted on an individual basis, but they are sometimes issued on behalf of a large number of people.[88] In 1795, for example, George Washington declared a general pardon or amnesty for those who had participated in the Whiskey Rebellion in Pennsylvania.[89] Although Article II, section 2 does not mention the dispensing or the suspending power, some have suggested that the Pardon Clause in effect grants these powers by allowing the president to dispense with the laws through individual pardons and to suspend them across the board through a blanket pardon or amnesty.[90] Yet it is a mistake to read Article II as giving the president either of these prerogatives, for the power conferred by the

Pardon Clause is far narrower in scope than either the dispensing or the suspending power.

The "prerogative . . . of pardoning offences," as Blackstone described it, was one of the powers still retained by the English Crown at the end of the eighteenth century.[91] It was this power that the Founders granted to the president in Article II.[92] As the Supreme Court explained in 1855:

> At the time of the adoption of the constitution, American statesmen were conversant with the laws of England, and familiar with the prerogatives exercised by the crown. Hence, when the words to grant pardons were used in the constitution, they conveyed to the mind the authority as exercised by the English crown. . . . At that time both Englishmen and Americans attached the same meaning to the word pardon. In the convention which framed the constitution, no effort was made to define or change its meaning, although it was limited in cases of impeachment.[93]

The pardon power differed in a number of critical respects from the former royal dispensing and suspending powers.[94] First, the power to pardon could be applied only to criminal laws, whereas the dispensing and suspending powers could be used to abrogate criminal as well as noncriminal statutes. Second, the pardon power could not be exercised until after a person had violated a law; by contrast, the powers to dispense with and suspend the laws were usually applied prospectively to shield conduct that had not yet taken place. Finally, a pardon merely relieved a person of the penal consequences of activity that was still deemed to be illegal, while the dispensing and suspending powers nullified the law and thereby legalized the conduct in question. The pardon power was thus much less destructive of the law than were dispensations or suspensions, for the law remained on the books as a potential deterrent to everyone. Since a pardon could not be issued in advance, few would be hardy enough to violate the law on the assumption that they would later be granted clemency.

That the pardon power was viewed as being quite distinct from the dispensing and suspending powers is evidenced by the fact that the Bill of Rights of 1689 abolished the latter two powers but left the pardon power intact. After the break with England, some of the American states denied their governors all three of these powers, though others—including Delaware, Maryland, and North Carolina—followed the English model and withheld the dispensing and suspending powers while permitting the governor to issue pardons.[95] The Federal Constitution likewise gave the president the power to issue pardons but not the authority to either suspend or dispense with the laws.

The pardon power conferred by Article II is thus not the equivalent of a dispensing or suspending power. It can come into play only with respect to laws of a penal nature. If a president believes that such a law is unconstitutional, he may pardon those who have violated the measure. It was on this basis that Thomas Jefferson, upon assuming office in 1801, pardoned those who had been prosecuted under the Sedition Act of 1798.[96] Clemency may be granted, however, only after a person has violated the law. To issue a pardon or amnesty before an offense has been committed would be to cross the line that separates the pardon power from the dispensing and suspending powers.[97] Moreover, the pardon power is of no use whatsoever to a president when the allegedly unconstitutional law is not of a penal nature.

THE SUSPENDING POWER AND THE BILL OF RIGHTS

If the Founders were opposed to giving the president the authority to suspend the laws, one may wonder why they failed to include a prohibition against this power in the Bill of Rights of 1791. Many states, in writing new constitutions after the break with England, copied the English Bill of Rights by expressly denying the executive a power to suspend the laws.[98] The Virginia Declaration of Rights of 1776 was typical; it provided in Article VII "[t]hat all power of suspending laws, or the execution of laws, by any authority, without consent of the representatives of the people, is injurious to their rights, and ought not to be exercised."[99] As of 1908, the constitutions of twenty states still provided that laws may be suspended only by the legislature or by authority derived from it.[100] Why was no comparable provision placed in the Federal Bill of Rights? The answer is that not even the most ardent Anti-Federalists feared that the Constitution of 1787 had given the president a power to suspend the laws. As a result, while many other state bill of rights provisions found their way into the federal Constitution, a proscription of the suspending power was not among them.

The state ratifying conventions proposed more than 200 amendments to the Federal Constitution. These included proposals from Virginia and North Carolina to expressly deny the president authority to suspend a law.[101] In June 1788, the Virginia ratifying convention recommended that the Constitution be amended to add a Bill of Rights that closely tracked its Declaration of Rights—including a prohibition against the suspending power.[102] A short time later, the North Carolina convention "adopted, word for word, the Virginia amendments," including the ban on the suspending power.[103] In Maryland, a similar provision was proposed but was not approved by the ratification convention.[104]

The Virginia and North Carolina conventions appear to have included the suspending power merely as part of a formal recitation of Virginia's Declaration of Rights. After listing virtually all of the rights found in the Virginia Declaration, both conventions proposed twenty other amendments to the body of the Federal Constitution.[105] Thomas Jefferson later wrote that the Virginia delegates had annexed the state's Bill of Rights to their ratification "not by way of Condition, but to announce their attachment to them."[106] This may explain the curious fact that in the Virginia debates, not a single delegate expressed a belief that the Constitution had given the president a suspending power. No one in the Virginia proceedings defended the need for the suspending power ban, and the only delegates who addressed the matter urged that the provision was unnecessary. In North Carolina, the prohibition against the suspending power was not discussed at all.

Several Virginia delegates urged that there was no need for a federal bill of rights or a specific ban against the suspending power, since it was clear from the Constitution that the president did not possess this power. George Nicholas, one of the Virginia delegates, noted that the Constitution gives the federal government only those powers that are enumerated, in contrast to England and Virginia whose governments possessed all powers that were not expressly withheld from them. As a result, "[i]n England, in all disputes between the king and people, recurrence is had to the enumerated rights of the people, to determine[:] Are the rights in dispute secured? Are they included in Magna Charta, Bill of Rights, &c.? If not, they are, generally speaking, within the king's prerogative."[107] The same was true in Virginia where "all powers were given to the government without any exception."[108] In such cases, a bill of rights was essential to limiting the authority of government. By contrast, said Nicholas, at the federal level, "the reverse of the proposition holds. Is the disputed right enumerated? If not, Congress cannot meddle with it."[109] In this sense, he said, the "Constitution itself contains an English Bill of Rights," including a built-in prohibition against the suspending power. "The English Declaration of Rights provides that no laws shall be suspended. The Constitution provides that no laws shall be suspended, except one, and that in time of rebellion or invasion, which is the writ of *habeas corpus*."[110] While Nicholas did not specify which branch could suspend the writ of habeas corpus, no one disputed his assumption that the president was not given a general authority to suspend the laws.

Edmund Randolph, who had been a Virginia delegate to the Federal Convention, agreed that there was a critical distinction between an "ordinary legislature, having no limitation to their powers, and another body arising from a compact, and with certain delineated powers. Were a bill of rights necessary in the former," he said, "it would not be in the latter; for the best security that can be in the latter is the express enumeration of its powers."[111] Randolph sought to demonstrate that all of the rights contained in the proposed bill "were either provided for in the Constitution itself, or could not be infringed by the general government, as being unwarranted by any of the powers which were delegated therein; for that it was in vain to provide against the exercise of a power which did not exist."[112]

Another member of the Virginia convention, John Marshall, concurred in Nicholas's and Randolph's assessment that the Constitution had not given the president a power to suspend the laws. Anticipating the decision he would write for the Supreme Court in *Marbury v. Madison* fifteen years later,[113] the future chief justice noted that it was the federal judiciary that would offer protection should Congress exceed its powers under the Constitution. "If they were to make a law not warranted by any of the powers enumerated, it would be considered by the judges as an infringement of the Constitution which they are to guard. . . . They would declare it void."[114] Moreover, he said, the federal judiciary was the only branch that could provide relief in these instances. "To what quarter will you look for protection from an infringement on the Constitution, if you will not give the power to the judiciary? *There is no other body that can afford such a protection*."[115] Marshall thus implicitly rejected the idea that the president could block an unconstitutional law by suspending or refusing to honor it.

Despite the objections of Nicholas and Randolph that it was unnecessary, the suspending power ban remained part of Virginia's proposed federal bill of rights. In its closing hours, the Virginia convention enjoined the state's congressional delegation "to exert all their influence, and use all reasonable and legal methods" to secure adoption of the forty amendments sought by the convention.[116] However, the suspending power provision was one of the few Virginia proposals for which its senators and representatives did not press when the first Congress convened in 1789.

Virginia's proposed amendments were of special importance to James Madison. Not only had he been a member of the Virginia convention, but his election to the House of Representatives was based on a campaign promise to vigorously support the amendments desired by his state.[117] In June 1789, Madison fulfilled this promise by offering Congress a set of proposed amendments that included twenty-five of the forty changes desired by Virginia. He excluded "the political generalities set forth in the first seven articles, and in the Tenth and Twelfth."[118] The omission of Article VII's suspending power ban strengthens the conclusion that Madison and the other members of Virginia's convention did not believe the president had been given a suspending power and that the proposed ban had been offered merely as a formality.

This conclusion draws further support from the conduct of Virginia's U.S. senators after the proposed federal Bill of Rights emerged from the House. According to a contemporary observer, it was "the Virginians who have been the great movers in amendments."[119] The state's senators, William Grayson and Richard Henry Lee, sought to add to the amendments approved by the House all but two of the Virginia convention recommendations that Madison had left out.[120] They chose to abandon Articles VI and VII, both of which were copied from the Virginia Bill of Rights. Article VI declared that the election of legislators should be free and frequent, that men with sufficient attachment to the community should enjoy the right to vote, and that there should be no taxation or legislation without representation.[121] Each of these principles was honored by the Constitution and was therefore superfluous in the federal context. It seems likely that Article VII was dropped for the same reason. There was simply no perceived need to bar the president from exercising a suspending power when the Constitution gave him only a qualified veto and expressly commanded him to "take care that the laws be faithfully executed."

In short, the failure of the first Congress to include a prohibition against the suspending power in the federal Bill of Rights did not reflect a belief that such authority rightfully belonged to the president. Instead, it appears that there was a widespread understanding that the Constitution had not given the executive a suspending power of any kind. As Edmund Randolph had counseled the Virginia delegates, there was no need "to provide against the exercise of a power which did not exist."[122]

THE SILENCE OF THE ANTI-FEDERALISTS

As the foregoing discussion of the Bill of Rights suggests, some of the evidence that the Founders did not intend to give the president the authority to ignore allegedly unconstitutional laws is negative in character—inferences to be drawn from claims that were not made. Sherlock Holmes once drew Watson's attention to the "curious fact" that "[t]he dog did nothing in the night-time."[123] The same observation may be made here. If there had been the least suspicion that a suspending power lurked in the shadows of the Constitution, the Anti-Federalists would have been sure to bark.[124] While some of them complained that the presidency was too weak, most Anti-Federalists opposed the Constitution on the ground that the president would have powers that equalled or exceeded those of the English Crown. Professor Forrest McDonald has found that the "Anti-Federalists, in their efforts to persuade voters that the Constitution posed grave threats to their liberties, interpreted its clauses in ways that justified their greatest fear, the maximization of the power of the central government and especially that of the president."[125] Yet in all of the debates that accompanied adoption of the Constitution, not a single Anti-Federalist charged publicly that the president had been given the authority to suspend an allegedly unconstitutional law. The only direct references to such a power came from a Federalist who championed a strong presidency, and from an Anti-Federalist who alluded to the matter in a private letter. In addition, in *The Federalist Papers*, James Madison made a statement that some have cited as supporting the president's authority to ignore an "unconstitutional" law, though Madison did not in fact endorse such a power.

The only clear public claim that the president had been given the power to ignore allegedly unconstitutional laws was made by James Wilson, a Federalist who was a delegate to the Federal Convention and a leading member of the Pennsylvania ratifying convention. At the Federal Convention, Wilson had urged that "[t]he Executive ought to have an absolute negative. Without such a Self-defence the Legislature can at any moment sink it into nonexistence."[126] His motion to this effect was unanimously defeated,[127] and a similar motion by George Read was rejected by every state but Delaware.[128] Yet Wilson continued to advance these views when the Constitution came before his state's ratifying convention. Addressing the Pennsylvania body on December 1, 1787, he declared that the president would have the same right as the judiciary to reject unconstitutional laws.

> [T]he legislature, when acting in that capacity, may transgress the bounds assigned to it, and an act may pass, in the usual mode, notwithstanding that transgression; but when it

comes to be discussed before the judges,—when they consider its principles, and find it to be incompatible with the superior power of the Constitution,—it is their duty to pronounce it void; . . . In the same manner, the President of the United States could shield himself, and refuse to carry into effect an act that violates the Constitution.[129]

In stating that the president would possess an absolute veto over laws that he thought were unconstitutional, Wilson was a voice in the wilderness. His views on this issue were not shared by the Federalists, who had opposed giving the president an absolute veto even as to laws that infringed on the executive domain. Nor, as we shall see, were his views shared by the Anti-Federalists. Indeed, Wilson's claim that the president may disregard an allegedly unconstitutional law appears not to have been seconded *by anyone* during the public debates concerning the Constitution. In light of his unsuccessful efforts on behalf of an absolute veto at the Federal Convention, Wilson's remarks may have been partly a case of wishful thinking. In addition, because Pennsylvania's Anti-Federalists had raised doubts about whether the presidency would be strong enough to resist domination by the Senate, Wilson may have sought to allay their concerns by exaggerating the president's powers, especially when it came to defending against encroachments by Congress.[130] These factors may account for Wilson's idiosyncratic views.

The only other direct suggestion that the president might ignore a law on constitutional grounds appeared in the private correspondence of William Symmes, an Anti-Federalist. In a letter written two months before the Massachusetts ratifying convention, which he attended as a delegate, Symmes expressed fear that under the Take Care Clause, the president might refuse to follow Congress's directions as to how a law should be executed.

Can we exactly say how far a faithful execution of the laws may extend? or what may be called or comprehended in a faithful execution? . . . And should the legislature direct the mode of executing the laws, or any particular law, is he obliged to comply, if he does not think it will amount to a faithful execution? For to suppose that the legislature can make laws to affect the office of President, is to destroy his independence, and in this case to supersede the very constitution. Is there no instance in which he may reject the sense of the legislature, and establish his own, and so far, would he not be to all intents and purposes absolute?[131]

Unlike Wilson, Symmes did not believe the president had been given a general power to suspend allegedly unconstitutional laws. Rather, his concern was that the president might claim a right to ignore statutory provisions that "direct the mode of executing laws," with the result that he might implement them in a manner different from that provided for by Congress. These fears were apparently put to rest. During the Massachusetts convention, Symmes spoke to other issues.[132] In the end, he voted in favor of ratification, announcing that the Constitution and the amendments proposed by the state had his "unreserved assent";[133] none of the proposed amendments pertained to the powers of the president.[134]

Finally, some have said that in *The Federalist* No. 44, Madison endorsed the principle that the president may ignore laws that he believes are unconstitutional.[135] Addressing concerns that Congress might "exercise powers not warranted by" the Constitution, Madison wrote: "In the first instance, the success of the usurpation will depend on the executive and judiciary departments, which are to *expound and give effect to* the legislative acts; and in the last resort a remedy must be obtained from the people, who can, by the election of more faithful representatives, *annul* the acts of the usurpers."[136] In this passage, Madison does not say that the president may refuse to honor allegedly unconstitutional laws. Such a position would have been surprising in light of Madison's opposition at the Constitutional Convention to proposals for an absolute veto and in light of his early opposition to judicial review. Madison was in fact careful to distinguish between the power of the president (and the judiciary) to "expound and give effect to" the laws, and the power of the people to "annul" them. Only by ignoring this distinction can Madison be said to have supported a *presidential* power to annul allegedly unconstitutional laws. Instead, he appears to have suggested that through their power to "expound and give effect to" the laws, the president and the courts may construe ambiguous laws to keep them within constitutional bounds. Yet, in contrast to James Wilson, Madison did not claim that the executive may take the further step of refusing to honor a clearly worded statute whenever the president believes that it is unconstitutional.

Aside from the statements of James Wilson and William Symmes, the debates that accompanied the framing and ratification of the Constitution are devoid of any reference to a presidential power to suspend the laws. Given the common Anti-Federalist strategy of claiming that the presidency "would be a kingship in everything but name,"[137] this silence is overwhelming in its implications. The authority to suspend the laws—including laws that the king claimed violated the royal prerogative—was one of the most reviled prerogatives ever possessed by the English Crown. Anti-Federalist propagandists would have been quick to attribute this power to the president were there the least ground for doing so.

Those who have canvassed the Anti-Federalist literature have identified numerous grounds on which the presidency came under attack. None of these involved a charge that the president would have the power to suspend the laws or to ignore those that he claimed were unconstitutional.[138] For example, in 1787 and 1788, the *New York Journal* published a prominent series of Anti-Federalist essays known as the "Letters of Cato." One of these sought to demonstrate that the president would possess a host of "direct prerogatives" resembling those of the kings of England. Notably absent from Cato's list was a presidential power to suspend the laws—either generally or in cases where the laws were said to be unconstitutional.[139]

Similarly, the "Essays of An Old Whig," published in Philadelphia's *Independent Gazetteer* in 1787 and 1788 and later printed separately, charged that the president was "clothed with such powers as are dangerous." The Old Whig, after cataloging these powers, declared that to possess such authority "is in reality to be a KING as much a *King as the King of Great-Britain*, and a King too of the worst kind:—an elective King.''[140] Yet the catalog of powers did not include a power to ignore allegedly unconstitutional laws.

In the same vein, the ''Address of the Albany Antifederal Committee,'' printed in the *New York Journal* in 1788, decried ''[t]he vast executive power vested in one man . . . who, though called President, will have powers equal if not superior to many European kings''—including that ''of negativing all laws, resolutions and votes, thereby to prevent their passing unless agreed to by two thirds of both houses of the legislature.''[141] The committee did not suggest that there were any circumstances under which the president might disregard a law if it were passed over his veto.

Finally, a series of essays by ''The Impartial Examiner,'' published in the *Virginia Independent Chronicle* in 1788, attacked the executive, including the president's power to veto bills. The author agreed, though, that the veto ''will not be so decisive in its nature as the king's *negative*. True it is, this power of rejecting does not extend so far as primarily to produce an entire overthrow of any law, which has passed those *two houses*: but it may be expected that in many instances this negative will amount to a final and conclusive rejection.''[142] Once again, the qualified veto was perceived as being the sole means by which the president could block a law; there was no suggestion that he could refuse to enforce a measure once it was enacted over his veto.

THE TRANSLATIONIST ARGUMENT FOR EXECUTIVE REVIEW

Some modern presidents and commentators have asserted that the White House may legitimately object to selected portions of a bill in order to compensate for congressional practices that have supposedly undermined the president's veto power.[143] These claims implicitly adopt the view that fidelity in interpreting the Constitution requires that we pay attention to both the text of the document and the context in which it was written. Since the meaning the Founders sought to convey was determined in part by the setting in which they wrote, a faithful modern translation of their words must take into account intervening changes in the relevant context.[144] As Professor Lawrence Lessig has described the method of ''translation,'' once he or she identifies the original meaning of a constitutional provision, ''the translator then constructs a text—*a reading*—that in the current context has the same meaning as the original text in its original context. Contexts change, so readings must change. The aim of the translator is to find a reading that neutralizes the change in context.''[145] Yet as we will see, the translationist approach does not support the notion that presidents may refuse to honor an allegedly unconstitutional law.

Those who defend the executive's right to ignore selected parts of a law claim that this is necessary to offset legislative practices that make it impossible for a president to employ the veto in the manner originally contemplated. The practices to which they object are bundling and tacking. *Bundling* entails grouping together, in one omnibus bill, separate appropriations items or unrelated substantive provisions. *Tacking* involves attaching nongermane substantive provisions as ''riders'' to an appropriations bill.[146] In both situations, the president is presented with a bill containing items that may be unrelated to one another and that may cover a variety of subjects. Had the items not been lumped together, the president could have vetoed them selectively. With bundling or tacking, however, the president may be unable to block the objectionable provisions, including those he believes are unconstitutional, for the bill in which they are embedded may be too important to kill.

The White House has claimed that constitutionally based signing statements constitute a proper remedy for this situation. Signing statements allow the president to in effect ''unbundle'' a bill by signing it into law while at the same time objecting to those provisions that he thinks are invalid. While this may be tantamount to an item veto, it has been defended on the ground that such a veto ''arguably does no more than restore the veto power to the scope originally intended by the framers.''[147]

The Reagan administration acknowledged that its extensive use of constitutionally based signing statements was designed to give the White House an item veto that would counteract perceived congressional inroads on the veto power. The administration's principal spokesperson on this issue was Douglas Kmiec, who, during the Reagan years, worked in the Office of Legal Counsel, which drafts presidential signing statements. Kmiec explained that ''the signing statement initiative grew as Congress continued the practice of lumping together numerous unrelated provisions in omnibus bills, often inserting the most controversial provisions in emergency appropriations measures passed at, or after, the fiscal deadlines. This practice effectively denied the President his constitutionally provided veto authority.''[148] It was the ''increasing impracticability of a veto,'' said Kmiec, that caused the White House to ''place renewed emphasis upon presidential signing statements to articulate constitutional concerns.''[149]

Presidents George Bush and Bill Clinton repeated Ronald Reagan's claims. Bush complained that it was ''often impractical to veto a tremendous bill, a major bill, especially an appropriations bill'' due to the presence of ''unrelated riders that would never stand a chance on their own.''[150] He charged that ''when Congress bundles up a series of unrelated measures and calls it a single bill, it frustrates the President's constitutional role in resisting the influence of special interests.''[151] Bush's attorney general later urged that it was appropriate for presidents to employ constitutionally based signing statements in these situations where ''it would be politically impossible simply to veto a bill.''[152] When Bill Clinton signed the 1996 Line Item Veto Act, he declared that ''[t]he modern congressional practice of presenting the President with omnibus legislation reduces the President's ability to play the role in enacting laws that the Constitution intended''; the statutory item veto, he said, ''brings us closer to the Founders' view of an effective executive role in the legislative process.''[153]

In fact, the legislative practices to which Reagan, Bush, and Clinton objected are not "modern" and do not entail a departure by Congress from the context in which the Constitution was framed. These practices were centuries old at the time of the eighteenth century and were well known to the framers, who nevertheless decided to neither prohibit them nor give the president a more versatile veto.[154] Thus, the fact that Congress employs omnibus bills and riders today cannot, under the banner of "translation," justify efforts to enhance the executive's veto power by allowing the president to ignore selected portions of a statute.

Since the 1600s, the British House of Commons routinely included in money bills "certain preliminary conditions to their money grant, a haybag dangled before the hungry monarchical nose."[155] Like today's presidents, the Crown was forced to take the bitter with the sweet, for it could not veto the conditions tacked to the bill without also losing the desired funds. As a leading scholar of the British Constitution observed, "although the English people have never been slow to shed blood in defense of liberty, most of the limitations by which at different times they have succeeded in binding the royal power have been purchased with money; many of them by stipulated payments."[156] The practice of tacking nongermane riders to money bills gradually disappeared in England during the eighteenth century, not because of the position in which it placed the Crown, but due to its coercive impact on the House of Lords. Since money bills had to originate in the House of Commons and could not be amended by the Lords, the Lords were forced to accept or reject such bills *in toto*.[157] In order to protect the Lords' role in the lawmaking process, the use of tacking by the Commons was eventually abandoned.

In creating the federal Constitution, the Founders expressly recognized that the House of Representatives might "engage in the practice of tacking foreign matter to money bills."[158] Tacking was not only well known in England but was widely employed by American colonial assemblies prior to 1776, even though they were officially prohibited from passing bills that contained clauses foreign to their title or that dealt with more than one subject. Indeed, tacking and bundling were favorite devices by which these popular assemblies had attempted to neutralize the absolute veto exercised by colonial governors.[159]

Delegates at the Federal Convention voiced concern that if money bills could originate only in the House, and if the Senate, like the Lords, was unable to amend such bills, the House might use nongermane riders to undermine the Senate's role in the legislative process. This was of particular concern to smaller states who would enjoy equal representation in the Senate but not in the House.[160] The framers might have protected the Senate's independence in the same manner that England later protected the Lords, that is, by prohibiting the House from attaching nongermane items to appropriations bills. This approach would have had the added effect of enhancing the executive's veto power, for the president could then not be put in the position of having to accept the bitter with the sweet. Yet instead of following the English model by banning the use of riders, the convention dealt with the issue simply by allowing the Senate to amend money bills.[161] Article I, section 7 provides: ''All Bills for raising Revenue shall originate in the House . . . but the Senate may propose or concur with Amendments as on other Bills.'' Under this scheme, the House was free to attach riders to appropriations bills, and the Senate could either remove them or add additional riders of its own. The framers thus protected the Senate from coercion by the House but allowed Congress to use riders as a means of placing pressure on the president. The tacking of riders to appropriations bills, which the Founders' deliberately chose to permit, became commonplace after the Civil War.[162]

The convention's approval of tacking also means that the Founders necessarily contemplated that legislation might deal with more than a single subject, for tacking involves the addition of nongermane material to a bill. That this was part of the original understanding is evidenced by the fact that in 1789 the first Congress passed an omnibus bill that bundled together in one piece of legislation sums for the civil list, for the War Department, for invalids' pensions, and for debts incurred under the Confederation.[163] The following year, Congress approved another omnibus appropriations bill that lumped such disparate items as funds for the War Department, the cost of a new lighthouse at Cape Henry, expenses of the old office of foreign affairs, and payments for services rendered by Roger Alden and Jehoiakim M'Toksin.[164] George Washington, who had presided over the Federal Convention, signed both of these bills without objection. He also acknowledged that in such situations, the president cannot pick and choose among a bill's provisions. ''From the nature of the Constitution,'' he said, ''I must approve all the parts of a Bill, or reject it in toto.''[165]

There is thus no merit to presidential claims that riders and omnibus bills represent a departure from the original context and that the executive's refusal to comply with selected portions of a law is a legitimate means of neutralizing the situation.[166] The framers, though fully aware of the restrictive impact that riders and omnibus bills could have on the president's use of the veto, nonetheless chose to allow these practices. Indeed, as others have noted, to the extent that the context has changed since the drafting of the Constitution, the net effect has been to enhance rather than diminish the president's power in the lawmaking process.[167]

Finally, even if there were merit to the contention that nongermane riders and omnibus bills pose a novel threat to the executive veto, this would not justify the claimed right of the president to ignore allegedly unconstitutional laws. While it may at times be necessary to translate constitutional principles in order to remain true to the Founders' conception, translation must do no more than neutralize or offset departures from the original context. By refusing to honor those parts of a law that are said to be unconstitutional, the White House grossly overcompensates for the supposed congressional encroachment on the presidential veto. The principle of translation would only justify the president's selective veto of an offending provision if (1) the provision was a rider to an appropriations bill or part of an omnibus bill, and (2) Congress was afforded an opportunity to override the president's action. Yet none of the presidents who have claimed the authority to ignore allegedly unconstitutional laws has suggested that this power should be limited in either of these ways. In the name of translation, the executive has instead asserted a right that far surpasses what would be needed to neutralize the alleged encroachment on the president's veto power.

LOGICAL ARGUMENTS FOR EXECUTIVE REVIEW

It has been argued that the president should, as a matter of logic, possess the same right as the judiciary to review the constitutionality of acts of Congress and to refuse execution to laws that the president believes are invalid.[168] Yet whatever merit these claims may have as a matter of logic, they cannot—absent a constitutional amendment or a willingness to totally disregard original intent—justify a presidential practice that the Founders clearly rejected.

The logical argument for so-called presidential or executive review builds on *Marbury v. Madison*, which held that the judiciary may not enforce a law that in the court's view violates the Constitution.[169] Just as the federal courts must treat the Constitution as a paramount law that trumps any statute in conflict with it, so the president, in "taking care" to execute the laws, must place the Constitution first. As Judge Frank Easterbrook summarized the argument, the lesson of *Marbury* "was essentially: 'Every man for himself.' Each official owes the same duty to the hierarchy and must make his own decision." Therefore, "the President can't kowtow to Congress' view any more than the Court will. Especially given the unique presidential oath to . . . [']preserve, protect, and defend the Constitution of the United States.' Nothing there about executing laws while ignoring the Constitution!"[170] Yet as we noted earlier, it does not follow, even as a matter of logic, that the president's oath to uphold the Constitution necessarily allows him to ignore the laws—not if the Constitution requires him to execute the laws regardless of what he may think of their constitutionality.[171] Judge Easterbrook used "history" to supplement what he described as an argument based on "arid logic." However, that history consisted of James Wilson's previously discussed statement to the Pennsylvania ratifying convention and an unpublished memo written by James Madison in 1834 stating that each branch of government "must, in the exercise of its functions, be guided by the text of the Constitution according to its own interpretation of it."[172]

Professor Michael Paulsen also makes what he describes as a "Euclidian" argument for executive review. His "thesis is that executive review follows logically as consequence of the structural premises the framers embraced, whether they intended it or not."[173] The basic premise that he derives from the writings of James Madison and James Wilson is one of "coordinacy" or equality among the three branches in terms of their authority to interpret the Constitution.[174] "[A] logical consequence of this Madisonian-Wilsonian statement of the coordinacy principle is that the executive, no less than the judiciary, has, within the sphere of its powers, independent authority to review the acts of the other two branches.''[175] As part of this interpretive autonomy, the president ''may decline to execute acts of Congress on constitutional grounds, even if . . . those grounds have been rejected by the courts.''[176]

In contrast to Judge Easterbrook, who relies on the Founders' intent to supplement his logical proof for presidential review, Paulsen invokes Wilson and Madison to support the basic premise of coordinacy upon which his logical proof is built. While Wilson, Madison, and others did see the president as having the general right to interpret the Constitution for himself,[177] the critical question is whether this interpretive authority extends to refusing to enforce the laws. James Wilson thought so, but as we saw earlier his position on this issue was idiosyncratic.[178] Paulsen also cites Madison, writing in *The Federalist* No. 44, but he fails to note the distinction that Madison drew between the president's duty to ''expound and give effect to the legislative acts'' and the power of the people to ''annul'' them.[179] While the executive may certainly construe an ambiguous statute in order to avoid an unconstitutional reading, Madison, unlike Wilson, stopped short of proclaiming that the president may annul or suspend the laws. As with Judge Easterbrook, Paulsen's citations to history do not support the conclusion that, as a matter of original intent, the president may refuse to comply with a law because he believes it is unconstitutional.

Moreover, insofar as the executive's authority to ignore ''unconstitutional'' laws is concerned, Paulsen's theory contains the seeds of its own destruction. He acknowledges that there are exceptions to his general theory of executive review. In those cases where the ''best reading'' of the Constitution restricts the executive's authority to enforce its own understanding of the Constitution or laws, ''the President may not constitutionally act without the concurrence of the judiciary.''[180] In determining when the ''best reading'' of the Constitution warrants such an exception, one may look to ''textual, historical, or structural evidence.''[181] On the basis of historical evidence, Paulsen recognizes an exception with respect to a president's duty to honor the writ of habeas corpus. Though the rule of executive interpretive autonomy normally allows a president to refuse to execute or comply with judicial decrees,[182] Paulsen states that ''[t]he Great Writ dates back to Magna Charta. It is an ancient and revered procedural check against the exercise of arbitrary executive power. . . . As such, the power of courts to issue writs of habeas corpus, directed to executive officers, is an important exception to the rule that the executive need not obey judicial decrees.''[183]

Paulsen fails to note that the Founders adopted another ''ancient and revered'' restriction against ''arbitrary executive power,'' namely the prohibition against the suspending power enshrined in the Bill of Rights of 1689. As we have seen, under the ''best reading'' of the Constitution, the Founders wished to deny the president a royal prerogative that had been used by the English Crown for centuries to thwart execution of the laws. Paulsen does not cite any of this history. Yet once it is taken into account, his own theory dictates that the president's authority to interpret the Constitution for himself does not encompass the power to ignore a law whenever the president believes that it is unconstitutional.

The logical arguments for executive review are totally divorced from the scheme that the Founders envisioned and created. If we were to examine the Constitution without taking a holistic view of the text, without the light shed by the records of the Federal Convention, without the input of the state ratifying conventions, and without even a glance at the British history from which the Founders drew inspiration—in short, if we were to read the Constitution in a vacuum—the logic of *Marbury* might suggest that we are to "equate the President with the judges in ability and authority to set the Constitution over a statute."[184] Yet this was not the plan adopted by the convention. The Founders did not write on a clean slate, but on one that contained the indelible traces of 400 years of English constitutional history. In a case like this, as Justice Oliver Wendell Holmes once said, "a page of history is worth a volume of logic."[185]

There is no doubt that the Founders viewed the Constitution as a paramount law that would trump measures inconsistent with it.[186] Alexander Hamilton, writing in *The Federalist* No. 78, explained that "every act of a delegated authority, contrary to the tenor of the commission under which it is exercised, is void. No legislative act, therefore, contrary to the Constitution, can be valid."[187] In the same vein, Chief Justice Marshall declared for the Court in *Marbury v. Madison* that "a law repugnant to the constitution is void."[188]

Given this vision of the Constitution as higher law, the Founders might have created a structure in which the executive and the judiciary would each have the right to ignore acts of Congress they thought violative of the Constitution. This was not the plan they adopted. While the Founders repeatedly and clearly recognized that the federal courts could refuse to honor unconstitutional laws,[189] the record contains but a shred of public evidence suggesting that the president would enjoy a similar power. That shred is James Wilson's statement before the Pennsylvania ratifying convention.[190] As we noted earlier, Wilson's views appear to have been a product of wishful thinking; they were not shared by any other delegates at the federal or state conventions, nor were they echoed by the Anti-Federalists, who would have seized upon such a presidential prerogative had there been any basis for believing that it existed.

Alexander Hamilton and John Marshall, both of whom agreed that laws contrary to the Constitution are void, also noted that the competence to make such findings is reserved for the courts. In *The Federalist* No. 78, after stating that a law in conflict with the Constitution "is void," Hamilton noted that there is "no other way than through the medium of courts of justice" to effect this determination.[191] John Marshall, addressing the Virginia convention, likewise observed that while the courts could declare an act of Congress to be unconstitutional, "[t]here is no other body that can afford such a protection."[192]

The same understanding is reflected in the debates of the Federal Convention concerning the proposed Council of Revision. Under the proposal, an unspecified number of Supreme Court justices would have exercised the veto power jointly with the president. Some delegates thought it inappropriate to give the justices two opportunities to reject a law, first as members of the council and then in a judicial role. Elbridge Gerry, a delegate from Massachusetts, expressed "doubts whether the Judiciary ought to form a part of it, as they will have a sufficient check against encroachments on their own department by their . . . power of deciding on their Constitutionality."[193] Luther Martin of Maryland likewise objected that "as to the Constitutionality of laws, that point will come before the Judges in their proper official character. In this character they have a negative on the laws. Join them with the Executive in the Revision and they will have a double negative.[194] Virginia's George Mason, on the other hand, was untroubled by the fact that the judges would have "a double negative," since as judges "they could impede in one case only, the operation of laws. They could declare an unconstitutional law void. But with regard to every law however unjust or pernicious, which did not come plainly under this description, they would be under the necessity as Judges to give it a free course."[195] The delegates decided against giving the courts a double negative and instead vested the veto power in the president alone.

If the delegates had envisioned that the president would possess a suspending power that allowed him to disregard laws that he thought unconstitutional, the same "double negative" objection would surely have been raised as to him. The president would have "two or more bites at the apple" if he could invoke the Constitution first in deciding whether to veto a bill and then in determining whether to comply with the measure once it has become law.[196] Yet no one suggested that in addition to his right to assert a qualified veto, the president could also block an allegedly unconstitutional law by declining to enforce it. Instead, under the plan of the convention, the executive and the judiciary were each given one means of checking measures that they believe to be unconstitutional: through the qualified veto, the president may seek to prevent a bill from becoming law; and by exercising judicial review, the courts may refuse to enforce such a law in cases coming before them.

The executive and the judiciary might have stood on more equal footing if the president had been given an absolute veto, for each department would then have had an unqualified right to block measures they thought were unconstitutional: the president by preventing a bill from becoming law, the judges by refusing to enforce a law. The two branches might also have enjoyed parity had the Council of Revision plan been adopted. James Madison believed that if the judiciary had thus been allowed to share the veto power with the president, the convention would have denied the courts a second chance to pass on the validity of laws through judicial review. The Council of Revision plan, said Madison, would have given judges "a qualified negative on Legislative *bills*. Such a control, restricted to Constitutional points, . . . would have precluded the question of a judiciary annulment of Legislative *acts*."[197] By instead opting to give the president merely a qualified veto, while recognizing the courts' power to disregard unconstitutional laws, the convention created a scheme in which the federal judiciary was to play a unique and in some ways superior role in the process of constitutional review. This disparity reflected the Founders' unwillingness to give the president a power to suspend "unconstitutional" laws.

THE FOUNDERS' CONCEPTION: A SUMMARY

The claim that a president may refuse to enforce a law on the ground that it is unconstitutional is but a reincarnation of the royal prerogative of suspending the laws, a prerogative of the Crown's that was abolished in England by the Bill of Rights of 1689. Though the American Constitution does not expressly deny such authority to the president, a fair and holistic reading of that document, of the history that preceded it, and of the debates surrounding its adoption makes clear that the Founders did not intend to confer this power on the president of the United States. The grant to the president of a qualified rather than an absolute veto; the assumption implicit in Article I, section 9 that the suspending power belongs to Congress; the president's Article II duty to ensure that the laws are "faithfully executed"; the Founders' conception of "the executive power"; the fact that the pardon power granted by Article II was perceived as being entirely distinct from a power to suspend the laws; the absence of any pressure to include a ban against the suspending power in the Bill of Rights; and the failure of even the staunchest Anti-Federalists to object that the president had been entrusted with a suspending power all point to one verdict: The Constitution does not give the president a power to suspend the laws, not even when the chief executive may think that a particular law is unconstitutional.[198]

Thomas Jefferson endorsed this view. As secretary of state in 1791, he urged President Washington to veto a bill to create the Bank of the United States. After urging that the bill was unconstitutional, Jefferson advised the president that his only option when presented with such a measure was to exercise the veto. "The negative of the President is *the* shield provided by the constitution to protect against the invasions of the legislature: 1. [Of] [t]he right of the Executive. 2. Of the Judiciary. 3. Of the States and State legislatures."[199] There was no suggestion on Jefferson's part that in addition to "*the* shield" provided by the veto, the president also had the option of ignoring the measure should it become law.

This was also the conclusion reached by the U.S. Circuit Court in *United States v. Smith*, an 1806 decision written by Supreme Court Justice William Paterson.[200] Paterson had been a leading member of the Constitutional Convention as a delegate from New Jersey.[201] The *Smith* case involved a prosecution for violating the Neutrality Act in which defendants claimed that their conduct was lawful because it had been authorized by President Jefferson. In an effort to prove this authorization, they subpoenaed Secretary of State James Madison and several other Cabinet members. When none of these witnesses appeared, the defense moved to have the trial postponed until they were made available.[202] The government objected that the defendants' argument

> proceeds altogether upon the idea that the executive may dispense with the laws at pleasure; a supposition as false in theory as it would be dangerous and destructive to the constitution in practice. . . . Among the powers and duties of the president . . . he is expressly required to "take care that the laws be faithfully executed." They will not venture to contend that this clause gives the president the right of dispensing with the laws. . . . He has a qualified veto, before the law passes. . . . When it has become a law . . . it is his duty to take care that it be faithfully executed. He cannot suspend its operation, dispense with its application, or prevent its effect, otherwise than by the exercise of [his] constitutional power of pardoning, after conviction. If he could do so, he could repeal the law, and would thus invade the province assigned to the legislature, and become paramount to the other branches of the government.[203]

The court agreed with the government and denied the motion. Since the president cannot suspend or dispense with the laws, even if Jefferson had authorized the defendants' conduct, this would have been no defense to the crime. In his opinion for the court, Justice Paterson noted that the law under which the defendants were charged

> imparts no dispensing power to the president. Does the constitution give it? Far from it, for it explicitly directs that he shall "take care that the laws be faithfully executed." . . . True, a nolle prosequi may be entered, a pardon may be granted; but these presume criminality, presume guilt, presume amenability to judicial investigation and punishment, which are very different from a power to dispense with the law.[204]

In sum, wrote Paterson, "The president of the United States cannot control the statute, nor dispense with its execution, and still less can he authorize a person to do what the law forbids. If he could, it would render the execution of the laws dependent on his will and pleasure; which is a doctrine that has not been set up, and will not meet with any supporters in our government."[205]

The decision in *Smith* accurately reflected the thinking of the times. The Constitution provides for other checks against unconstitutional laws short of the president's refusing to honor them. As Madison, Jefferson, and Hamilton recognized, the first line of defense against such laws is the executive's qualified veto. That this may, as some have complained, be an "imperfect defense" against unconstitutional laws,[206] is beside the point. The Founders repeatedly refused to give the president a perfect defense against such measure, that is, an absolute veto. If the qualified veto fails to prevent enactment of an unconstitutional law, the Founders provided a second line of defense in the form of judicial review. However, this power to declare laws unconstitutional was given to the courts, not to the president.

PRESIDENTIAL INVOCATION OF THE CONSTITUTION

To say that the president may not ignore laws that he thinks are unconstitutional is not to render meaningless his oath to "preserve, protect and defend the

Constitution." *Marbury* rightly noted "that courts, as well as other departments, are bound by that instrument."[207] Though the president cannot invoke the Constitution as a basis for refusing to honor or enforce acts of Congress, there are many ways in which the Constitution may legitimately serve as a guide to executive action. Presidents have taken the Constitution into account in a wide variety of settings. Some of these involve situations unrelated to the adoption and enforcement of laws.

Appointments

In 1793, President Washington withdrew his nomination of William Paterson as associate justice of the Supreme Court upon realizing that the appointment violated Article I, section 6. The office of associate justice had been created by Congress while Paterson was a senator, and his Senate term had not yet expired. In his message of withdrawal, Washington stated: "I deem the nomination to have been null by the Constitution."[208] The president later renominated Paterson after his Senate term had ended.[209]

Pardons

As noted earlier, shortly after taking office in 1801, President Jefferson granted full and unconditional pardons to those convicted under the Alien and Sedition Acts, based upon his belief that the acts violated the free speech provision of the First Amendment.[210]

Congressional Resolutions

Presidents have frequently cited the Constitution in refusing to comply with resolutions passed by one house of Congress and which therefore do not qualify as laws. President Washington, in March 1796, decided to ignore a House resolution requesting documents pertaining to negotiation of the Jay Treaty, explaining that compliance would infringe on the executive's Article II treaty-making power.[211] President Madison likewise declined, on constitutional grounds, to honor a Senate resolution asking that he confer with a Senate committee concerning the nomination of a minister to Sweden.[212]

Even in connection with legislation, a president has a range of legitimate options for dealing with bills or laws that he believes are unconstitutional, short of refusing to honor or comply with a statute on these grounds.

Shaping Legislation

The president can use his enormous prestige and influence with Congress, including the threat of a veto, to help ensure that unconstitutional measures never reach his desk.[213] John F. Kennedy successfully lobbied Congress to delete a provision from a military procurement bill that would have "directed" the Air Force secretary to spend "not less than $491 million during Fiscal Year 1963" on the B-70 bomber. Kennedy, who opposed development of this aircraft, argued that such mandatory language infringed on his authority as commander in chief. As finally approved, the act "authorized" rather than "directed" expenditure of the sum in question.[214]

Vetoes

Numerous presidential vetoes have rested on constitutional grounds.[215] The first veto, issued by George Washington in 1792, rejected a bill apportioning the House of Representatives because it did not comply with the requirements of Article I, section 2.[216] James Madison vetoed three public bills, all for constitutional reasons; two of these were measures to support churches,[217] while the third involved internal improvements.[218] Congress has sometimes responded to a constitutionally based presidential veto by passing a new bill that cures the alleged constitutional defect. For example, twelve days after he vetoed an army appropriations bill on constitutional grounds, Woodrow Wilson signed a revised bill from which the offending provision had been removed.[219]

Withholding Signature

Instead of vetoing a bill to which he has constitutional objections, a president may hold the bill for ten days so that it becomes law without his signature.[220] In doing so, the president might identify the alleged constitutional defect that caused him not to sign the measure. While the White House has issued statements indicating why the president chose to let a bill become law without his signature,[221] I was unable to find any case where the reason for doing so was that the law was unconstitutional.

Signing Statements

Presidents have frequently signed bills into law and at the same time issued statements explaining that, in their view, portions of the law were unconstitutional. As we shall see in chapters 5 through 7, the use of signing statements, though rare in the nineteenth century, became a commonplace in the latter half of the twentieth century.

Amendment or Repeal

Article II, section 3 of the Constitution authorizes the president to "recommend . . . such Measures as he shall judge necessary and expedient. . . ." This power may be used to urge the amendment or repeal of laws that the executive believes are unconstitutional, including laws that were enacted during a prior administration. For example, a number of presidents urged Congress to repeal the Tenure of Office Act, adopted during Andrew Johnson's presidency, arguing that it unconstitutionally limited the executive's power to remove federal officers.[222] Such efforts may also be directed at laws that were enacted over the president's veto or that he signed with constitutional reservations. Harry Truman, believing that a legislative ban against paying salaries to two federal employees amounted to a bill of attainder in violation of Article I, section 9, signed the measure into law but then persuaded Congress to drop the ban.[223]

Judicial Review

A president who believes that a law is unconstitutional may seek to have the measure overturned by the federal courts. The Nixon administration took this approach with the 1970 Voting Rights Act Amendments, which Nixon signed despite constitutional reservations.[224] When the statute was later challenged in court, the solicitor general offered a "lackluster and unenthusiastic" defense.[225] He "conceded that its validity was 'a very close question' " and informed the Supreme Court that both the Justice Department and the president opposed the measure on constitutional grounds.[226] Not surprisingly, the Justices held that portions of the act were unconstitutional.[227] The executive has also refused to defend a statute in court and even argued that a law was unconstitutional.[228] While some of these options raise difficulties of their own, all stop short of a president's taking the extreme step of refusing to honor the law.

PART II

Presidential Practice, 1789–1981

3

Presidential Practice: Introduction

TWO CONSTITUTIONS

In Part I, we saw that the Founders rejected the notion that a president may refuse to honor those laws that he believes are unconstitutional. Neither the text of the Constitution nor the understanding of those who drafted and ratified it supports the existence of such a presidential prerogative. Yet though this was the original understanding, the meaning of the Constitution is subject to change over time. As John Marshall wrote in 1819, the Constitution was "intended to endure for ages to come, and consequently, to be adapted to the various crises of human affairs."[1] Such adaptation may come about either through a constitutional amendment or through the case-by-case process of judicial interpretation.

Neither of these formal routes has led to a departure from the original understanding. The Constitution has not been amended to allow the president to ignore allegedly unconstitutional laws. There have been numerous proposed amendments that would have given the president an item veto, but none of these has been approved by Congress or submitted to the states for approval.[2] In 1996, Congress did give the president a temporary line-item veto that can be applied to cancel certain taxing and spending provisions. Even if this statutory grant of authority is found to be constitutional, it does not purport to give the president a general right to ignore allegedly unconstitutional laws. The statutory line-item veto may be used only with respect to fiscal provisions and may be overridden by a two-thirds majority in Congress. The statute does not sanction a presidential refusal to comply with a measure once it has become law.[3]

Neither has the Supreme Court construed the Constitution to give the president such authority. In 1838, the Court in *Kendall v. United States ex rel Stokes* found that the postmaster general had improperly refused to comply with a law requiring that certain monies be awarded to a postal contractor.[4] While the postmaster's refusal was not based on constitutional grounds, the Justices categorically rejected the existence of an executive prerogative to disregard acts of Congress. "To contend that the obligation imposed on the President to see the laws faithfully executed, implies a power to forbid their execution, is a novel construction of the Constitution, and entirely inadmissible."[5] To recognize such a power, said the Court, "would be vesting in the President a dispensing power, which has no countenance for its support in any part of the constitution; and is asserting a principle which, if carried out in its results to all cases falling within it, would be clothing the President with a power entirely to control the legislation of Congress, and paralyze the administration of justice."[6]

In *Myers v. United States*, a suit challenging President Wilson's refusal to comply with a law that barred the removal of certain postmasters without Senate approval, the Court in 1926 held that Congress's attempt to limit the president's removal power was unconstitutional and that the firing of Postmaster Frank S. Myers was therefore not unlawful.[7] Some have urged that *Myers* stands for the proposition that the president may defy a law that he believes is unconstitutional, reasoning that the Court otherwise would have found the dismissal to have been improper.[8] However, the *Myers* majority refrained from addressing the specific issue of whether a president may defy an allegedly unconstitutional law. This issue was not presented to the Court either in the briefs or at oral argument. The only member of the Court who even alluded to the matter was Justice James C. McReynolds who rejected the idea that the president could invoke the appointment provisions of a law but then repudiate those parts dealing with removal. There was, he wrote, a "certain repugnance" to "the suggestion that the President may ignore any provision of an Act of Congress under which he has proceeded. He should promote and not subvert orderly government."[9] Yet even McReynolds did not consider the question of whether the president's constitutional objection to a law entitled him to disobey it. The Court has often said that it is not bound by prior decisions like *Myers* that failed to "directly confront" an issue and instead dealt with it *sub silentio*.[10]

As we will see in chapter 10, the Supreme Court has yet to recognize a presidential prerogative to ignore "unconstitutional" laws. The Constitution as construed by the Court still adheres to the original understanding that the president may not defy acts of Congress that he believes are unconstitutional.

There is often a difference, however, between the formal Constitution and the actual practices of government. In this sense we have two constitutions.[11] The first, consisting of the text as authoritatively construed by the Supreme Court, may at times be little more than a "paper description," while the second or unofficial Constitution may provide a more accurate picture of "living reality."[12] Just as a house may be built in a way that departs from the original drawings, so, too, there may be a marked contrast between what Woodrow Wilson called the "literary theory" of the Constitution and the "actual machinery" of government.[13] It is to this second or unofficial Constitution—to the realities of presidential practice—that we turn in Part II.

THE UNOFFICIAL CONSTITUTION: A MAP OF REALITY

The unofficial Constitution is important for a number of reasons. First, it may provide us with a much more realistic description of how government operates than that portrayed by the literary theory of the Constitution. This point was brought home to Alexander Bickel when he testified before a House subcommittee during the Vietnam War. After Professor Bickel noted that Article I, section 8, clause 12 requires Congress to limit military appropriations to no more than two years, he was advised that Congress had in fact allowed the executive to carry over funds from year to year with the result that there was then more than $200 billion in the pipeline available to the president from prior military appropriations.[14]

Governmental practices that are not authorized by the text of the Constitution or by the original understanding may continue for decades before they are ultimately validated or rejected by the Court. This was true, for example, of the legislative veto device by which Congress reserved to one or both of its houses, or to designated congressional committees, the right to approve or reject certain actions of the executive branch. Though the practice was nowhere sanctioned by constitutional theory, it was employed for fifty years before the Court finally ruled that it was unconstitutional.[15] Yet even this ruling did not close the gap between official constitutional theory and the realities of governmental practice, for Congress has continued to enact statutes that contain legislative veto provisions.[16]

It is also possible that the judiciary may never address the validity of certain governmental practices, in which case the disparity between the official and unofficial Constitutions will persist indefinitely. This has proved to be the case with the executive's claimed authority to initiate hostilities without a declaration of war from Congress. According to the literary theory of the Constitution as spelled out in Article I, section 8, clause 11, the power to declare war belongs to Congress. Modern presidents have nevertheless asserted that this power now belongs to them and that they may go to war without the consent of Congress.[17] The Supreme Court could seek to eliminate this divergence between the official and unofficial Constitutions by ruling on the validity of the executive's claim, but the Court has so far declined to do so by finding that the issue is not justiciable.[18] Thus, with respect to the war power, the unofficial Constitution offers a far clearer picture of how the government actually operates than one would glean from looking only at the text, the original understanding, and decisions of the Court.

THE POTENTIAL IMPACT OF PRACTICE ON THEORY

Government practices are also important because of their potential impact on the literary theory of the Constitution. Through the process of judicial interpretation, the literary theory of the Constitution is constantly evolving. In this process of giving meaning to the Constitution, the Supreme Court often takes into account the actual workings of government. To the extent that the Court upholds practices that are not part of the original understanding and that would not be sanctioned by a strict reading of the text, the Court brings about a convergence of the two Constitutions. In such cases, the official Constitution is influenced by the unofficial, as theory is adapted to reality.[19]

There are a number of ways in which government practices may shape the evolution of constitutional theory. First, practices that were engaged in around the time the Constitution was adopted may provide " 'contemporaneous and weighty evidence' of the Constitution's meaning,"[20] since many of those who participated in drafting or ratifying the Constitution sat in the first Congress or held other office under the new government. In construing the Constitution, the Court may therefore look to practices that date from the early years of the federal government as providing insight into the original understanding.[21]

Second, the manner in which government actually conducts itself may shape the literary theory of the Constitution by causing the Court to validate those practices even when they do not comport with the original understanding. The conduct at issue may have made its appearance after the Constitution was adopted and yet have become so well established as to warrant official recognition from the Court. In 1803, the Court thus noted that the Constitution's meaning may be "fixed" by "practice and acquiescence under it for a period of several years."[22] Some of the Founders, including James Madison, agreed that long-standing practice may alter the meaning of the Constitution by a process of prescription.[23] As Madison put it, "a course of practice of sufficient uniformity and duration to carry with it the public sanction shall settle doubtful or contested meanings."[24] Madison emphasized the importance of "early" practice.[25] When the Court has given dispositive effect to governmental practices, those practices have usually dated from the incipient years of the federal government.[26] Yet this is not always the case.[27] In *Dames & Moore v. Regan*, the Court in 1981 relied on congressional practices to sustain the president's use of an executive agreement to settle the Iran hostage crisis; the earliest of those practices, however, dated from 1868 and most of them occurred in 1949 or later.[28]

Third, the manner in which government actually operates may subtly distort the literary theory of the Constitution without purporting to change it. The Court may uphold practices that are incompatible with the text or with the original understanding, but without noting the inconsistency or acknowledging that the formal Constitution is being altered. For example, the literary theory of the Constitution prohibits Congress from delegating its lawmaking power to the executive branch. Though the Court continues to pay lip service to this principle, it routinely upholds laws that confer broad policy-making authority on the executive, employing the fiction that Congress has laid down an "intelligible principle" to which the executive must conform.[29]

Finally, governmental practices may undermine the literary theory of the Constitution if the Court, in order to protect conduct that departs from its terms, insulates that conduct from judicial review.[30] While this makes it unnecessary for the Court to alter the legal theory of the Constitution in order to sustain deviant practices, it weakens the formal Constitution by neutralizing its commands. The constitutional provisions in question are no longer judicially enforceable and thus cease to operate as legal restraints on the conduct of government. The Court, for example, has invoked the doctrines of standing, ripeness, and political question to dismiss challenges to presidential war making in situations where there has been no congressional declaration of war as required by Article I, section 8.[31] The same fate has befallen other constitutional provisions.[32] By shielding constitutional theory from collisions that might alter it, the Court preserves that theory but at the expense of its integrity.

For all of these reasons, governmental practice is extremely important, both in its own right and because of its potential impact on the formal Constitution. In chapters 4 through 9, we will explore this unofficial Constitution as it is reflected in the practices of American presidents in dealing with laws that they believe are unconstitutional.

ASCERTAINING PRESIDENTIAL PRACTICE

The task of identifying instances where presidents have refused to comply with allegedly unconstitutional laws is, on its face, fairly straightforward. One must first locate those acts of Congress to which a chief executive has taken constitutional issue. As to each of these measures, we then ascertain whether or not the objecting president proceeded to disregard the law. Yet the simplicity of the undertaking is deceptive. Unless the White House has elected to publicize its refusal to comply with a statute on constitutional grounds, both the president's objection and any ensuing decision to ignore the measure may both remain hidden from view. Moreover, even in those cases where the president has announced his constitutional objection to a law, the fate of the disputed provision may not be easy to determine. The best one can do is attempt to trace the fate of those laws to which the chief executive has made his constitutional objections known.

Presidents may register their constitutional disagreement with congressional enactments in a variety of ways. The first method—and that envisioned by the Founders—is by exercising the veto power. To invoke this, the executive returns a bill "with his Objections" to the House where it originated, which enters his "Objections . . . on their Journal." The bill can then become law only if it is repassed by a two-thirds majority of both houses.[33] By examining the veto messages for all vetoes that were overridden by Congress, it is possible to identify those that involved constitutionally based objections.[34] The extent to which these laws were then honored by the president is explored in chapter 4. This discussion applies only to ''regular'' as opposed to ''pocket'' vetoes. If a bill is sent to the White House less than ten days before Congress adjourns, the president may kill the measure simply by refusing to sign it,—in effect, slipping it into his pocket. The bill never returns to Congress for a possible override vote and thus cannot become law. While no reason need be given for such vetoes, modern presidents frequently explain the reasons for their action.[35] Pocket vetoes are irrelevant to this study, since the bills in question were never enacted into law.

A second group of laws to which presidents have taken constitutional issue can be identified by reviewing presidential signing statements, a more recent means by which presidents have taken issue with the validity of statutes.[36] As their name implies, signing statements are usually issued at the time a president affixes his signature to a bill, though they sometimes appear days or even months later. Franklin Roosevelt, for example, signed the Urgent Deficiency Appropriations Act on July 12, 1943;[37] the following September, he issued a message noting that one section of the Act constituted a bill of attainder in violation of Article I, section 9.[38]

The record of presidential signing statements is fairly complete. They are included in the two major series of presidential papers commissioned by Congress. The first series, *A Compilation of the Messages and Papers of the Presidents*, covers the period from 1789 through January 4, 1926.[39] The second series, *Public Papers of the Presidents of the United States*, covers Herbert Hoover and every president from Harry Truman to the present time. Together these series between them offer complete coverage of all of the presidents except Calvin Coolidge (missing years 1926–1929) and Franklin Roosevelt. For Coolidge and Roosevelt, some signing statements are printed in the *Congressional Record*. Roosevelt's signing statements also appear in *The Public Papers and Addresses of Franklin D. Roosevelt*,[40] though the collection is probably incomplete, since it does not even contain all of FDR's veto messages.[41] Presidential signing statements issued since mid-1965 also appear in the *Weekly Compilation of Presidential Documents*, and those issued since 1986 are included in the *United States Code Congressional and Administrative News*. By reviewing all of the available presidential signing statements, one can identify those that raise constitutional objections to parts of a law. Chapters 5 through 7 examine the use of signing statements and the extent to which presidents ultimately complied with those statutory provisions to which they took constitutional issue.

While veto messages and signing statements offer the best leads in searching for laws that the executive has claimed are unconstitutional, they do not provide an exhaustive list. If a measure was passed during a prior administration, neither of these devices is available to the president. In such cases, the executive's constitutional objection to the statute is likely to come to light only if the president announces his intention not to enforce the measure or urges Congress to repeal it, or if a lawsuit is brought challenging the administration's refusal to honor the statute. The instances of presidential objection to laws adopted during a prior administration are explored in chapter 8.

In examining each of these categories—vetoes, signing statements, and objections to previously enacted laws—we will seek to determine the fate of the statutes that presidents have opposed on constitutional grounds. Of the range of options available to the executive, our goal is to discover the extent to which presidents from George Washington through Jimmy Carter took the extreme step of refusing to honor the law. It may not always be possible to determine with absolute certainty whether or not a particular statutory provision was implemented. As Arthur S. Miller observed:

> Congress has delegated large chunks of governing power to the public administration. About four hundred public laws are enacted each year. There is no way, at least no *known* way, that either Congress or the judiciary can oversee the implementation of the details of the statutes in the United States Code. . . . In any event, it requires no documentation (for it is common knowledge) that different political administrations approach statutes in different ways. Some enforce them to the hilt; others casually ignore them.[42]

The visibility problem that Congress and the judiciary face also confronts the historian. Yet by reviewing congressional hearings and reports, presidential papers, newspaper archives, and a variety of other sources, it is surprising how often an answer to the enforcement question may be found. Only on rare occasions was the search in vain.

4

Laws Enacted over a Constitutionally Based Veto

From 1789 to 1981, American presidents vetoed 462 public bills. Of this number, only eighty-seven—or fewer than 20 percent—became law over the executive's objection.[1] These figures cover only regular vetoes of public bills and do not include either pocket vetoes, which Congress has no opportunity to override, or vetoes of private bills.[2] While most of the eighty-seven overridden vetoes rested solely on policy grounds, in twenty-seven cases, the president's opposition was based at least in part on constitutional concerns.

Table 4.1 summarizes these twenty-seven cases, showing the nature of the statute, the general basis for the veto, and whether the law was executed by the president who unsuccessfully vetoed it. As the table indicates, all but six of these constitutionally based vetoes occurred during the nineteenth century. The constitutional ground most often invoked was federalism; in two-thirds of the cases, presidents claimed that Congress had exceeded the scope of its enumerated powers. Five vetoes stemmed from a separation of powers concern that Congress had invaded the executive's domain. The Bill of Rights played a role in six cases, in one case forming the sole basis for the president's veto.

On the question most pertinent to this study, in only one of the twenty-seven instances where a constitutionally based veto was overridden is there evidence that the president failed to honor the law. That case involved Andrew Johnson's alleged defiance of the Tenure of Office Act, a move that precipitated his impeachment. In none of the other twenty-six cases, involving nine different presidents, did the chief executive elect to disregard the statute.

Table 4.1
Statutes Enacted over President's Constitutionally Based Veto (1789–1981)

President	Nature of Bill and Statutory Citation	Constitutional Basis of Veto[a]	President's Response[b]
Pierce (5)	River & Harbor Appropriations ch. 54, 11 Stat. 24 (1856)	Federalism	Executed
	River & Harbor Appropriations ch. 55, 11 Stat. 25 (1856)	Federalism	Executed
	River & Harbor Appropriations ch. 56, 11 Stat. 25 (1856)	Federalism	Executed
	River & Harbor Appropriations ch. 121, 11 Stat. 44 (1856)	Federalism	Executed
	River & Harbor Appropriations ch. 126, 11 Stat. 51 (1856)	Federalism	Executed
A. Johnson (14)	Civil Rights Act ch. 31, 14 Stat. 27 (1866)	Federalism	Executed
	Freedmen's Bureau Act ch. 200, 14 Stat. 173 (1866)	Federalism; Bill of Rights	Executed
	Franchise for Blacks in D.C. ch. 6, 14 Stat. 375 (1867)	Spirit of the Constitution	No response required
	Admission of Nebraska ch. 36, 14 Stat. 391 (1867)	Federalism	No response required
	First Reconstruction Act ch. 153, 14 Stat. 428 (1867)	Federalism; Bill of Rights	Executed
	Tenure of Office Act ch. 154, 14 Stat. 430 (1867)	Separation of Powers	Arguably Defied
	Second Reconstruction Act ch. 6, 15 Stat. 2 (1867)	Federalism	Executed
	Third Reconstruction Act ch. 30, 15 Stat. 14 (1867)	Federalism; Bill of Rights; Separation of Powers	Executed
	Reconstruction Res. No. 39, 15 Stat. 30 (1867)	Federalism	Executed
	Supreme Court Jurisdiction ch. 34, 15 Stat. 44 (1868)	Separation of Powers	No response required
	Admit Arkansas to Congress ch. 69, 15 Stat. 72 (1868)	Separation of Powers	Executed
	Admit 6 States to Congress ch. 70, 15 Stat. 73 (1868)	Federalism	No response required
	Freedmen's Bureau ch. 245, 15 Stat. 193 (1868)	Federalism	No response required
	Electoral College Exclusion Res. No. 58, 15 Stat. 257 (1868)	Federalism	No response required

Table 4.1 (*continued*)

Arthur	River & Harbor Appropriations ch. 375, 22 Stat. 191 (1882)	Federalism	Executed
Cleveland	River & Harbor Appropriations ch. 314, 29 Stat. 302 (1896)	Federalism	Executed
Taft	Webb-Kenyon Act ch. 90, 37 Stat. 699 (1913)	Federalism	No occasion to respond
Wilson	National Prohibition Act ch. 85, 41 Stat. 305 (1919)	Federalism	Executed
Truman (2)	Internal Security Act ch. 1024, 64 Stat. 987 (1950)	Bill of Rights	Executed
	Immigration & Nationality Act ch. 477, 66 Stat. 163 (1952)	Bill of Rights; Separation of Powers	Executed
Nixon	War Powers Resolution Pub. L. No. 93-148 87 Stat. 555 (1973)	Separation of Powers	No response required
Ford	Freedom of Information Act Amends., Pub. L. No. 93-502 88 Stat. 1561 (1974)	Separation of Powers	No occasion to respond

a. *Federalism* means that a law exceeds the scope of the national government's powers and/or invades the province of the states; *Separation of Powers* means that a statute usurps or interferes with the functions of the Executive or the Judiciary; *Bill of Rights* means that the law violates the rights of individuals.

b. *No response required* means that the law could be carried out without any action on the part of the Executive; *No occasion to respond* means that the President left office before any opportunity to honor or enforce the law arose.

This chapter will examine the presidents' responses to these twenty-seven laws adopted over a constitutionally based veto.

FRANKLIN PIERCE: FIVE RIVER AND HARBOR BILLS

Franklin Pierce was the first president to have a constitutionally based veto overridden by Congress. In 1856, he unsuccessfully opposed five river and harbor appropriations bills.[3] Like many nineteenth century presidents, he believed that federal expenditures for so-called internal improvements were unconstitutional as falling neither within Congress's power to spend for the general welfare nor its power to regulate commerce among the states.[4] However, once each of these bills became law, Pierce faithfully executed them, undertaking the authorized improvements as promptly as weather conditions permitted.[5]

ANDREW JOHNSON: FOURTEEN ASSORTED VETOES

Johnson's Adherence to the Principle of Compliance

Andrew Johnson has the distinction of having had more public bill vetoes overridden than any other president in U.S. history.[6] Of the fifteen laws passed by Congress over his objection, fourteen were opposed by Johnson on constitutional grounds.[7] Most of these measures dealt with Reconstruction, a process that Johnson believed fell within the executive's province rather than that of Congress. According to Johnson, the eleven rebellious states never left the Union and were therefore entitled to immediate representation in the House and Senate once the Civil War had ended. The Republican Congress thought otherwise. Through a series of statutes enacted over Johnson's veto, the former Confederacy was placed under military rule.[8] Many of Johnson's vetoes rested on the premise that Congress could not validly legislate for the southern states at a time when their representatives were excluded from the House and the Senate.[9]

Though Johnson's constitutional opposition to these measures was deeply felt,[10] he more than once acknowledged that if a veto is overridden by Congress, the president is bound to enforce the statute despite his constitutional misgivings. In 1866, after the Civil Rights Act was passed over his veto, Johnson explained that since the measure was "now a law of the land," it "will be faithfully executed so long as it shall remain unrepealed and may not be declared unconstitutional by courts of competent jurisdiction."[11] In 1867, Attorney General Henry Stanbery appeared in the Supreme Court on Johnson's behalf and explained that though the president had vetoed the Reconstruction Acts as being unconstitutional, "when the President did that he did everything he intended to do in opposition to these laws. From the moment they were passed over his veto there was but one duty in his estimation resting upon him, and that was faithfully to carry out and execute these laws."[12] Finally, in his State of the Union Message to Congress in 1867, Johnson addressed the question of how far a president could go "in opposing an unconstitutional act of Congress" and concluded that because presidential defiance could lead to "civil war," such action is inappropriate if measures "which are peaceable remain open to him or to his constituents." He noted that the "reconstruction acts, though as plainly unconstitutional as any that can be imagined, were not believed to be within the class last mentioned" because the people still had the power to redress the situation at the polls. On the other hand, said Johnson, the executive's refusal to comply with an unconstitutional law might be proper "if there be neither judicial remedy for the wrongs it inflicts nor power in the people to protect themselves."[13]

Had Johnson wished to adopt a more confrontational stance, he would have had the support of his attorney general. Shortly after Johnson became president, his attorney general, James Speed, advised the secretary of the treasury that:

> The Constitution is the supreme law—a law superior and paramount to every other. If any law be repugnant to the Constitution, it is void; in other words, it is no law. It is the peculiar province and duty of the judicial department to say what the law is in particular cases. But before such cases arise, and in the absence of authoritative exposition of the law by that department, it is equally the duty of the officer holding the executive power of the Government to determine, for the purposes of his own conduct and action, as well the operation of conflicting laws as the constitutionality of any one.[14]

Yet, with the possible exception of the Tenure of Office Act, Johnson rejected this position and adhered to the principle that the president must enforce a law even if he believes that it is unconstitutional.

Six of the fourteen measures that became law over Johnson's constitutionally based veto were such that they took effect without any action on the executive's part. As a result, there was nothing the president could have done to prevent the measures from becoming operative. This was true of the statutes extending the franchise to blacks in the District of Columbia, admitting Nebraska to the Union, excluding certain southern states from the electoral college, narrowing the Supreme Court's jurisdiction in habeas corpus cases, and restoring some of the southern states to representation in Congress.[15]

Johnson grudgingly complied with seven other statutes that dealt with the Freedmen's Bureau and Reconstruction, despite his constitutional objection to them. At the same time, he urged that the measures be repealed.[16] In addition, he did everything he could to frustrate Congress's Reconstruction program, but did so by exercising discretionary powers in ways that in a "strained and nominal sense" adhered to the letter of the law.[17] At least until the Tenure of Office Act episode, "Johnson had broken no law; he had limited himself strictly to the exercise of his constitutional powers."[18] Had it been otherwise, not only would the House have impeached him much earlier, but the Articles of Impeachment would have rested on more than Johnson's debatable refusal to comply with the Tenure of Office Act. The House of Representatives, which finally voted to impeach Johnson on February 24, 1868, had been searching for grounds to do so since late 1866. Three earlier impeachment drives failed in the House for want of "charges that contained legal substance."[19] The articles of impeachment approved by the House contained only one allegedly illegal act—Johnson's dismissal of Secretary of War Edwin Stanton without the Senate's consent. This action was alleged to violate the Tenure of Office Act as well as several other Reconstruction measures.[20]

The Debatable Case of the Tenure of Office Act

It is far from clear that Andrew Johnson failed to comply with the Tenure of Office Act. That statute, enacted over his veto on March 2, 1867, provided that the secretary of war and other Cabinet members "shall hold their offices respectively for and *during the term of the President by whom they may have been appointed* and for one month thereafter, subject to removal by and with the advice and consent of the Senate.''[21] Johnson had vetoed the measure on the ground that it interfered with the president's power of removal, a position vindicated by the Supreme Court many years later in *Myers v. United States*.[22]

Johnson's alleged violation of the Tenure of Office Act stemmed from his efforts to remove Edwin Stanton as secretary of war. Stanton, a holdover from Lincoln's Cabinet, sympathized and cooperated with the Radical Republicans in Congress, and acted to thwart Johnson in a host of ways. As secretary of war, Stanton occupied a strategic position in carrying out Congress's plan for military reconstruction. For Johnson, gaining control of the War Department was critical to being able to implement his own more lenient approach to Reconstruction.[23] In August 1867, after Stanton refused the president's request that he resign, Johnson suspended him as secretary of war and appointed General Ulysses S. Grant as interim secretary. Because Congress was not in session at the time, the president's action was in accord with the Tenure of Office Act, which allowed for interim suspensions subject to the Senate's later concurrence. When the Senate disapproved the suspension in January 1868, Grant immediately relinquished the office to Stanton.

This attempt to displace Stanton having failed, Johnson, on February 21, 1868, issued an order removing Stanton as secretary of war and naming General Lorenzo Thomas as his interim replacement. The House responded three days later, voting to impeach Johnson by the overwhelming margin of 126 to 47.[24] Of the eleven Articles of Impeachment later approved by the House, ten related to the president's firing of Stanton in alleged violation of the Tenure of Office Act. Only Article X, dealing with Johnson's public criticism of Congress, was unrelated to the removal of Stanton.[25]

Yet as House Democrats noted in Johnson's defense, because Stanton had been appointed by President Lincoln, he was not covered by the Tenure of Office Act.[26] Indeed, when the final version of the act was being debated in the Senate, it was noted without contradiction that while the act would tie Johnson's hands with respect to Cabinet members that he had appointed, ''the Secretary of War . . . according to the terms of this provision, may be removed by him tomorrow.''[27]

Andrew Johnson's firing of Stanton was thus not a case where a president, believing a law to be unconstitutional, chose not to comply with it. While Johnson was convinced that the Tenure of Office Act was unconstitutional, he did not think that removing the secretary of war was in violation of it. As Johnson told the Senate a day after dismissing Stanton, ''Whether the act were constitutional or not, it was always my opinion that it did not secure him from removal.''[28] In Johnson's view, ''It would be a violation of the plain meaning of this enactment to place Mr. Stanton upon the same footing as those heads of Departments who have been appointed by myself. As to him, this law gives him no tenure of office.''[29] At the same time, Johnson acknowledged ''that there were doubts as to the construction of the law,''[30] and that many people, including some members of Congress, thought it shielded Stanton.[31] This perception may have arisen from the fact that Stanton would have been covered had the act's wording not been altered at the last minute by a joint conference committee whose report received little scrutiny in the House.[32]

The House managers who served as prosecutors in the impeachment trial before the Senate contended that because Johnson had first suspended Stanton in accord with the Tenure of Office Act, he was estopped from later claiming that the act did not cover Stanton.[33] Yet a president who was determined to remove Stanton might first seek to do so in accord with a law that many regarded as applicable; only after that effort failed was Johnson forced to adopt a more confrontational stance by asserting that Stanton was not in fact covered by the act and that even if he were, the measure was unconstitutional.

In the impeachment trial before the Senate, the president's counsel ably refuted the charge that Johnson had violated the Tenure of Office Act in removing the secretary of war.[34] The House prosecutors argued that Johnson was serving out Lincoln's term, rather than his own, and that Stanton was thus covered by the act, since he was dismissed "during the term of the President by whom [he was] appointed." However, even if Johnson's term was deemed to be a continuation of Lincoln's, Stanton was appointed during Lincoln's first term, which expired in 1865, rather than during his uncompleted second term.[35]

Yet, perhaps mindful of the inefficacy of such statutory arguments in the earlier House impeachment proceedings,[36] Johnson's lawyers also claimed that a president may sometimes ignore an unconstitutional law where he seeks to have the issue resolved by the courts.[37] One of the president's attorneys, Thomas Nelson, declared that "if a law is unconstitutional in the view of the President it is no law at all, and he is not bound to follow it";[38] a similar argument was made by Attorney General Henry Stanbery.[39] Nelson emphasized that Johnson had not sought to settle the question by his "own strong hand," but had tried to "submit it to the judicial tribunals of the country."[40] Another of the president's attorneys, William Groesbeck, urged that in "doubtful cases" such as that involving the Tenure of Office Act, a President may ignore a law if he seeks to "test the accuracy of the new interpretation in the forum which is the highest and final interpreter of such questions."[41] Only if a "law be upon its very face in flat contradiction to plain express provisions of the Constitution," said Groesbeck, may a President ignore it "without going to the Supreme Court."[42]

The most careful elaboration of this "test-case defense" was advanced by Benjamin Curtis. In his opening argument for the defense, the former Supreme Court justice conceded that as a general rule the president "is not to erect himself into a judicial court and decide that the law is unconstitutional, and that therefore he will not execute it."[43] The only time a president may refuse to comply with a law, said Curtis, is when "a question arises whether a particular law has cut off a power confided to him by the people through the Constitution, and he alone can raise that question, and he alone can cause a judicial decision to come between the two branches of the Government to say which of them is right, and . . . when he takes the needful steps to raise that question and have it peacefully decided.[44]

Though the president's lawyers were probably unaware of it, the principle they were advancing was recognized by one of the leading constitutional analysts of the day, John Norton Pomeroy. In a treatise published in 1868, but written prior to Johnson's impeachment, Pomeroy stated that the president normally may not disregard a law, even if he believes it to be unconstitutional. Yet there was an exception to this "general rule":

> A statute may be passed of such a form and character as to be addressed directly to the President; it assumes to regulate his official action; no private person and no subordinate officer is affected by its provisions. If the Chief Magistrate enforces this law, no question as to its validity can be raised, no opportunity can be given to deny the power of the legislature. . . . In such a case the President, unless he chooses to acquiesce, may plainly exercise an independent judgment, and act upon his own separate convictions.[45]

Pomeroy noted that the Tenure of Office Act fell into this category, for unless the president ignored this law, no one would be able to bring a lawsuit challenging its validity. "The law, therefore, must stand unquestioned, unless the President should disregard its commands and proceed to remove from office without consulting the Senate."[46]

The House managers did not contend that there was any way of testing the Tenure of Office Act short of dismissing Stanton.[47] However, they vehemently denied the premise that a president may ignore an allegedly unconstitutional law where this is necessary to securing a judicial ruling as to its validity. In his opening argument for the House, Benjamin Butler echoed the Founders:

> All the power or right in the President to judge upon any supposed conflict of an act of Congress with the paramount law of the Constitution is exhausted when he has examined a bill sent him and returned it with his objections. If then passed over his veto it becomes as valid as if in fact signed by him. . . . After that he and all other officers must execute the law, whether in fact constitutional or not.[48]

Representative George Boutwell likewise denied that Johnson "had a right to violate this law for the purpose of obtaining a judicial determination."[49] According to Boutwell,

> The constitutional duty of the President is to obey and execute the laws. He has no authority under the Constitution, or by any law, to enter into any schemes or plans for the purpose of testing the validity of the laws of the country, either judicially or otherwise. . . . Nor is it any answer to say . . . that "there never could be a judicial decision that a law is unconstitutional, inasmuch as it is only by disregarding a law that any question can be raised judicially under it." If this be true, it is no misfortune.[50]

John Bingham, who concluded the case for the House, urged that Andrew Johnson and King James II presented "the most remarkable parallel that I have ever read in history," for the "charges against James are substantially the charges presented against this accused President . . . that he has suspended the laws and dispensed with the execution of the laws."[51]

The impeachment trial of Andrew Johnson squarely raised the issue of whether a president may refuse to honor an allegedly unconstitutional law in order to obtain a judicial determination as to its validity. The Senate vote to convict was 35–19, one shy of the two-thirds majority needed to remove the president from office.[52] To what extent did Johnson's acquittal rest on the Senate's acceptance of his claim that the chief executive may disregard an act of Congress where this is the only way to test its constitutionality in court?

Johnson's test-case defense was recognized in principle by Chief Justice Salmon P. Chase. The Chief Justice presided over the impeachment trial but could not vote on the ultimate question of whether to convict the president. Though Chase did not reveal his views publicly, senators could easily deduce it from his consistent rulings to admit evidence concerning Johnson's belief that the Tenure of Office Act was unconstitutional and the executive's efforts to test it in court. In private, the Chief Justice was quite explicit as to his position, even during the trial. On April 19, 1868, ten days after Johnson's attorneys first raised the test-case defense, Chase wrote to a friend:

> The President had a perfect right and indeed was under the highest obligation to remove Mr. Stanton, if he made the removal, not in wanton disregard of a constitutional law, but with a sincere belief that the Tenure of Office Act was unconstitutional and for the purpose of bringing the question of its constitutionality before the Supreme Court. Plainly it was then a proper and peaceful, if not the only proper and peaceful mode of protecting and defending the Constitution.[53]

However, Chase added that such an approach was proper only where, as in the case of the Tenure of Office Act, the law in question "directly attacks and impairs the Executive power confided to him by the Constitution. In that case it seems to me to be the clear duty of the President to disregard the law, so far at least as may be necessary to bring the question of its constitutionality before the Judicial Tribunals."[54]

Despite the Chief Justice's views, the fact that nearly two-thirds of the Senate voted to convict Johnson might seem a clear repudiation of the claim that presidents may ignore a law in order to test its validity. As students of Johnson's impeachment have noted, however, the case was as much a political trial as a legal proceeding.[55] Many Republicans, who made up more than three-quarters of the Senate, were prepared to convict the president regardless of the evidence.[56] Many Democrats were equally determined to see him acquitted. A middle group of Senators that included seven conservative Republicans who crossed party lines to vote for Johnson's acquittal may have made a genuine effort to set political prejudice aside. Yet even these so-called recusants did not necessarily accept the test-case defense and may have voted to acquit for other reasons. One possible consideration was the fact that if Johnson were removed from office he would have been succeeded by Ohio Senator Benjamin Wade, a fiery radical whom the conservatives had reason to fear.[57] Moreover, to the extent that their votes rested on legal grounds, some of the Republican holdouts concluded that Stanton was not protected by the Tenure of Office Act; as a result, they had no need to reach the issue of whether Johnson would have been justified in violating the act in order to test its validity in court.[58]

Our ability to interpret the impeachment proceedings would have been greatly enhanced had all of the Senate's fifty-four members issued written opinions explaining their votes; as it was only twenty-nine did so. Of these, twenty senators addressed the president's claimed right to ignore laws where necessary to test their validity—eight recognizing such a right and twelve rejecting it.[59] These twenty opinions represent the views of barely a third of the Senate, making it difficult to distill from the outcome of Johnson's impeachment trial a precedent on the issue of whether presidents are ever justified in refusing to comply with allegedly unconstitutional laws.

Professor Michael Les Benedict has suggested a potentially more fruitful approach that focuses on the Senate's evidentiary rulings rather than on the outcome of the case.[60] While the Senate voted 29–20 to exclude evidence tending merely to show that Johnson and his Cabinet thought the Tenure of Office Act was unconstitutional,[61] it agreed by votes of 29–21, 27–23, and 26–25 to admit evidence that Johnson desired to obtain a judicial ruling on the act's constitutionality.[62] Thirty-two different senators—a clear majority—voted for at least one of these motions to admit, and twenty-one senators supported all three. The Senate was thus much more willing to acknowledge a narrow right of noncompliance, limited to situations where such action is necessary to create a test case, than it was to recognize a general presidential right to ignore laws that the executive believes are unconstitutional.

Though a majority of the Senate was willing to hear evidence of the president's efforts to obtain a judicial ruling on the Tenure of Office Act, this does not necessarily mean that they accepted the legitimacy of such a defense. Senators John Sherman and Charles Sumner, for example, voted to admit this evidence but ultimately concluded that the president should not be allowed to ignore a law even if this is the only way to test its validity in court.[63] Others may have felt likewise, helping to explain why, of the thirty-two senators who agreed to hear evidence supporting the test-case defense, thirteen voted to convict the president.[64]

It is also likely that some who accepted the test-case defense in principle were in the end unpersuaded that Johnson had violated the Tenure of Office Act in order to obtain a judicial ruling as to its validity.[65] The president on several occasions said he wished to obtain a court determination of the question.[66] Moreover, when he first suspended Stanton and named Grant to be interim secretary,

Johnson apparently did so believing that if the Senate disapproved the suspension, Grant would not surrender the office as required by the Tenure of Office Act, thus allowing a suit by Stanton. Johnson reportedly even offered to pay the $10,000 fine that Grant risked by violating the act, in order to create a possible test case. Grant upset these plans by yielding the office as soon as the Senate voted to disapprove Stanton's suspension.[67] As Johnson later told the Senate, "My order of suspension in August last was intended to place the case in such a position as would make a resort to a judicial decision both necessary and proper. My understanding and wishes . . . were frustrated, and the late order for Mr. Stanton's removal was a further step toward the accomplishment of that purpose."[68]

More significant steps to test the Tenure of Office Act occurred six months later after Johnson ordered Stanton's removal and named General Thomas to replace him. Stanton refused to give up the office and instead brought criminal proceedings against Thomas in the District of Columbia Supreme Court. After Thomas was arrested and charged with violating the Tenure of Office Act, the president hired Walter S. Cox, a private attorney, to represent Thomas.[69] The president instructed Cox that "he desired the necessary legal proceedings to be instituted without delay to test General Thomas's right to the office and to put him in possession."[70]

At this point, there were three avenues by which Cox might have obtained a ruling on the validity of the Tenure of Office Act. First, he could have filed a habeas corpus action seeking Thomas's release from custody on the ground that the act he was charged with violating was unconstitutional. Second, Cox could have raised the issue of the act's validity as a defense to the criminal action. Third, he could have arranged to have a quo warranto proceeding brought to challenge Stanton's right to remain in office. None of these avenues was pursued with diligence. The first two were quickly eliminated when Cox asked the court to discharge his client; to Cox's purported surprise, the judge did so, putting an end to the criminal suit and to any chance of filing a habeas petition.[71] Quo warranto proceedings could be brought only by the government with the consent of Attorney General Stanbery.[72] Cox presented quo warranto papers to the local district attorney who refused to sign them "without instructions or a request from the President or the Attorney General."[73] Though Cox passed this information on to Stanbery, nothing further occurred, perhaps because Johnson had by then been impeached, making it unlikely a federal court would intervene in the matter.[74]

This evidence of Cox's ineptitude and of the attorney general's inaction seriously undermined the president's claim that he sought to have the constitutionality of the Tenure of Office Act resolved by the judiciary.[75] Instead, it may have appeared to the Senate that Johnson was trying to clothe his political objectives in the more respectable garb of the Constitution. The House managers repeatedly noted that the president could easily have instituted a test case had he wished to do so.[76] Several senators who agreed to admit evidence supporting the test-case defense but who later voted to convict cited Johnson's vacillating efforts to place the question before the courts.[77] In the absence of any serious attempt to create a test case, Johnson was in effect claiming that presidents may ignore any allegedly unconstitutional law, a prerogative that he and his defense counsel repeatedly disavowed and to which Congress was firmly opposed.

In sum, Andrew Johnson's dismissal of Secretary Stanton was probably not a case where a president chose to violate a law to which he had constitutional objections, for Johnson was on solid ground in believing that the Tenure of Office Act did not protect Stanton. Yet because Congress treated the incident as one of presidential noncompliance, the impeachment proceeding sheds light on the perceived legitimacy of such executive conduct. While there is evidence that the Senate rejected the broad assertion that a president may ignore any law that he thinks is unconstitutional, a majority of the Senate may have accepted a more limited right of noncompliance in cases where such defiance is necessary to produce a test case.

The Johnson impeachment also makes clear that a president who seeks to invoke this right bears a heavy burden of persuasion. He cannot, as Johnson sought to do, merely assert his belief that a law is unconstitutional. Instead, the chief executive must make every effort to ensure that the issue is presented to the federal courts for final resolution. Without such a requirement, the president could routinely invoke the Constitution as a means of suspending laws that he opposes on policy grounds. In the veto context at least, Andrew Johnson's impeachment appears to have had a chastening effect. It was not until more than a century later, when Ronald Reagan refused to comply with the Comprehensive Anti-Apartheid Act of 1986,[78] that another president dared to ignore a law that was passed over his constitutionally based veto.[79]

CHESTER A. ARTHUR: RIVER AND HARBOR IMPROVEMENTS

On August 2, 1882, Congress overrode President Arthur's veto of an $18.7 million river and harbor improvements bill, then the largest such appropriation ever.[80] Arthur opposed the measure as an "extravagant expenditure of public money" and on the ground that "it contains appropriations for purposes not for the common defense or general welfare, and which do not promote commerce among the States."[81]

The president's veto message did not specify which of the hundreds of projects covered by the bill were allegedly unconstitutional. Senator George Hoar later stated that Arthur objected to "a very few items only, amounting altogether to a very few thousand dollars."[82] Hoar's account is substantiated by a report that the president submitted to Congress in January 1884, in response to a request that he "inform the House whether any moneys have been appropriated or expended in the improvement of rivers or harbors not navigable" and hence not within the scope of Congress's power to regulate interstate commerce.[83] The report, which covered the period "from the beginning of the Government to the present time," identified three projects that did not involve navigable waters: Lake Winnipesauke in New Hampshire, the North Carolina stretch of the Yadkin River, and the French Broad River in North Carolina.[84] Only the latter two projects were funded by the 1882 act. The amounts appropriated for these two projects were small: $25,000 for the Yadkin River and $5,000 for the French Broad River.[85]

The act did not require that the funds be spent within a set period of time. Despite his constitutional objections, President Arthur began implementing the act even as to the disputed projects. During the 1883 fiscal year, the secretary of war spent $9,061 on the Yadkin River project and $1,364 on improving the French Broad River.[86] At the same time, the administration spent all of the funds that remained from previous appropriations for Lake Winnipesauke, even though Arthur had expressed constitutional concerns about this project as well.[87]

GROVER CLEVELAND: RIVER AND HARBOR IMPROVEMENTS

Grover Cleveland, like Chester Arthur, unsuccessfully vetoed a major river and harbor improvements bill. The act of June 3, 1896, directly appropriated $12.6 million for 417 projects, and authorized the War Department to contract for an additional $62 million in improvements to be funded by future appropriations.[88] It is not absolutely clear that Cleveland's objections rested on constitutional grounds. His veto message gave nine reasons for rejecting the bill. The first was that some of the projects "are not related to the public welfare, and many of them are palpably for the benefit of limited localities or in aid of individual interests."[89] By this, the president may have meant that the measure violated Article I, section 8, which limits Congress's spending power to "provid[ing] for the common Defence and general Welfare." The president's remaining objections reflected his belief that if the federal government became a "giver of gifts" it would "stimulate a vicious paternalism."[90] This concern, too, may have had constitutional roots. According to one of his biographers, Cleveland "proposed to confine the government to its proper functions as prescribed in the Constitution—which Cleveland believed did not include paternalistic aid to any group or individual."[91]

Even assuming that Cleveland's river and harbor veto rested on constitutional grounds, there is no evidence that he refused to spend the appropriated funds. Cleveland left office in March 1897, nine months after the bill became law. During this interim, the War Department began to carry out the authorized improvements.[92] Although the administration sought to limit a few of the disbursements under the act, it did so based on the peculiar wording of the statute, not under a claimed right to ignore projects that were thought to be unconstitutional.[93] In fact, Cleveland's attorney general advised the secretary of war that the act did not "leave anything to your discretion with respect to the expenditure of the sum appropriated.''[94] Rather, ''[t]he intention of Congress was, except in instances where a contrary intent is manifested . . . that you should proceed with the projects specified to the extent of the appropriations without inquiry as to their wisdom.''[95] I was unable to find anything to indicate that the secretary of war failed to heed this advice.

WILLIAM HOWARD TAFT: INTERSTATE SHIPMENT OF LIQUOR

The Webb-Kenyon Act, passed by Congress over President William Howard Taft's veto in 1913, outlawed the interstate shipment of intoxicating liquor if it was intended for use contrary to the laws of the state of destination.[96] This act enabled states for the first time to enforce local prohibition laws by barring the importation of liquor. Taft vetoed the measure on the ground that ''it is in substance and effect a delegation by Congress to the States of the power of regulating interstate commerce in liquors which is vested exclusively in Congress.''[97] However, Taft never faced the question of whether or not to implement the act, for he turned the White House over to Woodrow Wilson three days after the measure became law.

WOODROW WILSON: THE WAR-TIME PROHIBITION ACT

During World War I, the prohibition lobby, led by the Anti-Saloon League, capitalized on the need to conserve foodstuffs and on the prevailing spirit of self-sacrifice to push through Congress a series of laws, including the War-Time Prohibition Act, which turned the United States into a ''dry'' nation on July 1, 1919, more than six months before prohibition under the Eighteenth Amendment went into effect.[98] In October 1919—nearly a year after the armistice—the Anti-Saloon League induced Congress to again use its war powers to expand the War-Time Prohibition Act, even though that act would be displaced in January 1920 when the Eighteenth Amendment became operative.[99]

On October 27, 1919, President Woodrow Wilson vetoed the bill to expand the War-Time Prohibition Act, noting that ''[i]t has to do with the enforcement of an act which was passed by reason of the emergencies of the war and whose objects have been satisfied in the demobilization of the Army and Navy, and whose repeal I have already sought at the hands of Congress.''[100] Though Wilson's veto message was somewhat ambiguous, he seems to have believed that Congress was constitutionally barred from making peacetime use of its war powers to impose prohibition. The message cautioned that ''[i]n all matters having to do with the personal habits and customs of large numbers of our people we must be certain that the established processes of legal change are followed.''[101]

Congress overrode the president's veto on October 28.[102] The White House immediately announced that the expanded War-Time Prohibition Act would be fully enforced—a pledge to which the administration in fact adhered.[103] On January 5, 1920, eleven days before it was superseded by the Eighteenth Amendment, the Supreme Court ruled that the expanded War-Time Prohibition Act was constitutional.[104]

HARRY S. TRUMAN: TWO CONSTITUTIONALLY BASED VETOES

President Harry S. Truman issued two constitutionally based vetoes that were overridden by Congress. In both instances, his administration then implemented the disputed statute.

The Internal Security Act of 1950

One of the statutes that Truman unsuccessfully vetoed on constitutional grounds was the Internal Security Act of 1950. Title I of the act was designated as the Subversive Activities Control Act of 1950; Title II was the Emergency Detention Act of 1950.[105] In his veto message, Truman alleged that Title I, which required Communist front groups to register with the government, "would make a mockery of the 'Bill of Rights' and greatly chill expression."[106] He also opposed Title II, which allowed the president to declare an "internal security emergency" during which the government could then detain anyone whom the attorney general has "reasonable ground to believe . . . probably will engage in . . . acts of espionage or of sabotage." Truman objected to Title II on the ground that except in times when the writ of habeas corpus had been suspended, it was unconstitutional "to detain a man not charged with a crime."[107] Congress overrode the president's veto on September 23, 1950.[108]

The Truman administration proceeded to enforce Title I, despite the president's constitutional objections.[109] In October 1950, the attorney general issued regulations implementing the act's registration provisions.[110] A month later, he petitioned the Subversive Activities Control Board for an order compelling the Communist Party to register under the act.[111] Truman had no occasion to invoke the emergency detention provisions of Title II; however, the Justice Department did implement these provisions to the extent of rehabilitating six World War II installations for use as detention camps should an internal security emergency be declared.[112]

The Immigration and Nationality Act of 1952

The second law that Truman unsuccessfully vetoed on constitutional grounds was the Immigration and Nationality Act of 1952.[113] His veto message of June 25, 1952, though based mainly on policy concerns, noted that "serious constitutional questions" were raised by provisions of the act dealing with children's loss of citizenship, denaturalization procedures, and judicial review of administrative denials of citizenship.[114] In addition, Truman objected under the "doctrine of the separation of powers" to a section requiring the secretary of state and the attorney general to provide any information requested by a new Joint Congressional Committee on Immigration and Nationality.[115]

The joint committee could not submit any requests to the Truman administration, since it did not begin to function until after Truman left office.[116] The act's other provisions took effect on December 24, 1952,[117] less than a month before Truman's term ended. Nevertheless, his administration immediately began to enforce the act.[118] Implementing regulations published on December 19, 1952, contained no caveats or references to the president's constitutional objections.[119] In early January, Truman advised Congress that enforcing the act had increased the Justice Department's expenses, necessitating a supplemental appropriation for 1953.[120] Though Truman urged Congress to amend or repeal the act,[121] there is no evidence that he failed to carry out its provisions.

RICHARD NIXON: THE WAR POWERS RESOLUTION

The War Powers Resolution of 1973, requiring the president to consult and notify Congress if U.S. military forces are introduced into situations that involve actual or imminent hostilities, became law on November 7, 1973, over President Richard Nixon's veto.[122] In his veto message of October 24, 1973, the president asserted that the resolution unconstitutionally sought "to take away, by a mere legislative act, authorities which the President has properly exercised under the Constitution for almost 200 years."[123] He also objected that a section allowing Congress to compel the withdrawal of armed forces by concurrent resolution "denies the President his constitutional role in approving legislation,"[124] for concurrent resolutions require approval by the House and Senate but not the president.

Shortly after the War Powers Resolution was enacted, the Nixon administration indicated that it would comply with the measure despite the president's constitutional objections. "The law is on the books," said a White House source, and "we may just have to live with it."[125] However, in the nine months remaining of his presidency, Nixon did not use the military in situations falling within the resolution's consultation or notification requirements. By the time the resolution became law, American troops had been withdrawn from Indochina and the U.S. bombing of Cambodia had ceased.[126] Members of Congress twice questioned the Nixon administration's compliance with the resolution in other settings. At issue were the July 1974 use of Navy helicopters to evacuate U.S. and foreign nationals from Cyprus, and the airdrop of supplies to Cambodian villages under siege by Communist forces. Congress ultimately accepted the administration's position that the reporting requirement was not triggered in either of these situations because the aircraft in question were unarmed and did not operate in hostile areas.[127] While the United States later employed armed forces to evacuate American personnel and foreign civilians from Cambodia and Vietnam, these operations occurred after Nixon had resigned from office.[128]

GERALD FORD: THE FREEDOM OF INFORMATION ACT

Among the changes made by the 1974 Freedom of Information Act amendments was a provision allowing federal courts to review de novo a government agency's claim that requested information is exempt from disclosure, the agency having the burden of proving that it had a right to withhold the records in question.[129] In a veto message issued on October 17, 1974, President Gerald Ford objected to this amendment as it applied to classified material. "Such a provision would violate constitutional principles," he said, for "a determination by the Secretary of Defense that disclosure of a document would endanger our national security would, even though reasonable, have to be overturned by a district judge who thought the plaintiff's position just as reasonable."[130] The president's veto was overridden on November 21, 1974.[131]

There was no way that Ford could have directly refused to honor this provision for it was addressed to the federal courts, not to the executive branch. Not until 1986, long after Ford left office, did an appellate court uphold on the merits a decision rejecting an agency's classification claim.[132] Thus, the Ford administration had no occasion to indirectly defy the provision by refusing to honor a court order compelling disclosure of classified material.

With perhaps one exception, American presidents during the period from 1789 to 1981 acted on the premise that once a bill is passed over their veto, the executive must honor the measure despite the president's constitutional misgivings. In a few of these cases, private parties were able to challenge the statute in court and obtain a judicial determination as to the law's validity.[133] Yet in many of these instances, the president implemented the statute even though the effect of doing so was that no one would have standing to secure a judicial ruling as to its constitutionality. This was true, for example, of the internal improvements bills opposed by Presidents Pierce, Arthur, and Cleveland. Had these presidents instead defied the law by refusing to spend the money in question, the states for whom the funds were intended might have challenged the executive's action in court. Yet even the fact that Congress would thus have the last word as to a statute's validity was not deemed by these presidents a sufficient reason to refuse to honor an allegedly unconstitutional law.

5

Signing Statements: Introduction

ALTERNATIVES TO THE VETO

The Founders created a system under which the executive was expected to veto unconstitutional measures approved by Congress. As we have seen, presidents have often adhered to this scheme. Yet the veto authority given the president by Article I is a crude instrument that must be applied to a bill in its entirety. The veto cannot be employed in a surgical fashion to excise only those portions of a bill the president finds objectionable. This all-or-nothing quality of the veto has been a source of presidential complaints for more than a century.[1] Where, as is frequently the case, a bill combines the desirable with the undesirable, the White House may face the difficult choice of either rejecting the entire package or accepting the bitter with the sweet.

These difficulties would disappear if presidents had the authority to veto selective portions of a bill while signing the rest of the measure into law. There have been many proposals over the years for amending the Constitution to give the president just such an item veto; some of these would have been limited to appropriations bills while others would have allowed a surgical veto with respect to bills of all types.[2]

Though none of these efforts to amend the Constitution has succeeded, the 1996 Line Item Veto Act gave the president a more flexible negative than he possesses under Article I.[3] This statutorily conferred authority allows the president to sign a bill into law but then cancel or rescind certain items in the statute. The authority conferred by the act is narrow in scope. It may be exercised only with respect to new appropriations items, new spending programs, and tax benefits that assist no more than 100 beneficiaries.[4] Congress can override the president's action by a two-thirds vote of each house.[5] Unless renewed by Congress, the authority granted by the Line Item Veto Act will expire on January 1, 2005,[6] although the courts may declare the act unconstitutional before that date.[7]

During the period covered by this study, 1789 to 1981, presidents enjoyed no statutorily conferred item veto authority. It is, therefore, not surprising that they sought other means of registering their constitutional objections to bills without having to veto the entire measure. Indeed, with growing frequency, presidents have chosen to approve such bills while at the same time issuing a statement that identifies the measure's perceived constitutional defects.

This use of signing statements has by no means supplanted the veto of allegedly unconstitutional bills. If the executive is opposed to a bill as a whole, or if its constitutional flaws are viewed as overriding, the president may still veto the measure and cite its constitutional difficulties as among the reasons for rejection. George Bush issued forty vetoes during his term in office, eleven on constitutional grounds.[8] Yet these eleven constitutionally based vetoes pale in comparison to the 116 bills that Bush approved despite constitutional objections that were spelled out in signing statements.[9]

From the president's standpoint, the all-or-nothing quality of the Article I veto, coupled with the lack (or limited scope) of a statutory item veto, render the signing statement a highly preferred option. Yet whether a constitutionally based signing statement will operate as a surgical veto ultimately turns on whether the president decides to honor or to ignore the statutory provision in question. Only where the constitutional objection is coupled with a presidential refusal to comply with the law does the signing statement become the equivalent of an item veto.

The balance of this chapter explores the evolution of presidential signing statements in general and their increasing use as a means of raising constitutional objections. While most so-called signing statements are issued at the time the president signs a bill into law, the term as used here also embraces statements issued after a bill is signed, as well as the occasional statement explaining why the president allowed a bill to become law without his signature. Chapters 6 and 7 will then examine the critical question of how presidents have dealt with laws to which they objected in signing statements: Did the chief executive honor the provisions despite his constitutional objections, or did he opt to defy the law?

THE EMERGENCE OF SIGNING STATEMENTS

The Constitution makes no mention of signing statements. Article I, section 7 states that if the president approves of a bill, "he shall sign it"; there is no indication that he is to offer any explanation for his action. Only where the chief executive elects to veto a measure does the Constitution provide that he set forth his reasons for doing so. Article I, section 7 thus states if the president does not approve a bill, "he shall return it, *with his Objections* to that House in which it shall have originated" (emphasis added).

In the early decades of the Republic, presidents seldom issued statements in connection with signing a bill. James Monroe twice issued statements, long after a bill became law, explaining his understanding of how the legislation should be implemented.[10] Actual signing statements were extremely rare. During the Constitution's first fifty years, only two such statements were issued, both by Andrew Jackson.[11] In 1842, when President John Tyler issued a statement expressing doubt about the validity of a bill he had just signed, Congress denounced his conduct as "a defacement of the public records and archives" and an "evil example for the future."[12] In 1848, James Polk apologized for issuing a signing statement, agreeing that while presidents customarily notified Congress upon signing a bill, "[t]he mode of giving this notification has been by an oral message by his private secretary."[13] Franklin Pierce was equally defensive about an 1854 signing statement, admitting that he had "deviate[d] from the ordinary course of announcing the approval of bills by an oral statement only."[14] As late as 1875, President Ullyses S. Grant acknowledged that his use of a signing statement was an "unusual method of conveying the notice of approval."[15]

Signing statements remained an anomaly well into the twentieth century. From 1789 until the Civil War, a total of only six such statements appeared. There was a slight surge during the Civil War and Reconstruction eras when Presidents Lincoln, Johnson, and Grant between them issued twelve such statements. From 1877 through 1900, only five signing statements appeared.[16] Signing statements were still an exception in the early 1900s: Theodore Roosevelt issued one,[17] and William Howard Taft issued but a few.[18]

By 1950, however, signing statements were a commonplace.[19] Harry Truman averaged almost sixteen signing statements a year.[20] As Table 5.1 indicates, the annual total has climbed steadily since that time. Gerald Ford and Jimmy Carter each averaged about sixty signing statements a year.[21] Carter holds the record for a single year, having issued ninety-two signing statements during his last year in office.[22] The annual rate fell to thirty-one during the Reagan years, but rose again to more than fifty under George Bush who issued eighty signing statements in 1992 alone.[23] During Bill Clinton's first term in office, the annual average declined but nonetheless remained at more than forty statements a year.[24]

The importance of signing statements today is also evident from the proportion of public laws that are now accompanied by such statements. In Harry Truman's day, signing statements were issued in connection with only 3.9 percent of the public laws enacted. By contrast, during Bill Clinton's first term in office, this figure reached an all-time high of 20.8 percent. While Truman used signing statements with respect to one in every twenty-five laws, Clinton issued them in connection with every fifth law.[25]

Presidents may issue signing statements for a variety of reasons. They sometimes play a purely political or ceremonial role, publicizing the enactment of a

Table 5.1
Presidential Signing Statements (1945–1997)

President	Signing Statements of All Types		Constitutionally-Based Signing Statements		
	Total	Annual Average	Total	Annual Average	As Percent of All Signing Statements
Truman (1945-53)	121	15.7	4	0.5	3.3%
Eisenhower (1953-61)	146	18.3	9	1.1	6.2%
Kennedy (1961-63)	37	12.8	1	0.3	2.7%
Johnson (1963-69)	171	33.5	9	1.8	5.3%
Nixon (1969-74)	146	26.1	9	1.6	6.2%
Ford (1974-77)	146	60.8	15	6.3	10.3%
Carter (1977-81)	229	57.3	30	7.5	13.1%
Reagan (1981-89)	247	30.9	87	10.9	35.2%
Bush (1989-93)	217	54.2	116	29.0	53.5%
Clinton (1993-97)	166	41.5	30	7.5	18.1%

Source: The data for Presidents Truman through Carter is drawn from the volumes of Public Papers of the Presidents of the United States covering their presidencies. The data for Presidents Reagan, Bush, and Clinton is drawn from the same series and from U.S. Code. Cong. & Admin. News volumes for 1981 through 1996, and from Weekly Comp. Pres. Docs. for 1981-97.

law and giving credit to those who were responsible for its passage.[26] Their political value in the eyes of the White House is suggested by the fact that there is usually a dramatic increase in signing statements in a re-election year. Richard Nixon issued forty-one signing statements in 1972, well above his average of twenty-six a year. Gerald Ford issued seventy-eight statements in 1976, more than twice his total in any prior year. Jimmy Carter averaged fifty-seven signing statements a year but released ninety-two in 1980. Ronald Reagan, who averaged thirty-one statements a year, issued forty-six in 1984. George Bush issued eighty signing statements in 1992, twenty more than his previous annual high. Bill

Clinton issued seventy-three signing statements in 1996, nearly two-and-a-half times his average for the previous three years.[27]

Signing statements may be issued for other reasons as well. In some instances, they identify policy shortcomings in a statute and urge the adoption of corrective legislation.[28] Presidents have also used them to promulgate their own interpretation of an ambiguous or controversial law, both as guidance for executive branch officials and with hope that the White House's views will be treated as part of the act's legislative history when the measure is later construed by the courts.[29] Ronald Reagan made extensive use of signing statements for this purpose. Indeed, in 1986, Attorney General Ed Meese arranged for presidential signing statements to be published in the "legislative history" section of *United States Code Congressional & Administrative News*,[30] triggering a vigorous debate as to the legitimacy of executive efforts to create legislative history.[31] Finally, signing statements may serve as a vehicle for expressing the president's constitutional disagreement with a law. These purposes are not mutually exclusive. Individual signing statements are frequently designed to promote a number of different goals.[32]

CONSTITUTIONALLY BASED SIGNING STATEMENTS

Since the end of World War II, signing statements have gradually emerged as the principal means for the White House to assert constitutional objections to acts of Congress. Prior to 1945, the number of signing statements raising constitutional issues was negligible. From 1789 to 1945, only fifteen constitutionally based statements were issued—an average of about one every decade.[33] As Table 5.1 reveals, from early 1945 through the end of Nixon's presidency in 1974, constitutionally based signing statements appeared at the rate of about one a year—ten times the previous rate.[34]

Since 1975, the frequency of such statements has jumped even further. During the Ford and Carter years, the number rose to between six and eight a year. The upward trend continued under Ronald Reagan who averaged eleven constitutionally based signing statements a year. His total of eighty-seven constitutionally based signing statements[35] nearly equaled that of all his predecessors combined: Presidents from George Washington through Jimmy Carter issued ninety-two constitutionally based signing statements, only five more than Reagan's individual total. During the next four years, George Bush almost tripled Reagan's annual output, averaging twenty-nine constitutionally based signing statements a year—a rate of more than one every two weeks. The rate fell during Bill Clinton's first term to 7.5 per year, the same frequency as during the Carter years. Yet even at the reduced Carter-Clinton rate, constitutionally based signing statements still appeared once every seven weeks, in marked contrast to the one-per-decade rate that prevailed before 1945.

The extent to which signing statements have become a vehicle for raising constitutional objections is further evidenced by the fact that between 1945 and

1974, the proportion of all signing statements that rested on constitutional grounds ranged between 3 and 6 percent. As Table 5.1 indicates, this figure has risen dramatically since the mid-1970s. The zenith may have been reached under George Bush when 53 percent of all signing statements were constitutionally based. During Bush's last two years in office, signing statements were used to raise constitutional objections to one out of every ten public laws that emerged from Congress.[36] Though the use of such statements declined during Clinton's first term in the White House, they were still far more prevalent than in the period prior to 1975.

THE CONSTITUTIONAL GROUNDS FOR OBJECTION

During the period from 1789 to 1981, presidents employed signing statements to challenge the constitutionality of a total of ninety-two different statutes. These statutes are identified in Table 5.2, broken down by the type of constitutional objection involved. If a president objected to more than one distinct provision in a statute, the statute will appear several times in the table. As a result, Table 5.2 contains 101 entries even though only ninety-two statutes were involved.[37]

Table 5.2 divides these statutes into three broad categories, based on whether the president's objection was one of federalism, separation of powers, or individual rights. For these purposes, *federalism* means that the statute allegedly exceeded the scope of the national government's powers or intruded on the rights of the states; *separation of powers* indicates that Congress aggrandized its own powers or encroached on the powers of another branch; and *individual rights* means that the law impaired the constitutional rights of individuals. Table 5.2 further subdivides each of these three categories based on the specific nature of the objection.

As Table 5.2 shows, the most frequent ground for objection was separation of powers. This formed the basis for 84 of the 101 constitutional objections raised, representing 83 percent of the total. In virtually every one of these cases, Congress was alleged to have usurped or intruded upon the authority of the president. More than half of the separation of powers objections involved "legislative veto" provisions giving one or both houses of Congress, or designated congressional committees, the right to approve or disapprove actions taken by the executive branch. Presidential claims that a law violated individual rights made up 11 percent of the objections, while federalism was the issue in only 6 percent of the cases.

Table 5.2 also indicates the nature of the president's response to each of the statutory provisions whose validity was objected to in a signing statement. The record of executive compliance or noncompliance with these laws is explored in the next two chapters.

Table 5.2
Statutes Objected to in Signing Statements: Grounds for Objection and Nature of President's Response (1789–1981)

PRESIDENT	DATE AND CITATION OF STATUTE	PRESIDENT'S RESPONSE[a]
FEDERALISM (6)		
Exceeds scope of National Power (2)		
Jackson	May 31, 1830, ch. 232, 4 Stat. 427	NO OCCASION
Cleveland	Aug. 2, 1886, ch. 840, 24 Stat. 209	COMPLIED
Intrudes Upon Other Rights of States (4)		
Tyler	June 25, 1842, ch. 47, 5 Stat. 491	NO OCCASION
A. Johnson	July 24, 1866, Res. No. 73, 14 Stat. 364	NO OCCASION
A. Johnson	Mar. 2, 1867, ch. 170, §6, 14 Stat. 485, 487	NO OCCASION
Nixon	June 22, 1970, PL 91-285, 84 Stat. 314, 318	COMPLIED
SEPARATION OF POWERS (84)		
Appointment and Removal Power (8)		
Arthur	Jan. 16, 1883, ch. 27, 22 Stat. 403, 404	DISREGARDED
Nixon	Aug. 15, 1970, PL 91-379, 84 Stat. 796-98	COMPLIED
Nixon	Nov. 16, 1973, PL 93-153, §404, 87 Stat. 576, 590	NO OCCASION
Nixon	Nov. 16, 1973, PL 93-153, §405, 87 Stat. 576, 590	COMPLIED
Ford	Oct. 23, 1974, PL 93-463, 88 Stat. 1389, 1390	DISREGARDED
Ford	Dec. 20, 1975, PL 94-158, 89 Stat. 844	AVOIDED
Ford	Jan. 2, 1976, PL 94-201, 89 Stat. 1129, 1130	COMPLIED
Carter	Dec. 12, 1980, PL 96-515, 94 Stat. 2987, 2998-99	DISREGARDED
Members of Congress Holding Other Office (2)		
Ford	Oct. 20, 1975, PL 94-118, 89 Stat. 603, 604	DISREGARDED
L. Johnson	Oct. 8, 1964, PL 88-638, §1(10), 78 Stat. 1035, 1036	COMPLIED
Commander-in-Chief (7)		
Buchanan	June 25, 1860, ch. 211, 12 Stat. 104, 106	DISREGARDED
A. Johnson	Mar. 2, 1867, ch. 170, §2, 14 Stat. 485, 486-87	COMPLIED
L. Johnson	Sept. 12, 1966, PL 89-568, 80 Stat. 739, 757	COMPLIED
L. Johnson	Apr. 4, 1967, PL 90-8, 81 Stat. 8, 9	COMPLIED
L. Johnson	Oct. 21, 1967, PL 90-110, §809, 81 Stat. 279, 309	COMPLIED
L. Johnson	Oct. 21, 1967, PL 90-110, §1001, 81 Stat. 279, 310	COMPLIED

Table 5.2 (*continued*)

PRESIDENT	DATE AND CITATION OF STATUTE	PRESIDENT'S RESPONSE[a]
Power to Pardon (1)		
Carter	Aug. 2, 1977, PL 95-86, 91 Stat. 419, 444[b]	DISREGARDED
Conduct of Foreign Relations (10)		
Grant	Aug. 15, 1876, ch. 288, 19 Stat. 170, 175	COMPLIED
Wilson	June 5, 1920, ch. 250, 41 Stat. 988, 1007	DISREGARDED
Truman	Sept. 6, 1950, ch. 896, 64 Stat. 595, 758	COMPLIED
Eisenhower	Aug. 2, 1955, ch. 491, 69 Stat. 435	COMPLIED
Eisenhower	July 31, 1956, ch. 803, 70 Stat. 733-34	COMPLIED
Eisenhower	Aug. 8, 1956, ch. 1036, 70 Stat. 1119, 1123	COMPLIED
Eisenhower	July 29, 1958, PL 85-568, 72 Stat. 426, 432	DISREGARDED
Ford	Apr. 13, 1976, PL 94-265, 90 Stat. 331, 339-40	AVOIDED
Carter	Aug. 17, 1977, PL 95-108, 91 Stat. 871-72	COMPLIED
Carter	Aug. 15, 1979, PL 96-60, §108, 93 Stat. 395, 397	DISREGARDED
Legislative (and Committee) Veto: Disapproval Power (32)		
Eisenhower	July 13, 1955, ch. 358, 69 Stat. 301, 321	COMPLIED
Eisenhower	Aug. 6, 1956, ch. 972, 70 Stat. 1044, 1045	AVOIDED
Eisenhower	Aug. 6, 1959, PL 86-137, 73 Stat. 280, 282	AVOIDED
Eisenhower	July 14, 1960, PL 86-648, 74 Stat. 504	NO OCCASION
Kennedy	Oct. 23, 1962, PL 87-872, 76 Stat. 1163, 1164	COMPLIED
L. Johnson	July 17, 1964, PL 88-379, 78 Stat. 329, 331	AVOIDED
L. Johnson	Oct. 8, 1964, PL 88-638, §1(8), 78 Stat. 1035, 1036	COMPLIED
Nixon	Aug. 5, 1974, PL 93-365, 88 Stat. 399, 408	NO OCCASION
Ford	Aug. 21, 1974, PL 93-380, 88 Stat. 484, 545	NO OCCASION
Ford	May 26, 1975, PL 94-25, 89 Stat. 90, 91	COMPLIED
Ford	Aug. 9, 1975, PL 94-88, 89 Stat. 433, 436-37	NO OCCASION
Ford	May 11, 1976, PL 94-283, 90 Stat. 475, 477	COMPLIED
Ford	June 30, 1976, PL 94-329, 90 Stat. 729, 743	NO OCCASION
Ford	Sept. 14, 1976, PL 94-412, 90 Stat. 1255	NO OCCASION
Ford	Oct. 15, 1976, PL 94-502, 90 Stat. 2383, 2397-98	NO OCCASION
Carter	July 27, 1977, PL 95-75, 91 Stat. 308	NO OCCASION
Carter	Aug. 4, 1977, PL 95-92, 91 Stat. 614, 622-23	NO OCCASION
Carter	Dec. 28, 1977, PL 95-223, 91 Stat. 1625, 1628	NO OCCASION
Carter	Mar. 10, 1978, PL 95-242, 92 Stat. 120, 123	NO OCCASION
Carter	Sept. 18, 1978, PL 95-372, 92 Stat. 629, 641, 668	NO OCCASION
Carter	Oct. 5, 1978, PL 95-421, 92 Stat. 923, 925-26	NO OCCASION
Carter	Oct. 6, 1978, PL 95-424, 92 Stat. 937, 956	NO OCCASION
Carter	Aug. 15, 1979, PL 96-60, §408, 93 Stat. 395, 405-06	NO OCCASION
Carter	Mar. 5, 1980, PL 96-199, 94 Stat. 67, 73	NO OCCASION
Carter	May 23, 1980, PL 96-247, 94 Stat. 349, 352-53	NO OCCASION

Table 5.2 (*continued*)

PRESIDENT	DATE AND CITATION OF STATUTE	PRESIDENT'S RESPONSE[a]
Carter	May 28, 1980, PL 96-252, 94 Stat. 374, 393-96	NO OCCASION
Carter	Aug. 29, 1980, PL 96-332, 94 Stat. 1057	NO OCCASION
Carter	Oct. 17, 1980, PL 96-464, 94 Stat. 2060, 2067	NO OCCASION
Carter	Dec. 12, 1980, PL 96-515, 94 Stat. 2987, 3004	NO OCCASION
Carter	Dec. 16, 1980, PL 96-533, 94 Stat. 3131, 3136, 3142	NO OCCASION
Carter	Dec. 17, 1980, PL 96-539, 94 Stat. 3194, 3195	NO OCCASION
Carter	Dec. 24, 1980, PL 96-592, 94 Stat. 3437, 3449-50	NO OCCASION
Legislative (and Committee) Veto: Approval Power (12)		
Truman	July 5, 1949, ch. 296, 63 Stat. 405, 406	COMPLIED
L. Johnson	Dec. 31, 1963, PL 88-257, 77 Stat. 844, 847	COMPLIED
L. Johnson	Oct. 13, 1964, PL 88-643, 78 Stat. 1043	COMPLIED
L. Johnson	Oct. 27, 1965, PL 89-298, 79 Stat. 1073	AVOIDED
Nixon	May 27, 1972, PL 92-306, 86 Stat. 163, 175	AVOIDED
Nixon	June 16, 1972, PL 92-313, 86 Stat. 216, 217, 220	COMPLIED
Nixon	July 9, 1973, PL 93-66, 87 Stat. 152, 158-59	COMPLIED
Ford	Feb. 9, 1976, PL 94-212, 90 Stat. 153, 161-62	COMPLIED
Ford	June 30, 1976, PL 94-330, 90 Stat. 771, 773-74	COMPLIED
Carter	Sept. 30, 1978, PL 95-405, 92 Stat. 865, 877	NO OCCASION
Carter	Nov. 10, 1978, PL 95-625, 92 Stat. 3467, 3549	COMPLIED
Carter	Sept. 8, 1980, PL 96-342, 94 Stat. 1082-83	AVOIDED
Recommending Measures to Congress (2)		
Taft	Aug. 23, 1912, ch. 350, 37 Stat. 360, 415	DISREGARDED
L. Johnson	Sept. 7, 1966, PL 89-556, 80 Stat. 689, 690	COMPLIED
Executive Privilege (2)		
Eisenhower	July 24, 1959, PL 86-108, 73 Stat. 246, 253-54	AVOIDED
Nixon	Nov. 18, 1969, PL 91-120, 83 Stat. 203	COMPLIED
Execution of Laws and Supervisory Power (8)		
Wilson	June 23, 1913, ch. 3, 38 Stat. 4, 53	AVOIDED
F. Roosevelt	June 17, 1944, ch. 262, 58 Stat. 280	NO OCCASION
F. Roosevelt	June 17, 1944, ch. 262, 58 Stat. 280, 281-82	COMPLIED
Nixon	Dec. 18, 1973, PL 93-190, 87 Stat. 736-37[c]	NO OCCASION
Carter	Dec. 9, 1977, PL 95-205, 91 Stat. 1460-61	COMPLIED
Carter	Oct. 1, 1980, PL 96-369, 94 Stat. 1351, 1356	COMPLIED
Carter	Dec. 12, 1980, PL 96-515, 94 Stat. 2987, 2999	NO OCCASION
Carter	Dec. 12, 1980, PL 96-516, 94 Stat. 3007	NO OCCASION

Table 5.2 (*continued*)

PRESIDENT	DATE AND CITATION OF STATUTE	PRESIDENT'S RESPONSE[a]
RIGHTS OF INDIVIDUALS (11)		
Punishment for Treason (1)		
Lincoln	July 17, 1862, ch. 195, 12 Stat. 589	AVOIDED
Bill of Attainder (3)		
F. Roosevelt	July 12, 1943, ch. 218, 57 Stat. 431, 450	COMPLIED
Truman	June 29, 1948, ch. 754, 62 Stat. 1112, 1126	COMPLIED
Truman	May 12, 1949, ch. 101, 63 Stat. 67	COMPLIED
First Amendment (5)		
Ford	Oct. 15, 1974, PL 93-443, 88 Stat. 1263-64	COMPLIED
Carter	Nov. 2, 1978, PL 95-567, 92 Stat. 2405	DISREGARDED
Carter	Nov. 10, 1978, PL 95-629, 92 Stat. 3635, 3636-39	DISREGARDED
Carter	Jan. 8, 1980, PL 96-187, 93 Stat. 1339, 1367	NO OCCASION
Carter	Dec. 24, 1980, PL 96-593, 94 Stat. 3452	NO OCCASION
Due Process (1)		
Hoover	Mar. 23, 1932, ch. 90, 47 Stat. 70-71	NO OCCASION
Equal Protection (1)		
Carter	Oct. 8, 1977, PL 95-126, 91 Stat. 1106	COMPLIED

If in a signing statement the President objected to more than one distinct provision of a statute, the statute appears more than once in this table. As a result, while Presidents during this period issued 92 constitutionally-based signing statements, there are 101 entries in this table.

a. The following terms are used in this column of the table:

"Avoided" indicates the President was able to avoid the allegedly unconstitutional provision by securing its prompt repeal or amendment, or by lawfully bypassing it;

"Complied" indicates the President complied with the allegedly unconstitutional provision;

"Disregarded" indicates the President disregarded the allegedly unconstitutional provision by failing to honor or enforce it;

"No occasion" indicates the President had no occasion to honor or ignore the provision because the Executive was not required to take any action with respect to it, the President left office before an opportunity to respond to the law arose, or the provision did not otherwise come into play during the balance of the President's term.

b. Carter also asserted that the statute constituted a bill of attainder and that it denied due process.

c. Non-signing statement explaining why President allowed bill to become law without his signature.

6

Signing Statements: Acquiescence, Avoidance, and Compliance

As we saw earlier in reviewing constitutionally based vetoes, it is one thing for a president to assert that a law is unconstitutional, and quite another for him to actually ignore it. The same distinction has held true with respect to signing statements. Of the 92 statutes and 101 distinct statutory provisions whose validity was challenged in presidential signing statements between 1789 and 1981, only 12 statutory provisions were disregarded by the president. (See Table 5.2.) In the remaining cases—involving 80 statutes and 89 statutory provisions—the chief executive: (1) had to acquiesce in the measure because there was no occasion to defy it; (2) found a legal way to avoid the provision; or (3) honored the statute despite his constitutional objections.

COMPELLED ACQUIESCENCE

In more than a third of the cases where presidents used signing statements to challenge the validity of a statute, circumstances beyond the president's control forced him to acquiesce in the contested law. Thus, in 37 of the 101 cases involved, presidents had no choice but to accept the statutory provision despite its claimed invalidity. In the righthand column of Table 5.2, these cases appear as "No Occasion." In some of these instances, the law was such that the president had no role to play in its execution. In other cases, the president either left office shortly after the law was enacted or the provision simply never came into play during the balance of the president's term.

No Presidential Role in Executing a Law

Most federal laws require implementation by the president or by someone else within the executive branch. Yet, occasionally, a law is such that the executive plays no role in its execution. This was true of five statutory provisions to which presidents took constitutional objection in signing statements. In each of these cases, the president never faced the issue of whether to honor or defy the law in question.

The first such instance involved an 1842 signing statement by President John Tyler in which he expressed doubt that Congress could constitutionally require states to establish single-member districts for electing Representatives to Congress.[1] Since Article I, section 5 provides that "[e]ach House shall be the Judge of the Elections, Returns and Qualifications of its own Members," there was nothing Tyler could do if the House of Representatives refused to seat persons not elected from single-member districts.

Andrew Johnson objected to the constitutionality of two statutory provisions that he had no role in enforcing. The first was an 1866 joint resolution "restoring Tennessee to her relations in the Union."[2] Johnson disagreed with statements in the resolution concerning Congress's claimed authority to decide when a state is entitled to representation in the House and the Senate.[3] Yet, since Article I, section 5 gives Congress the discretion to admit or continue to exclude a state's chosen representatives, Johnson realized that there was nothing he could do in connection with the measure. The following year, Johnson issued a signing statement attacking the constitutionality of a law that ordered all militia forces in the former Confederate states disbanded and that barred their reorganization without Congress's approval.[4] Since this provision operated directly on the states, the President had no responsibility in connection with its enforcement.

Another instance of compelled acquiescence involved the Norris-LaGuardia Act of 1932.[5] When President Herbert Hoover signed the act, he released a letter from his attorney general noting that the act might be unconstitutional because it prohibited federal courts from enforcing "yellow dog contracts" in which employees agreed not to belong to a labor union.[6] Because this part of the statute was addressed to the federal courts, there was nothing the president could have done to block its implementation.

The final case in which a president had no role to play in implementing an allegedly unconstitutional law involved a 1973 statute that authorized a federal court to hear suits brought by the Senate Select Committee on Presidential Campaign Activities. President Richard Nixon allowed the bill to become law without his signature but issued a non-signing statement declaring that the measure gave Congress enforcement "authority which properly resides exclusively in the executive branch."[7] Implementation of the statute, however, rested entirely with the Senate and with the federal courts.

President Left Office Shortly after Law Was Passed

On nine occasions, the president was forced to acquiesce in an allegedly unconstitutional law because he left office shortly after the measure was passed and before any action could be taken in connection with it. The first of these concerned a bill permitting the House or the Senate to terminate the attorney general's authority to parole certain refugees into the United States.[8] President Dwight D. Eisenhower signed the measure in July 1960 but challenged the validity of the one-House veto provision.[9] This veto could be exercised only after the attorney general had submitted a report to Congress, which was not due until January 15, 1961; each House then had ninety days in which to interpose a veto. Since Eisenhower left the White House on January 20, 1961, it was virtually impossible for Congress to invoke the challenged provision during the balance of his term in office.

Time also ran out for Richard Nixon who, on August 5, 1974, issued a signing statement challenging, on separation of powers grounds, a provision allowing Congress by concurrent resolution to override presidential decisions authorizing certain exports.[10] Nixon resigned the presidency four days later before Congress could take action under the disputed provision.

In October 1976, three months before he left office, Gerald Ford signed a veterans' education bill. The measure would terminate in five years unless, by June 1, 1981, the president recommended an extension and neither the House nor the Senate disapproved that recommendation within sixty days.[11] Though Ford objected that this one-House veto provision was unconstitutional and "a nullity,"[12] the provision would not be triggered, if at all, until years after his presidency had ended.

Jimmy Carter left the White House before six laws to which he constitutionally objected could come into play. One of these was a funding bill for the National Science Foundation for the 1981 fiscal year. The bill was accompanied by congressional committee reports directing the foundation to take certain actions. Carter issued a signing statement on December 12, 1980, objecting that "committee reports are not law and should not be treated as though they were."[13] However, Carter left the White House January 20, 1981, well before the 1981 fiscal year began. Another Carter-era measure amended the National Labor Relations Act to provide that workers who conscientiously opposed joining or supporting labor unions did not have to do so. In a signing statement dated January 2, 1981, Carter warned that the law might violate the Establishment Clause, but in the three weeks that remained of his presidency, little could be done in response to the provision.[14] Finally, between December 12 and December 24, 1980, Carter issued signing statements objecting to legislative veto provisions contained in four different laws.[15] Congress adjourned on December 16, 1980, with the result that the disputed veto authority was not exercised before Carter left office.

Provision Not Triggered During President's Term

Even when a president did not leave office shortly after registering his objection to a statute, there were many occasions when the disputed measure did not come into play during his term; therefore, the president never had to confront the issue of whether or not to comply with the law.

Of the twenty-three such cases between 1789 and 1981, all but five involved legislative veto provisions through which Congress reserved to one or both of its houses, or to specified congressional committees, the right to approve or veto actions taken by the executive branch. In 1983, the Supreme Court ruled that the legislative veto was unconstitutional,[16] but for decades before this, presidents had objected that the device violated the principle of separation of powers, as well as Article I, section 7's bicameralism and presentment requirements.[17]

All of the legislative vetoes at issue here involved Presidents Ford and Carter. Ford objected to such provisions in four statutes,[18] and Carter protested their inclusion in fourteen statutes.[19] In none of these cases did the executive agree in advance to comply with a veto. Nor was the provision triggered during the president's term in office. Either no veto was exercised by the House, the Senate, or the specified committee, or the executive took no action requiring approval from these congressional bodies.

Though these legislative veto provisions were not triggered during the president's term of office, they may nonetheless have had an impact on the executive branch. For even if no formal veto or approval action was taken by Congress, the executive often treated the provision as a ''report-and-wait'' requirement, delaying any action on its part until Congress had an opportunity to consider the matter. As Jimmy Carter explained to Congress in 1978, where legislative vetoes are included ''in bills I must sign for other reasons, the Executive Branch will generally treat them as 'report-and-wait' provisions. In such a case, if Congress subsequently adopts a resolution to veto an Executive action, we will give it serious consideration, but we will not, under our reading of the Constitution, consider it binding.''[20]

There were five other instances, not involving legislative vetoes, in which a president objected to the constitutionality of a measure that did not come into play during his term in office. One of these was an internal improvements bill passed during Andrew Jackson's administration. Jackson objected to an item appropriating $8,000 ''[f]or continuing the road from Detroit to Chicago.'' He signed the bill ''with the understanding that the road authorized by this section is not to be extended beyond the limits of the [Territory of Michigan].''[21] Jackson's signing statement did not specify that his concern was constitutional, but his veto of the Maysville Road Bill three days earlier made clear his view that Congress had authority to fund internal improvements only in the territories and not within the limits of a state.[22] In the case of the Chicago Road, however, it seems that Jackson's concern was premature, for it was not until several years after this appropriation was spent that the road reached the boundary between the Michigan Territory and the State of Indiana.[23]

Franklin Roosevelt objected in a 1944 signing statement to the validity of a provision in the Elk Hills Oil Bill requiring an authorization from Congress through a joint resolution before the executive could allow production from the government's naval petroleum reserves.[24] On the same day this statute was enacted, Congress approved and Roosevelt signed a joint resolution that authorized such production until December 1, 1945.[25] Thus, the challenged provision was effectively suspended beyond April 1945 when Roosevelt's presidency ended.

On November 16, 1973, President Richard Nixon signed a bill that required Senate confirmation of the incumbent director of the Office of Energy Policy John A. Love.[26] In a signing statement, Nixon asserted that the director occupied such an "intimate staff relationship" that the president must be able to select him without Senate intervention. Moreover, he said, Congress cannot impose new confirmation requirements on incumbent officers.[27] The constitutional issues posed by this provision were mooted by Love's resignation on December 3, 1973, before the Senate could confirm or reject him. Had the president sought to replace Love, the provision would have come into play, but Nixon instead abolished the Office of Energy Policy and replaced it with a new Federal Energy Office.[28]

In January 1980, Jimmy Carter issued a signing statement objecting to an amendment to the Federal Election Campaign Act that barred federal workers from contributing to their employers' campaigns even if the contribution was voluntary.[29] Carter, backed by his attorney general, asserted that the prohibition violated the First Amendment rights of federal workers and urged that it be promptly repealed or amended.[30] The statute nevertheless remained on the books. Carter never said that he would not enforce the provision while it was in effect. I found no evidence that any prosecutions were brought under the statute during Carter's remaining year in office, though this may have been because no violations occurred during that time. This is one of the few cases where I was unable to determine how the president responded to an allegedly unconstitutional law. In the absence of any evidence of defiance, the case is treated here as one in which the president had no occasion to enforce the measure though research may one day reveal that this was not the case.

The final statutory provision that was not triggered during the term of the president who challenged its validity also involved Jimmy Carter. In mid-December 1980, he issued a signing statement challenging a law that allowed the Advisory Council on Historic Preservation to conduct litigation on its own behalf.[31] Carter left office a month and a half after signing this bill. There is no evidence that during this brief period the council sought to litigate on its own rather than with the Justice Department.[32]

AVOIDANCE THROUGH REPEAL OR BY-PASS

Not every instance where the executive lacked occasion to enforce a disputed law was foreordained. A president who would prefer not to enforce a statute he thinks unconstitutional but who is uncomfortable with the idea of ignoring the law may be able to escape this dilemma by adopting a middle course. During the period from 1789 to 1981 there were ten such cases; they are marked "Avoided" in the far right column of Table 5.2.

Amendment or Repeal of the Offending Provision

One means of avoidance is for the president to persuade Congress to amend or repeal the provision in question. Many signing statements asserted that the White House would seek corrective action from Congress, but the very fact that the provision was adopted in the first place suggests that such efforts will often be ineffectual. Yet in a few cases, involving Presidents Lincoln, Eisenhower, Nixon, and Carter, the White House secured prompt legislative action curing the perceived constitutional defects in bills the president had signed.

President Lincoln had planned to veto the Second Confiscation Act, which passed Congress in July 1862. His principal objection was that the act provided for the forfeiture of rebel property beyond the life of the guilty party, in violation of Article III, section 3. However, the president worked closely with Congress and secured a joint resolution that explained that the act should not "be so construed as to work a forfeiture of the real property of the offender beyond his natural life." Lincoln signed the act and the joint resolution on the same day. What had been drafted as a proposed veto message instead became a signing statement.[33]

Though Lincoln holds the record for the fastest amendment of a constitutionally objectionable law, President Eisenhower ranks a close second. On August 6, 1959, Eisenhower signed a bill concerning the Tennessee Valley Authority but objected to the validity of a provision giving Congress a legislative veto over certain TVA projects. The president explained that he was approving the bill with the understanding that "legislation will be passed swiftly by both Houses deleting this objectionable feature."[34] Eight days later, Eisenhower signed into law an amendment that removed the legislative veto provision.[35]

Eisenhower also took advantage of the amendment route with respect to a 1959 bill that required the executive, upon request from either the General Accounting Office or a congressional committee, to furnish information concerning the International Cooperation Administration and the State Department's Office of the Inspector General and Comptroller.[36] In signing the bill, Eisenhower objected that if the measure were deemed to mandate disclosure under all circumstances, it would violate "the recognized Constitutional duty and power of the Executive with respect to the disclosure of information"; accordingly, the President said he would read the statute as requiring "the fullest possible information consistent with the public interest.''[37] Although Eisenhower did not specifically ask that the law be amended, his objection led Congress to relax the disclosure requirement for the balance of his presidency. Appropriations acts covering the 1960 and 1961 fiscal years gave the president a choice of either furnishing the requested information or certifying that he had forbidden the disclosure.[38] Eisenhower invoked the certification option three times.[39] On the last of these occasions, in December 1960, the comptroller general—an agent of Congress—ruled that despite the certification, Eisenhower had no right to refuse disclosure of information about the State Department. The comptroller general accordingly advised the State Department that some of its funding would be terminated.[40] Yet as the attorney general noted, the president had complied with the law by issuing the requisite certification.[41] Eisenhower proceeded to ignore the comptroller general and directed that the State Department's funding continue uninterrupted for the month that remained of his presidential term.[42] This was not a case where the president had defied an allegedly unconstitutional law, for the law in question had been modified by the two appropriations acts to meet the president's constitutional objections.

In 1972, President Nixon signed a bill appropriating funds for the construction of three federal buildings but objected to the constitutionality of a ''coming into agreement'' provision that allowed the money to be spent only after the executive obtained approval from the House and Senate Public Works Committees.[43] Nixon promised to obtain a repeal of this provision. Six weeks later he signed such an amendment into law.[44]

President Carter also secured the repeal of a provision that he had approved despite constitutional misgivings. The statute in issue allowed the secretary of defense to waive certain limits on the percentage of military recruits who had low test scores but only if the waiver was approved by concurrent resolution of Congress.[45] In a signing statement issued in September 1980, Carter objected to this two-house legislative veto and advised the secretary of defense to treat it as a report-and-wait provision.[46] Less than a month later, Congress eliminated the constitutional difficulty by amending the act so as to delete the waiver provision.[47]

By-passing the Contested Provision

In other cases, instead of obtaining amendment or repeal of an allegedly unconstitutional law, presidents found a way to by-pass the disputed provision without engaging in conduct that amounted to noncompliance. One of these involved a $300,000 appropriation to cover the Justice Department's enforcement of the antitrust laws during the 1914 fiscal year. The statute contained a proviso barring any use of the funds to prosecute labor unions, workers, or farmers.[48] President Wilson signed the bill but suggested that this attempt by Congress to interfere with the executive's enforcement of the law was unconstitutional. Wilson noted, however, that because the statute only restricted the use of a "single small additional fund," it would not "in fact limit the opportunity or the power of the Department of Justice to prosecute violations of the law, by whomsoever committed."[49] In fact, during the 1914 fiscal year, it appears that several antitrust prosecutions were initiated against coal miners, but there is no evidence that the Wilson administration spent any of the restricted funds for this purpose.[50]

Gerald Ford was able lawfully to by-pass a 1975 statute that assigned executive functions to the Federal Council on the Arts and the Humanities. Under the statute, four of the council's members were not appointed in accord with Article II, section 2, and, contrary to Article I, section 6, one could be a member of Congress.[51] In a signing statement objecting to these provisions, Ford noted that another law allowed him to alter the council's membership. He immediately exercised this authority by ordering that when the council performed executive functions, the members in question could not participate.[52]

In the legislative veto context, presidents were sometimes able to circumvent the veto provision by not engaging in the conduct for which congressional approval was required. In August 1956, President Eisenhower signed a bill authorizing the secretary of the interior to provide federal assistance for small reclamation projects in the western United States.[53] In doing so, the president declared that the measure was unconstitutional insofar as it gave two congressional committees the power to block execution of contracts made by the secretary. Eisenhower warned that unless this legislative veto provision was deleted the secretary would not enter into any contracts under the act.[54] No such contracts were made until Congress had amended the law in June 1957 to remove the committee veto.[55] During this ten-month interval, Eisenhower by-passed the act but without defying its terms. He was not guilty of impounding funds, since the 1956 statute merely authorized an appropriation; Congress did not actually appropriate funds for the projects until August 1957,[56] nor did the secretary's failure to enter into contracts violate the act, for the statute gave him discretion in this matter.

Lyndon Johnson adopted a similar strategy with respect to a legislative veto provision in the 1964 Water Resources Research Act.[57] In a signing statement, Johnson objected to a provision of the act that barred the secretary of the interior from funding any project under Title II that was disapproved by either of two congressional committees.[58] While the act authorized up to $1 million a year to be spent on these projects, no funds had been appropriated, and Johnson ordered the secretary not to request any. Congress might have amended the president's budget to include such funding,[59] but it failed to do so. As a result, Johnson did not begin implementing Title II until after Congress amended the statute in 1966 to delete the committee approval requirement.[60]

Johnson later used the same approach to steer clear of a legislative veto clause written into the Flood Control Act of 1965.[61] In a signing statement, he challenged a requirement that House and Senate committees approve every project the army wished to undertake. Johnson sidestepped the provision by ordering the secretary of the army not to exercise his authority under the act until Congress deleted the provision.[62] Congress failed to amend the statute, with the result that as of late 1968, this part of the act had still not been implemented.[63] The president's action did not amount to a refusal to comply with the law, however, for the act authorized but did not direct the army to pursue these projects. Moreover, the act was so worded as not to appropriate any funds until after a proposal had been approved by the committees,[64] thus precluding a charge that the president had impounded funds that Congress had directed him to spend.[65]

COMPLIANCE

In the situations we have been examining, the president did not face a choice between honoring and defying an allegedly unconstitutional law. Instead, he was either compelled to acquiesce in the disputed provision or was able to avoid a confrontation by having the law repealed or by finding a lawful means of bypassing it. These cases of acquiescence or avoidance account for 47 of the 101 statutory provisions that were the basis for constitutionally based signing statements. In the remaining 54 cases, presidents confronted the issue of whether or not to comply with the law. In 42 of these cases—or 78 percent of the time—the president chose to honor the law despite his constitutional reservations. The balance of this chapter examines these cases of compliance; they are marked "Complied" in Table 5.2. The next chapter will explore the twelve instances where presidents defied a law to which they had objected in a signing statement.

Compliance Coupled with Other Means of Resolution

In many cases where the president honored an allegedly unconstitutional law, he at the same time sought to resolve the problem in other ways. In some instances, the White House took steps to have the constitutional issue resolved by the courts. In other instances, the chief executive asked Congress to amend the law in question, sometimes submitting an administration bill to this effect.

Obtaining Judicial Resolution

On at least five occasions, the executive complied with a law while seeking a judicial ruling as to its validity. The first of these involved Franklin Roosevelt who, in July 1943, approved an urgent deficiency appropriations bill that contained a rider prohibiting the government, after November 15, from continuing to employ three particular individuals.[66] In mid-September, Roosevelt issued a post-signing statement charging that the rider was a bill of attainder in violation of Article I, section 9 and explaining that he had approved the measure only "to avoid delaying our conduct of the war."[67] While Roosevelt complied with the act, he made sure that the men would have standing to challenge it in court.[68] When they later filed suit, the Justice Department refused to defend the validity of the act, a task that fell to Congress participating as amicus curiae. After the Court of Claims found for plaintiffs without reaching the constitutional issue,[69] the Justice Department took the case to the Supreme Court where the attorney general successfully argued that the rider was unconstitutional.[70]

President Nixon turned to the courts to vindicate his constitutional opposition to the Voting Rights Act Amendments of 1970, which lowered the voting age to eighteen in federal, state, and local elections.[71] In a signing statement, Nixon announced that he had "directed the Attorney General to cooperate fully in expediting a swift court test of the constitutionality of the 18-year-old provision."[72] In order to produce a test case, the administration immediately undertook to enforce the law despite Nixon's opposition to the measure.[73] By the end of August, four cases involving the constitutionality of the amendments had been filed directly with the Supreme Court.[74] Although the Nixon Justice Department defended the act, its efforts were "lackluster and unenthusiastic."[75] At oral argument, Solicitor General Erwin Griswold informed the justices that both the president and the attorney general thought the voting rights amendments were unconstitutional, adding that even in his own mind their validity was "a very close question."[76] Nixon's efforts met with partial success. The Court held that the Voting Rights Act amendments were unconstitutional insofar as they purported to lower the voting age in state and local elections.[77]

Two of the other instances where presidents complied with a law while attempting to have its constitutionality determined by the courts involved Gerald Ford. In October 1974, Ford signed a bill that amended the Federal Election Campaign Act but which continued the act's limitations on individual contributions and candidate expenditures.[78] The president believed that the act might violate the First Amendment but expressed confidence that "such issues can be resolved in the courts."[79] When a suit was brought challenging the act's constitutionality, the Justice Department defended the measure despite the administration's doubts as to its validity.[80] The Supreme Court partially sustained Ford's position by holding that some of the expenditure limitations were unconstitutional.[81]

The same 1974 Federal Election Campaign Act amendments contained a one-house legislative veto provision to which Ford did not initially object when he signed the measure into law.[82] During 1975 and 1976, his administration frequently honored the provision, submitting proposed Federal Election Commission regulations to Congress where some of them were vetoed by the House or Senate.[83] Yet when the veto was carried over by the Federal Election Campaign Act Amendments of 1976,[84] Ford objected that it was unconstitutional. He instructed the attorney general "to challenge the constitutionality of this provision at the earliest possible opportunity."[85] The administration did so by having the United States intervene as a plaintiff in a suit that former Attorney General Ramsey Clark had brought against various defendants, including the Federal Election Commission, attacking the legislative veto provision.[86] However, the president failed to secure a judicial resolution of the issue for the case was dismissed on the ground that it was not ripe.[87]

Jimmy Carter also turned to the judiciary to determine the validity of a 1977 appropriations rider curtailing the Department of Health, Education, and Welfare's (HEW) authority to enforce Title VI of the 1964 Civil Rights Act.[88] Though Carter expressed doubts as to the restriction's constitutionality,[89] his administration complied by settling or dismissing administrative proceedings that HEW had brought against local school districts to compel busing.[90] When the provision was challenged in court the Justice Department, apparently satisfied that the case against its constitutionality would be argued capably by the plaintiffs, vigorously and successfully defended the provision.[91]

Encouraging Amendment or Repeal

In at least eight cases, presidents complied with an allegedly unconstitutional law while urging Congress to amend or repeal the provision in question. These were not situations in which the president was thereby able to avoid the question of compliance, for even if the law was eventually amended or repealed, there was a lengthy interim during which executive action was required.

The earliest of these cases involved an 1867 law barring the president from issuing military orders except through the General of the Army who was not to be removed, suspended, or assigned outside of Washington without prior approval from the Senate.[92] In a signing statement, Andrew Johnson protested that this restriction "deprives the President of his constitutional functions as Commander in Chief of the Army."[93] After the provision had been enacted, Johnson urged Congress that it be repealed.[94] Though one of the articles of impeachment voted by the House accused Johnson of *planning* to circumvent this command-of-the-army provision, there is no evidence that he actually violated it.[95]

In 1886, Grover Cleveland issued a signing statement in connection with a law taxing and regulating oleomargarine. He noted that parts of the measure might "interfere with the police powers of the States" and urged "an immediate amendment of the bill" if Congress agreed that the president's constitutional concerns were well founded.[96] When no amendment was forthcoming, the president saw to it that the statute was promptly enforced.[97]

Harry Truman sought the repeal of three statutory provisions that he had objected to as being unconstitutional. The first two involved riders to appropriations bills for fiscal year 1949. The riders sought to force the removal of two men from their positions with the Bureau of Reclamation by prohibiting the government from paying their salaries.[98] The men had drawn the wrath of special interests by vigorously enforcing laws that promoted family-size farms. In signing statements, Truman declared that the provisions amounted to unconstitutional bills of attainder.[99] Though he honored the laws by terminating the men's salaries, they continued to work for the bureau. In the meantime, Truman launched a campaign that resulted in Congress omitting a similar rider from the

1950 appropriations bill and in the passage of a law awarding the men back pay for 1949.[100]

Truman also urged repeal of part of a 1949 law that required the executive branch to have its printing done at the Government Printing Office unless a joint committee of Congress approved having the work done elsewhere.[101] In a signing statement, the president objected that the provision violated the principle of separation of powers by allowing "a committee of Congress [to] administer Executive functions"; he indicated that while he would comply with the law he would also recommend new legislation to "maintain the proper respective roles of the executive and the legislative branches."[102] It is unclear whether Truman sent such a proposal to Congress but if he did, the measure failed. Though the committee approval requirement remained the law throughout Truman's presidency,[103] there is no evidence that he failed to honor the provision.

Lyndon Johnson sought the repeal of two provisions in a 1966 law continuing the Food for Peace Program. One of the provisions gave House and Senate committees veto authority over executive actions involving foreign currency; the other required approval by an advisory committee composed partly of members of Congress before the president could make low-interest loans.[104] In a signing statement, Johnson complained that these provisions "represent a clear violation of the constitutional principle of separation of powers."[105] The administration submitted proposed legislation to cure these perceived defects, and in 1966, Congress amended the act to eliminate both requirements.[106] During the more than two years that the provisions were in effect, the Johnson administration appears to have complied with them to the complete satisfaction of Congress.[107]

Richard Nixon urged Congress to repeal or amend two statutes that contained what he believed were unconstitutional provisions. One of these created a Cost Accounting Standards Board as an "agent of Congress" with authority to impose binding standards on executive agencies.[108] Nixon objected that to vest these functions in a board that was independent of the executive violated separation of powers. He asked Congress to enact an amendment "to place the functions of the Board in the executive branch."[109] The administration introduced a bill to this effect, but it was not approved. Nixon nevertheless complied with the provision by cooperating fully with the board.[110]

President Nixon also sought the repeal of committee approval requirements contained in a law governing the lease and purchase of public buildings.[111] In a signing statement charging that the requirements were unconstitutional, he directed the General Services Administration (GSA) "to submit appropriate legislation to the Congress to eliminate the unconstitutional language."[112] The statute was not amended during Nixon's tenure in office. The GSA complied with the provision by submitting numerous projects for review by the House and Senate Public Works Committees.[113] There is no evidence that the GSA ever proceeded with a project without the committees' approval.

Simple Compliance

On most occasions when a president honored a statute with which he had taken constitutional issue in a signing statement, the administration complied with the law without seeking a ruling from the courts or remedial legislation from Congress. Nearly all of these cases involved a presidential objection involving some aspect of separation of powers although one dealt with individual rights.

President's Conduct of Foreign Affairs

There were seven instances of compliance with laws that allegedly violated separation of powers because they intruded on the president's authority to conduct foreign affairs. The earliest of these involved Ulysses S. Grant, who signed an 1876 appropriations act for the consular and diplomatic service but objected that one provision ordering the closure of certain diplomatic and consular offices was "an invasion of the constitutional prerogatives and duty of the Executive."[114] In his annual message to Congress in December 1876, Grant reported that he had immediately complied with the act by instructing U.S. representatives in the designated countries "to close their respective legations and consulates."[115]

Harry Truman likewise objected to a statutory provision on the ground that it impaired his authority to conduct diplomatic relations. The provision, part of a 1950 appropriations bill, required the government to lend Spain $62.5 million.[116] Truman, who strongly opposed the Franco regime, issued a statement that he would treat the provision as merely an authorization.[117] Newspapers read the president's objection to mean that the Spanish loan would not be made,[118] but within a few months, the administration agreed to lend Spain the full $62.5 million.[119]

Dwight Eisenhower twice took issue with congressional directives that foreign aid be extended to particular countries in specified amounts. In 1955, he approved an appropriations bill that mandated "at least" $50 million in aid to Spain and "not less than" $26.2 million to Greece, for the 1956 fiscal year.[120] In a signing statement, Eisenhower said that to construe these as directives rather than authorizations "would raise substantial Constitutional questions."[121] Yet the administration extended aid to Spain and Greece in amounts that satisfied the statutory criteria.[122] The same problem arose the next year with respect to a law specifying minimum amounts of aid for Spain and for Guatemala.[123] Though Eisenhower again balked at treating these as directives,[124] his administration honored the statute.[125]

Eisenhower also objected to the constitutionality of a law that required Interior Department officials to be included in the U.S. delegation to any international conference relating to fish and wildlife.[126] He explained that this requirement impaired "the authority of the President of the United States to conduct negotiations with other governments through agents designated by him or at his direction''; however, Eisenhower nonetheless agreed to comply with the provision because it seemed sensible.[127]

In 1976, Congress expressed its frustration with the slow pace of negotiations at the U.N. Law of the Sea Conference by ordering the administration to seek international recognition of a 200-mile fishery conservation zone by entering into bilateral treaties and agreements.[128] In a signing statement, Gerald Ford objected that this law ''encroach[ed] upon the exclusive province of the Executive relative to matters under international negotiations.''[129] Yet the administration promptly complied with the statute. By January 1977, it had signed agreements with seven countries recognizing the 200-mile fishery conservation zone.[130]

Jimmy Carter expressed concern that a 1977 arms control statute could interfere with the president's authority to conduct negotiations without interference from Congress. However, as he explained in a signing statement, the law gave Congress no role in or control over the negotiations, for it merely required the executive to report to Congress, something Carter agreed to do.[131] There is no indication that the administration reneged on its promise to respect the statute's reporting requirement.

President's Role as Commander in Chief

Lyndon Johnson honored five statutory provisions, contained in three different laws, that allegedly violated separation of powers by impairing his authority as commander in chief of the armed forces. The first of these was a 1966 law requiring that the Department of Defense notify Congress before it closed or abandoned any military base and that it then delay action until Congress had been in session for thirty continuous days.[132] In a signing statement, Johnson noted that the lengthy waiting period could undermine his ''responsibilities as President and Commander in Chief'' but suggested that he would comply with it and seek a ''revision of the restriction if future circumstances prove it to be inimical to the national interest.''[133] There is no evidence that the administration failed to honor the provision.

Johnson also objected on commander-in-chief grounds to a post–Vietnam War statute that sought to prevent the Department of Defense from deactivating three Air National Guard and eight Air Force Reserve groups.[134] The president contended that the law, which required these services to be kept at existing strength, deprived him of needed flexibility as commander in chief.[135] The administration nonetheless honored the provision and promptly sought additional funds from Congress to maintain the eleven groups it had planned to scrap.[136]

In 1967, Lyndon Johnson signed a military authorization bill containing three provisions that raised separation of powers concerns because of their alleged impact on his authority as commander in chief.[137] One of these barred the government from closing or disposing of any of the lands that constituted Fort DeRussy in Hawaii except pursuant to an act of Congress.[138] Despite Johnson's objection, the administration honored this prohibition.[139]

Johnson objected to another section of the same 1967 act that prohibited the Defense Department from selling the Naval Academy's dairy farm in Annapolis.[140] Pressure to close the dairy came from local milk producers who wished to supply the academy's dairy needs themselves.[141] In an objection that bordered on the frivolous, Johnson claimed that separation of powers questions were raised because "Congress, which has given the Navy Department authority over the world's most powerful fleet, has withdrawn the Department's authority over 380 cows."[142] However, the administration nevertheless respected the statute's ban by abandoning its plans to sell the dairy farm.[143]

A third provision of the 1967 act required that the Defense Department maintain the existing number of naval districts in the United States and that each district be commanded by an officer of no lower rank than rear admiral.[144] Even before the act cleared Congress, the department dropped its plan to reorganize the naval districts and urged that the statutory restriction was thus unnecessary. There is no evidence that the administration thereafter failed to honor the directive.[145]

Legislative Veto or Approval Provisions

One of the most frequent constitutional objections raised in signing statements dealt with statutes imposing legislative veto or approval requirements. As we saw earlier, these provisions were often not triggered during the objecting president's term in office. Yet in those cases where the provisions did come into play, the president almost always complied with them.

In 1955 Dwight Eisenhower signed a defense appropriations bill but objected to a section giving two committees of Congress a veto over Defense Department plans to discontinue military operations of a commercial nature and transfer them to the private sector.[146] Eisenhower declared the provision "an unconstitutional invasion of the province of the Executive" and stated that it "will be regarded as invalid . . . unless otherwise determined by a court of competent jurisdiction."[147] However, his administration in fact respected the provision. It submitted more than fifty proposals to the two committees and indicated that it would not implement any that were disapproved.[148]

Lyndon Johnson took issue with part of a 1963 statute that required the approval of two House and Senate committees before the Panama Canal Company could dispose of any interest in real property.[149] The measure was enacted after President John F. Kennedy and the president of Panama announced plans to transfer some of the company's property to Panama in order to alleviate pressures to nationalize the canal.[150] I found no evidence that the company transferred any interest in real property to Panama without the committees' approval during Johnson's presidency.

The 1964 CIA Retirement System Act contained a provision insisting that certain regulations of the Central Intelligence Agency (CIA) be approved by the chairmen and ranking minority members of the House and Senate Armed Services Committees before they could take effect.[151] President Johnson objected that the provision, which gave four members of Congress authority to veto actions of the executive branch, was in "violation of the principle of separation of powers."[152] Notwithstanding the president's objections, the CIA submitted proposed regulations to the committees and refrained from issuing them until it had received approval from the designated committee members.[153]

On July 9, 1973, Richard Nixon signed a law postponing the effective date of certain regulations issued by the Department of Health, Education, and Welfare. The regulations were to have taken effect July 1, 1973, but the new law delayed them until November 1st, unless an earlier implementation date was approved by two congressional committees.[154] Nixon objected that the committee approval requirement violated separation of powers.[155] However, HEW complied with the provision and postponed the effective date of the regulations until November 1, 1973.[156]

Gerald Ford objected to but honored several legislative veto provisions. The first was contained in a 1975 statute dealing with Amtrak, the National Railroad Passenger Corporation, and allowed either the House or the Senate to disapprove proposed route or service changes.[157] Ford noted in a signing statement that the "provision provides for an unconstitutional exercise of Congressional power,"[158] but Amtrak officials agreed to submit the proposed changes to Congress and to abide by its wishes.[159]

The following year, President Ford objected to part of an appropriations bill that required approval from several House and Senate committees before the army could build or modernize an ammunition plant for the production of certain artillery shells.[160] The army wished to build a new plant in Texarkana, Texas, but some members of Congress instead favored expanding an existing plant in St. Louis.[161] Ford said that because the approval requirement was unconstitutional he would treat it "as a complete nullity."[162] Though army officials likewise denied that formal committee approval was necessary, the army complied with the provision by submitting its proposal for the new plant and agreeing not to proceed until the committees could review it. When opposition later surfaced in one of the committees, the army decided to delay the plant's construction indefinitely.[163]

President Ford also took issue with a committee approval requirement that applied to certain federal expenditures dealing with the government's foreign assistance programs.[164] Ford rejected the proposition that congressional committees could exercise such authority but agreed to work with them "in a spirit of cooperation" and to "keep the Congress fully informed on a current basis on the execution of the laws."[165] The restriction was in effect for only ninety days. I found no evidence that the administration took any action inconsistent with the provision during this brief period.

Other Separation of Powers Concerns

Presidents raised a variety of other separation of powers objections to laws with which they ultimately complied. In 1944, Franklin Roosevelt objected to provisions in the Elk Hills Oil Bill compelling the secretary of the navy to consult with the House and Senate Naval Affairs Committees before condemning lands around the Elk Hills Naval Petroleum Reserve or entering into any contracts or leases pertaining to it.[166] Although the provision did not require the secretary to obtain the committees' approval, Roosevelt objected on the ground that the Constitution ''vest[ed] authority to carry out the laws in an independent executive and not in legislative committees.''[167] It is likely that Roosevelt honored the consultation requirement, for a short time earlier, his administration had agreed to comply with a similar law requiring the navy to secure approval from the same committees before it acquired or disposed of real property.[168]

Another separation of powers objection dealt with the president's Article II, section 3 power to recommend to Congress ''such measures as he shall judge necessary and expedient.'' Lyndon Johnson on this basis took issue with a statutory provision that barred him from proposing a budget for fiscal 1968 that included more than $15 million for agricultural research funded from certain sources.[169] Johnson asserted in a signing statement that the ''provision clearly intrudes upon the Executive function of preparing the annual budget.''[170] However, the budget that he submitted to Congress for fiscal 1968 scrupulously honored the restriction by recommending that ''not to exceed $15 million'' be spent on such agricultural research.[171]

Richard Nixon invoked the doctrine of executive privilege to object to part of a 1969 law requiring the director of the National Science Foundation (NSF) to keep two congressional committees ''fully and currently informed with respect to all of the activities of the [Foundation].''[172] The provision, which applied only to the 1970 fiscal year, did not reflect any dissatisfaction with the NSF's past reporting behavior,[173] nor is there anything in the committee reports indicating that it did not continue to keep them fully informed during fiscal 1970.[174] That the NSF probably complied with the provision is further suggested by the fact that Congress dropped the reporting requirement from the authorization act for the following year.[175]

Several presidents objected to but implemented statutory provisions that allegedly interfered with their Article II, section 2 power to appoint federal officers. Richard Nixon took issue with a 1973 law requiring the incumbent head of the Mining Enforcement and Safety Administration, James M. Day, to be confirmed by the Senate, although it allowed Day to continue serving until he was disapproved by the Senate.[176] The president charged that the provision ''raises constitutional difficulties because of the way it affects incumbent executive officials.''[177] Yet he complied with the measure by renominating Day and sending his name to the Senate.[178] Day was confirmed by the Senate but not until after Nixon had left office.[179]

Gerald Ford had Appointments Clause concerns with a law that created an American Folklife Center in the Library of Congress. The law provided for a Board of Trustees, some of whom were not appointed in a manner that accorded with Article II, section 2. In particular, eight of the trustees were to be named by members of Congress, an option not sanctioned by Article II.[180] In a signing statement, Ford expressed "serious reservations concerning the constitutional propriety" of the provision but indicated that he would go along with it "given historical practice and custom in the area of cultural and educational affairs and the potential of [the law] to enrich the cultural life of the Nation."[181]

In October 1980, Jimmy Carter signed an appropriations bill that contained a provision precluding the secretary of education prior to June 1981 from adopting or enforcing guidelines under Title VI of the 1964 Civil Rights Act to prevent discrimination against students with limited proficiency in English.[182] Carter objected that it was "inappropriate for the Congress to interpose itself between the courts and a Cabinet officer on this matter."[183] At the time the law was enacted, the secretary had already published proposed regulations, with public comments due by October 20, 1980.[184] In February 1981, however, the secretary announced that "[i]n light of the public comment regarding the proposed rules," they were being withdrawn.[185] Although the withdrawal was not said to be in response to Congress's directive, the administration complied with the statutorily mandated delay.

Individual Rights

All of the cases of simple compliance that we have discussed so far involved some aspect of separation of powers. However, there was one instance in which a president complied with a law that allegedly violated the constitutional rights of individuals. This involved a 1977 statute concerning eligibility for veterans benefits of those who had received less-than-honorable discharges but whose discharges were later upgraded. Many of these veterans had served in Vietnam and had been upgraded under a Special Discharge Review Program created by Jimmy Carter shortly after he became president. In October 1977, Congress passed a law denying automatic benefit eligibility to upgraded veterans who had been absent without leave for more than 180 days; these individuals could receive veterans benefits only if they showed "compelling circumstances" for their absence.[186] In a signing statement, Carter objected that "serious equal protection problems" were created by treating these upgraded veterans differently from others.[187] However, he complied with the provision. In April 1978, the Veterans Administration issued final regulations that implemented the 180-day ban on automatic benefit eligibility.[188]

Involuntary Compliance

Compliance with laws to which the president had objected was not always intentional. The president and the Office of Legal Counsel, which advises him concerning the constitutionality of all enrolled bills, have an interest in protecting executive authority and in preserving principles of separation of powers. Yet these abstract interests are not always shared by executive branch officials and agencies whose effective operation usually depends on maintaining good relations with Congress and its committees.[189] As a result of this tension between the president and lower-level officials, there may be occasions when the White House's attempt to defy an allegedly unconstitutional law is thwarted by subordinates in the executive branch. This occurred at least twice during the period from 1789 to 1981. Both cases involved legislative veto provisions that agency officials may have been reluctant to ignore for fear of congressional reprisal. As political scientist Louis Fisher has noted, ''Although the President may treat [such provisions] as having no legal force or effect, agencies have a different attitude. They have to live with their review committees, year after year, and have a much greater incentive to make accommodations and stick by them. Presidents and their legal advisors can indulge in confrontations with Congress on these issues. Agencies cannot risk these types of collisions with the committees that authorize their programs and provide funds.''[190]

The first of these instances arose from a January 8, 1963, memorandum in which President Kennedy, on the attorney general's advice, objected to the constitutionality of a committee veto provision in a law that he had signed the previous October.[191] In this post-signing statement, Kennedy instructed David E. Bell, head of the Agency for International Development to whose actions the veto applied, that Bell should treat the provision as a mere ''request for information'' by the congressional committees.[192] The agency nevertheless complied with the provision during the 1963 fiscal year when it was in effect. The agency did so, said Bell, because ''the Comptroller General gave an opinion that it was in the act, unconstitutional or not, and we had to abide by it as long as it was in the act.''[193] It is unclear whether Kennedy ever learned that this executive agency decided to ignore his instructions and the advice of the attorney general in favor of a conflicting legal opinion issued by the comptroller general, an agent of Congress.

President Carter was similarly frustrated when he attempted to ignore a two-house legislative veto provision contained in the 1978 National Parks and Recreation Act. One section of the act required the Department of Agriculture to obtain House and Senate approval in the form of a concurrent resolution before making land exchanges exceeding 6,400 acres in Montana's Gallatin-Beaverhead National Forest.[194] Carter's November 10, 1978, signing statement noted that both he and the Justice Department thought the section was unconstitutional. Carter directed the secretary of agriculture to listen to the views of Congress but to ''consummate any land exchanges . . . which are, in his opinion, otherwise authorized by statute, irrespective of the acreage involved.''[195] Senator John Melcher of Montana, who had sponsored this legislative veto provision, took the unprecedented step of appealing the president's action to the Justice Department and persuaded it that ''in spite of the President's direction, the Department [of Agriculture] and the Forest Service should cooperate with him and the Congress in processing these land exchanges.''[196] The Justice Department then advised the Department of Agriculture that, as a matter of policy, it could elect to comply with the two-house veto provision. On November 22, ten days after Carter had issued his directive to the contrary, the Agriculture Department ordered the Forest Service "to proceed as if [the section] were applicable, that is, that proposed exchanges exceeding 6,400 acres would have to be approved by concurrent resolution of Congress."[197] Seeing the writing on the wall, the Forest Service suspended all further consideration of the proposed land exchanges.[198]

This completes our discussion of the eighty-nine statutory provisions whose validity presidents challenged in signing statements but which the White House did not defy. In thirty-seven of these cases, the president never faced the issue of whether or not to comply with the disputed provision, either because the law gave the executive no role in its enforcement, the president left office, or the provision for some other reason did not come into play during the balance of the president's term. In ten of the eighty-nine cases, the president avoided a choice between compliance and defiance by securing a prompt repeal or amendment of the law, or by finding a lawful way to by-pass it. In the remaining forty-two cases, the president complied with the provision notwithstanding his constitutional objections. In nearly a third of these cases of compliance, the president also sought to bring the issue of the law's validity before the courts or to have the measure repealed. In the other twenty-nine cases, the executive complied with the law without taking any other action, though on several occasions the compliance appears to have occurred contrary to the president's wishes.

7

Signing Statements: Noncompliance

Between 1789 and 1981 there were twelve instances where the president failed to comply with a law whose constitutionality he had objected to in a signing or post-signing statement. As Table 7.1 shows, two-thirds of these incidents occurred in the last half of the twentieth century, and most of them (seven out of the twelve) did not take place until after 1973. To put it differently, from 1789 through 1973, executive noncompliance occurred on the average of once every thirty-six years, whereas between 1974 and 1981 it became an annual event. To the extent that there is now a developed a practice of presidents refusing to comply with laws based on constitutional objections raised in signing statements, it is a practice of extraordinarily recent vintage.

This chapter will explore each of these twelve episodes. In doing so, one of the things to be considered is the extent to which a president's defiance of the law was subject to check by either Congress or the courts. While every presidential refusal to carry out the law raises serious concerns, the dangers of defiance are mitigated if the executive's action can have no effect without the affirmative cooperation of Congress, or if there are people who have standing to challenge the president's action in court. In either of these cases, the other branches may be able to prevent the president from suspending a law that he claims is unconstitutional.

The doctrine of standing has evolved over time.[1] In its current form, a litigant will generally have standing to bring a suit in federal court if: (1) the litigant has suffered a present or imminently threatened injury; (2) the injury was caused by the government conduct being challenged; (3) the injury is likely to be redressed by a judgment in the litigant's favor; and (4) the litigant is asserting his

Table 7.1
Presidential Noncompliance with Laws to Which President Had Constitutionally Objected in a Signing Statement (1789–1981)

President	Statute	Nature Of Objection
Buchanan	Act of June 25, 1860, ch. 211, 12 Stat. 104, 106	Requiring Washington Aqueduct to be completed only under the supervision of Captain Meigs violates President's authority as Commander in Chief.
Arthur	Act of Jan. 16, 1883, ch. 27, 22 Stat. 403, 404	Chief Examiner of Civil Service Commission is an officer of the U.S. and cannot be chosen by Commission but must be appointed in accord with Article II.
Taft	Act of Aug. 23, 1912, ch. 350, 37 Stat. 360, 415	President has constitutional right to submit additional budget information to Congress in any form he chooses.
Wilson	Act of June 5, 1920, ch. 250, 41 Stat. 988, 1007	Congress may not direct that President terminate treaties.
Eisenhower	Act of July 29, 1958, Pub. L. No. 85-568, 72 Stat. 426	President may enter into executive agreements without the approval of the Senate.
Ford	Act of Oct. 23, 1974, Pub. L. No. 93-463, 88 Stat. 1389, 1390	Senate may not participate in the appointment of executive branch officials who are not appointed by the President.
	Act of Oct. 20, 1975, Pub. L. No. 94-118, 89 Stat. 603, 604	Members of Congress may not participate as voting members on a federal commission.
Carter	Act of Aug. 2, 1977, Pub. L. No. 95-86, 91 Stat. 419, 444	Congress may not prohibit the executive branch from spending funds to implement a presidential pardon.
	Act of Nov. 2, 1978, Pub. L. No. 95-567, 92 Stat. 2405	Federal ban on editorializing by public broadcasting stations violates the First Amendment.
	Act of Nov. 10, 1978, Pub. L. No. 95-629, 92 Stat. 3635, 3636-39	Establishment Clause prohibits government from spending money to restore and maintain the San Antonio Missions.
	Act of Aug. 15, 1979, Pub. L. No. 96-60, §108, 93 Stat. 395, 397	Congress may not direct the President to close certain U.S. Consulates abroad.
	Act of Dec. 12, 1980, Pub. L. No. 96-515, 94 Stat. 2997, 2988	Congress may not name members of an advisory council that performs executive functions.

or her own legal rights rather than the rights of someone else.[2] These abstract standing principles will become clearer as the doctrine is discussed in the context of specific cases.

JAMES BUCHANAN: THE CAPTAIN MEIGS AFFAIR

In June 1860, Congress appropriated $500,000 to complete the Washington Aqueduct, an Army Corps of Engineers project that was to carry water from the Great Falls of the Potomac to the cities of Washington and Georgetown. The measure specified that the funds were "to be expended according to the plans and estimates of Captain Meigs, and under his superintendence."[3] President James Buchanan signed the bill on June 25, but issued a statement objecting to the proviso that the monies had to be spent under the supervision of Montgomery C. Meigs, the army captain who had designed the aqueduct and who had overseen its construction from the outset. Because the proviso interfered with his authority as commander in chief, said Buchanan, he would treat it merely as an expression of Congress's "preference" and not as "intending to deprive the President of the power to order [Meigs] to any other army duty for the performance of which he might consider him better adapted."[4]

On September 1, 1860, after a long simmering quarrel between Meigs and Secretary of War John B. Floyd forced the president to choose between the two men, Meigs was relieved of his duties and sent to the Dry Tortugas in the Gulf of Mexico.[5] In February 1861, after Floyd had resigned from the Cabinet, Meigs returned to Washington to resume charge of the aqueduct project. During his six months' absence, the army paid out more than $150,000 of the funds Congress had insisted be spent only under Meigs's personal superintendence.[6]

In choosing to ignore this statutory provision, Buchanan was supported by his attorney general, Jeremiah S. Black, who advised the president that the Meigs proviso was unconstitutional because it deprived the commander in chief of the "right to decide according to [his] own judgment what officer shall perform any particular duty."[7] The attorney general added that if the president wished, he could spend the aqueduct funds and ignore the Meigs proviso "as if the paper on which it is written were blank."[8] By following this advice, Buchanan defeated the statute's purpose of forcing the president to spend the money under Meigs' supervision or not spend it at all.[9]

The Meigs proviso had not placed Buchanan in a situation where he was forced to either defy an act of Congress or surrender his perceived constitutional authority as commander in chief. Instead, Congress had left him with the option of not undertaking work on the aqueduct during the time Captain Meigs was not its supervisor. This alternative was not as unrealistic as it might seem. The administration had not requested funding for the aqueduct project in 1860. Congress appropriated the money at Meigs' request, for the captain feared that without further work in the Washington area, Secretary Floyd might carry out threats to send him to a distant post. Not only did Meigs initiate the appropriation, but it was also his idea to include the proviso that the funds must be spent under his supervision.[10] The project was thus not a priority with the administration. Since Congress had not insisted that the money be spent, the president's failure to do so would not have constituted a refusal to enforce the law through impoundment.[11]

Was Buchanan's action defensible on the basis that defiance constituted the only way to secure a judicial determination as to the act's validity? Although the president never sought to justify his conduct on this basis, if Buchanan had honored the proviso by spending the funds under Meigs's direction, it is doubtful that anyone would have suffered an injury sufficient to give them standing to challenge the measure in court. On the other hand, it was not clear that the prospects for judicial review would be enhanced by noncompliance. While Meigs was upset at being sent to the Tortugas, he suffered no legal injury as a result. The transfer did not cause a reduction in his pay or rank, nor did the act give him a right to remain in Washington. Congress had recognized the president's authority to transfer Meigs and simply provided that if he were shipped elsewhere, the money was not to be spent. Meigs thus lacked standing to challenge Buchanan's action. The president's conduct caused no injury to anyone else who could have challenged his action in court. Buchanan would therefore have been hard pressed to invoke the test-case defense.

Yet as things turned out, the president's defiance might have been subjected to judicial review. This possibility arose from the fact that when Meigs returned to Washington in February 1861, he refused to pay $5,600 in claims for work that had been performed on the aqueduct during his absence, on the theory that the contracts were void because they were made in violation of the law.[12] Those holding these claims could have sued in the Court of Claims, contending that because the statutory proviso was unconstitutional, their contracts with the government were valid and enforceable. If any such suits were filed, they were mooted by the act of June 14, 1862, passed at Meigs's request, that authorized payment of all the outstanding claims.[13]

CHESTER A. ARTHUR: APPOINTING THE CHIEF EXAMINER

When Congress created the U.S. Civil Service Commission in January 1883, it provided for the position of a chief examiner to be hired by the commission.[14] President Chester A. Arthur signed the bill without objection on January 16, but on March 1, he sent a message to the Senate objecting to the manner in which the chief examiner was to be chosen. Due to the nature of the position, said Arthur, "There is great doubt whether such examiner is not properly an officer of the United States," in which case allowing him to be named by the commission "is not in conformity with section 2, Article II of the Constitution."[15] Article II, section 2 states that officers of the United States must be appointed by the president with the advice and consent of the Senate, unless Congress vests the appointment "in the president alone, in the Courts of Law, or in the Heads of Departments." Arthur noted that his attorney general shared his concerns about this law.[16] Yet the attorney general cautioned Arthur against seeking to resolve the matter himself. "The question," he said, "is one which can not be settled by executive action. Whether the functions or duties and powers of the chief examiner constitute him an officer of the United States in the sense of the Constitution, is one that can only be authoritatively determined by the courts. But should the doubt appear well founded, it may be worthy of your consideration whether it is expedient to call the attention of Congress thereto."[17] The president ignored this advice. While he did bring the matter to Congress's attention, his March 1 message to the Senate defied the statutory procedure by "nominat[ing] Silas W. Burt, of New York, to be chief examiner of the Civil Service Commission."[18] When Burt promptly declined the post, Arthur named Edward O. Graves in his place.[19]

President Arthur's decision to ignore this allegedly unconstitutional law was in itself harmless, for it could have no effect unless the Senate acquiesced by confirming Graves. Had the Senate refused to do so it would have prevented the president from defying the law, clearing the way for the commission to make the appointment. Instead, on March 3, 1883, the Senate confirmed Arthur's nominee, at the same time passing a resolution declaring that "the Senate neither assent to nor dissent from the constitutional views concerning the appointment of an examiner, communicated by the president in his message of March 1, and consider its present action as affording no precedent for the future."[20] While the Senate may have avoided setting a precedent concerning the constitutional status of the chief examiner, it seems to have been unaware of the larger issue at stake, that is, whether the president may ignore a law whenever he believes it to be unconstitutional.

This was not a case where defiance was necessary in order to create the possibility of judicial review. Indeed, the attorney general had urged Arthur that the matter be resolved judicially rather than through executive action. This might have occurred had the president honored the statute and allowed the Civil Service Commission to appoint a chief examiner. The attorney general could then have instituted quo warranto proceedings to determine whether the appointment was one that the Constitution permitted Congress to place in the hands of the commission.

By taking the course he did, Arthur made it all but impossible to test the law in court. Once the Senate confirmed the president's nominee, the only person with standing to raise the constitutional issue would have been someone appointed chief examiner by the commission. If the government refused to pay the commission's appointee for services rendered, he or she could have sued in the Court of Claims, forcing a decision as to which appointee—the president's or the commission's—was entitled to the post. This improbable scenario never came about, no doubt because the civil service commissioners appointed by the president were unwilling to challenge the chief executive in this way. Though the Senate might have prevented it, the result was that the president had the last word as to the constitutionality of this law.

WILLIAM HOWARD TAFT: THE PRESIDENTIAL BUDGET

In his last week of office, President William Howard Taft refused to honor a law that prohibited him from submitting a national budget to Congress. Earlier, Taft had appointed a Commission on Economy and Efficiency whose final report, "The Need for a National Budget," was issued in June 1912.[21] The commission recommended that instead of having each executive department submit its own budget figures directly to Congress, they should report to the president who would then prepare and submit a coherent national budget.[22] Taft forwarded this report to Congress, urging that the law be amended to adopt the suggested procedure. Yet even without such an amendment, said Taft, he was constitutionally entitled to require that information be submitted to him in such form as he wished and to send Congress "a definite well-considered budget, with a message calling attention to subjects of immediate importance."[23] Taft instructed each department to prepare two sets of budget estimates, "one in accordance with the present practise and one substantially in accordance with . . . the report of the Commission."[24] Congress responded by adding a rider to a pending appropriations bill, directing that budget estimates be submitted "only in the form and at the time now required by law, and in no other form and at no other time."[25]

Taft signed this measure in August 1912. Six months later, he defied the prohibition by sending Congress both a national budget and budget figures in the form required by law. He defended his action on the basis that the Constitution places a duty on the president to send Congress " 'a regular statement and account of the receipts and expenditures,' " and to make such recommendations to Congress as " 'he shall judge necessary and expedient.' "[26]

The president's refusal to comply with this law could have no impact without the affirmative approval of Congress. While there was some additional expense in having executive departments prepare budget data both for the White House and for Congress, the statute did not prohibit the president from obtaining this information; it merely regulated the manner in which the material was to be sent to Congress.[27] The legislators were apparently concerned that Taft might propose lower levels of funding for certain projects in their districts than was sought in the departments' own budget estimates.[28] Yet no harm could result from the president's separate recommendations unless Congress chose to go along with them. The legislators were free to ignore Taft's model budget, as they ultimately did.[29]

With respect to judicial review, had the president complied with the ban by not submitting his own budget, it is unlikely that anyone would have had standing to challenge the statute's validity in court. To be sure, if Taft had desired more funding for some agency than was sought in the departmental estimates, but had declined to ask Congress for this due to the statutory prohibition, the agency might have had standing to challenge the constitutionality of the ban. However, this is an improbable scenario, for Taft's goal was to reduce rather than increase the federal budget.[30]

By disregarding the prohibition, Taft created at least a possibility of judicial review. If an agency or department learned in advance that the president was planning to recommend less funding than was requested in the departmental budget, this threatened injury might have given it standing to sue. In court, the agency or department could have invoked the statutory ban as a basis for enjoining the White House from submitting its own budget figures. The president might then have raised the statute's invalidity as a defense, thereby giving the court an opportunity to resolve the constitutional issue.

This may therefore have been a situation where presidential defiance was necessary to secure judicial review. Yet there is no evidence that Taft took any steps to facilitate this review, such as by providing details of his budget in advance to those who might be adversely affected by it. Though the president's final budget was not submitted to Congress until a few days before he left office, it would seem that a test case nonetheless might have been arranged earlier, in time to allow a court to rule on a request for injunctive relief.

WOODROW WILSON: THE TERMINATION OF TREATIES

Woodrow Wilson signed the Merchant Marine Act (also known as the Jones Act) on June 5, 1920. The act sought to strengthen the American shipping industry and its ability to compete with foreign shipping interests. To this end, section 28 of the act authorized domestic interstate carriers to charge lower freight rates for goods that were imported in American rather than in foreign vessels.[31] Because the United States had thirty-two treaties that barred such unequal treatment, section 34 of the act required that these treaties be terminated insofar as they prohibited the United States from discriminating against foreign vessels. Section 34 provided that "the president is hereby authorized and directed within ninety days" to notify the affected governments that our treaties with them would "terminate on the expiration of such periods as may be required for the giving of such notice by the provisions of such treaties."[32]

On September 2, 1920, a day before the ninety-day deadline was to run, Wilson advised the secretary of state that he would not comply with section 34. The matter, he said, was a "sacred" one involving "[t]he binding force of treaties and the reciprocal obligation which treaties imply." And, "inasmuch as it is clearly not the Constitutional right of Congress to direct the president to do anything whatever, particularly in regard to foreign affairs," Wilson concluded that he "ought to stand stiff upon the prerogatives of the presidential office."[33] Three weeks later, the State Department announced that "the president . . . does not deem the direction, contained in Section 34 of the so-called Merchant Marine Act, an exercise of any constitutional power possessed by the

Congress.''[34] Although this defiance produced ''congressional rumblings of impeachment,''[35] Congress was not then in session. By the time it reconvened in December 1920, Wilson had only three months left in office.

President Wilson's constitutional objection to section 34 was somewhat surprising. He signed the bill in June without complaint, after discussing it fully with the Cabinet.[36] Moreover, five years earlier, he had approved the La Follette Seamen's Act and complied with one of its provisions that ''instructed and directed'' him to send notices of treaty termination to seventeen countries.[37] On the other hand, in December 1919, Wilson opposed a proposed congressional resolution that would have directed him to sever diplomatic relations with Mexico, stating that ''the initiative in directing the relations of our Government with foreign governments is assigned by the Constitution to the Executive, and to the Executive only.''[38]

These inconsistencies simply illustrate the fact that constitutional objections, rather than being raised in a vacuum, are usually invoked to further other policy objectives.[39] Passage of the Jones Act had triggered protests and threats of retaliation from countries around the world. By September 1920, Wilson had developed second thoughts about taking action that the State Department said ''would amount to nothing less than the breach or violation of said treaties.''[40] Yet by refusing to send the termination notices required by section 34, Wilson risked exacerbating this very problem, for his refusal meant that if the United States engaged in the discrimination authorized by section 28, it would breach treaties that could otherwise have been lawfully terminated by the giving of timely notice.[41]

In the end, these treaty violations never occurred because the administration exercised its discretion not to allow the rate discrimination sanctioned by section 28. By its terms, section 28 could be suspended by the Interstate Commerce Commission (ICC) if the U.S. Shipping Board certified that there were not enough American ships to service the nation's import needs. The ICC invoked this authority four days after the Jones Act was passed, suspending section 28 for ninety days, and then indefinitely.[42] Though the suspension was based on the alleged inadequacy of U.S. shipping, the ICC's action appears to have been in response to the anger section 28 had provoked among foreign governments.[43] The section remained inoperative for the rest of Wilson's term in office.[44]

Even though the treaties were not violated, the president had refused to comply with section 34's directive that they be terminated. His refusal to implement section 34 was virtually insulated from judicial review. Those who were injured by the suspension of section 28 because they had to pay higher freight rates lacked standing to challenge the president's refusal to honor section 34. Their injuries were neither caused by the failure to send treaty termination notices, nor would those injuries necessarily be redressed by a judgment ordering Wilson to implement the statute. For even if treaty termination notices were sent in accordance with section 34, the ICC could continue its suspension of section 28 until U.S. shipping facilities were deemed to be adequate. The only injuries caused by noncompliance with section 34 would consist of those treaty violations that would occur if section 28 were implemented. While this might confer standing on foreign governments and their nationals whose treaty rights were violated, the constitutionality of section 34 would not arise in such proceedings. The only issue would be whether the federal government had violated the treaty, not whether Congress properly ordered the president to terminate the treaty.

On the other hand, the prospects for judicial review would not have much better had Wilson complied with section 34 and sent the treaty termination notices. No one could have claimed an injury from the mere transmittal of the notices, as distinct from an independent decision to implement section 28. While sending the notices might have increased the likelihood that section 28 might be implemented, any injury caused by this implementation would be highly speculative. Moreover, even a favorable ruling that the president should not have been forced by section 34 to send termination notices might not redress plaintiffs' threatened injury, for not only might the president elect not to withdraw the notices, but even if he did so, section 28 might be still be implemented anyway. For these reasons, it is highly unlikely that anyone would have had standing to challenge the validity of section 34 had Wilson instead decided to honor the provision.

The Jones Act episode illustrates the fact that there will be occasions when there is no one, under any plausible scenario, who will be in a position to trigger judicial review of a law the president claims is unconstitutional—whether the president complies with that law or refuses to comply with it.

DWIGHT D. EISENHOWER: THE AGREEMENT WITH CHILE

During the 1950s, Senator John Bricker led a campaign to amend the Constitution to restrict the president's ability to enter into agreements with foreign governments without obtaining ratification by the Senate. The campaign ended in November 1958 when Bricker was defeated for re-election to Congress.[45] Several months earlier, Congress had passed a bill creating the National Aeronautics and Space Administration (NASA). The measure authorized the president to cooperate with other nations in the fields of aeronautics and space exploration, but section 205 provided that any such international agreements were to be "made by the president with the advice and consent of the Senate."[46] President Dwight D. Eisenhower, who had strongly opposed the Bricker Amendment, signed the bill but objected to section 205, explaining: "I regard this section merely as recognizing that international treaties may be made in this field, and as not precluding, in appropriate cases, less formal arrangements for cooperation. To construe the section otherwise would raise substantial constitutional questions."[47]

Eisenhower ignored this statutory restriction on at least one occasion. Through an exchange of notes between the American ambassador to Chile and the Chilean minister of foreign affairs, the two countries entered into an agreement for a joint program of tracking and receiving radio signals from earth satellites and space vehicles, with NASA designated as the U.S. cooperating agency. According to the State Department, the agreement took effect immediately.[48] There is no evidence that it was ever approved by the Senate as required by section 205.

By defying this law, the president cut off any possibility of judicial review, for it is doubtful that anyone could claim a sufficient injury from the agreement to challenge its validity in court. If Eisenhower had instead complied under protest and sought approval from the Senate, there would have been a chance of obtaining judicial review. For had the Senate rejected the agreement, either NASA or the State Department might have had standing to sue Chile for a declaratory judgment as to whether the agreement was binding despite its rejection by the Senate.

GERALD FORD: THE POWER OF APPOINTMENT

President Gerald Ford objected to and refused to comply with two laws that provided for the appointment of executive branch officials in a manner that he believed to be violative of the Constitution.

The Commodity Futures Trading Commission

The first of these statutes involved the Commodity Futures Trading Commission (CFTC). The 1974 statute creating the CFTC allowed it to appoint an executive director "with the advice and consent of the Senate."[49] In a signing statement, Ford objected that the law violated separation of powers by "providing for an executive branch appointment in a manner not contemplated by the Constitution" and urged that this "be corrected by deletion of the request for Senate confirmation of the Executive Director."[50] Since Ford proposed having the appointment made by the CFTC alone, a method not sanctioned by Article II, section 2, he apparently viewed the executive director as being a federal employee, rather than an officer or inferior officer whose appointment is governed by Article II.[51] With respect to such employees, Ford evidently took the position that because nothing in the Constitution authorizes a Senate role in their appointment, the requirement of Senate confirmation was invalid.

The Ford administration arranged for corrective legislation to be introduced in Congress,[52] but the law was not amended to provide for appointment of the executive director by the CFTC alone until 1978, well after Ford left office.[53] In the interim, this part of the law was not executed. No one was appointed to the executive director's position; instead, the role was filled by a series of acting directors, none of whose names was submitted to the Senate.[54]

This was another case where the executive's refusal to comply with the law effectively precluded judicial review. Nobody had standing to challenge the CFTC's failure to appoint an executive director. As a study undertaken for the

House Appropriations Committee noted, if the president had instead directed the CFTC to submit a nominee to the Senate and that person had been confirmed, "actions of the appointee [might] be challenged as those of one not legally in office."[55] Or, the attorney general might have brought a quo warranto proceeding to determine whether the commission's executive director had been appointed in a constitutional manner.

The Japan–United States Friendship Commission

The second statute to which Gerald Ford objected because of its allegedly unconstitutional appointment provisions was a 1975 law creating the Japan-United States Friendship Commission.[56] In signing this measure, Ford complained that four commissioners were to be members of Congress, in violation of Article I, section 6, which prohibits congressional members from holding any other federal office. Ford announced that the congressional members of the commission "will serve in an advisory capacity, as nonvoting members."[57] The commission followed Ford's directive from the inception. According to its by-laws, "[t]he four members of Congress appointed to the Commission shall not be entitled to vote."[58] For all practical purposes, this action removed the congressional members from the commission, contrary to the requirements of the statute.

The president's refusal to honor this statute was not insulated from judicial review. The senators and representatives named to the commission could have sued to overturn the by-law that denied them the right to vote on the ground that it was inconsistent with the statute. The commission would then have asserted the act's unconstitutionality as a defense, permitting the federal courts to resolve the issue. Yet it was unnecessary for the president to defy this law to set up the possibility of judicial review. Instead, he might have allowed the members of Congress to assume their positions as full voting members of the commission and then had the attorney general institute a quo warranto proceeding to test their right to do so. Such a suit would not have been barred by the Speech or Debate Clause, for Article I, section 6 shields members of Congress from judicial proceedings only with respect to "legislative acts."[59]

JIMMY CARTER: FIVE INSTANCES OF DEFIANCE

Jimmy Carter holds the distinction of having refused to comply with five laws to whose constitutionality he objected in signing statements.

The Presidential Pardon for Draft Resisters

The first of these involved a protest by Congress against the "complete and unconditional pardon" that Carter had extended to Vietnam-era draft resisters immediately upon taking office early in 1977.[60] That summer, Congress attached a rider to an appropriations bill, barring the Justice Department from using any of the funds to carry out the president's pardon.[61] While the bill was pending in the Senate, Carter tried unsuccessfully to have the restriction removed.[62] He signed the bill on August 2, 1977, but objected that the restriction was unconstitutional because it interfered with the pardon power, constituted a bill of attainder, and denied due process of law.[63]

An executive order implementing the pardon had required the Justice Department to dismiss all pending indictments against the pardoned individuals, terminate any investigations concerning them, and permit entry into the United States of aliens who were otherwise excludable for having violated the Selective Service laws.[64] By the time the appropriations act took effect on October 1, 1977, the Justice Department had already dismissed all pending indictments and investigations.[65] The funding bar was, however, expected to have a severe impact on that part of the pardon allowing the admission of aliens, many of whom were draft resisters who had left the country and renounced their U.S. citizenship.[66] It was initially rumored that other funds might be available for this purpose, but the Justice Department later stated that the restriction would likely prevent the processing of re-entry applications for those who had been pardoned.[67]

In the end, the Carter administration ignored the spending restriction.[68] On November 18, 1977, less than two months after the ban took effect, the Immigration and Naturalization Service (INS) announced re-entry procedures for aliens seeking to take advantage of the president's pardon.[69] In May 1978, it was estimated that thousands of aliens may have been admitted under the amnesty program.[70] There is no evidence that the Justice Department underwrote these activities with other funds not subject to the restriction.

By refusing to comply with this spending limitation, Carter effectively precluded judicial review of the limitation and of his action ignoring it. A suit to enjoin implementation of the pardon was dismissed for lack of standing. None of the plaintiffs—who included present and former military personnel, two military wives, the child of a prisoner of war, a civilian, and two members of Congress—was found to have suffered an injury sufficient to confer standing.[71] Though the plaintiffs did not specifically allege that implementation of the pardon violated the statutory funding bar, this claim would likewise have been dismissed for lack of standing. Had the administration instead complied with the funding bar and refused to process re-entry papers for aliens who had been pardoned, they would have had standing to seek a judgment declaring the law unconstitutional and ordering the INS to carry out the pardon.[72] The government might even have helped to facilitate the filing of a test case by informing the affected individuals of their right to bring suit.

The Ban on Editorializing by Public Broadcasters

The second law that President Carter failed to honor on constitutional grounds was the 1978 Public Telecommunications Act.[73] This statute amended the Public Broadcasting Act of 1967 but retained section 399(a), which prohibited public radio and television stations from editorializing.[74] Carter, who had asked Congress to delete the ban, signed the 1978 act but objected that section 399(a) was invalid because "public broadcasters should have the same first amendment rights as other broadcasters."[75] The Federal Communications Commission (FCC) proceeded to enforce the ban only to the minimal extent necessary to permit a test case to be brought. After a suit challenging section 399(a) was filed in federal court, the Justice Department advised Congress that it would not defend the provision.[76] That task fell to the Senate, which intervened in the suit as amicus curiae.[77] However, the federal court dismissed the case on the grounds that it was not ripe and that plaintiffs lacked standing. The court noted that the FCC's "willingness to enforce the statute solely for the purpose of test litigation indicates that otherwise the FCC will not enforce the statute. It is, to the Commission, a nullity."[78] Since there was a "distinct likelihood that the FCC will not seek to penalize a broadcaster that violates Section 399(a)," said the court, plaintiffs could not show that the editorializing ban had caused them any present or threatened injury sufficient to confer standing.[79]

Carter's refusal to enforce this law thus prevented the federal courts from reviewing the measure's constitutionality. Ironically, it was only after the Reagan administration took office and announced that it would enforce and defend the editorializing ban that the judiciary was able to entertain a challenge to section 399.[80] In 1984, the Supreme Court held that the statute was unconstitutional.[81]

Restoration of the San Antonio Missions

The third statute that President Carter ignored due to its alleged unconstitutionality was an appropriations act provision that created the San Antonio Missions National Historical Park. The statute directed the secretary of the interior "to assure the protection and preservation of the historical and architectural values of the missions," by either acquiring the missions from the Catholic Archdiocese or making agreements with the Church through which the government would reconstruct and rehabilitate them.[82] When Carter signed the bill in November 1978, he objected that the provision violated the First Amendment because it "would lead to unacceptable entanglements of the Federal Government in the operations of active churches." He directed the secretary of the interior "to consider implementation of the portions of the bill relating to restoration and maintenance of the Missions only if they pass into secular ownership and use."[83] The Secretary heeded this directive. He informed a House committee in February 1979 that the administration opposed spending federal funds on the missions because "[t]he structures there are used currently and steadily and for the primary use of church services."[84]

The administration considered possibly acquiring the mission properties, but nothing came of this.[85] In the meantime, no federal money was spent on the missions. The matter was not finally resolved until after Carter left office. In 1983, a cooperative agreement was signed under which the Archbishop of San Antonio assumed responsibility for maintaining the missions while the United States agreed to repair and maintain the secular buildings and the mission grounds.[86] The statutory scheme whereby the federal government was to restore and maintain the missions was never implemented.

Carter's decision to disregard this law did not necessarily preclude judicial resolution of the issue. Once it became clear that the Interior Department would not restore and maintain the missions, the Archdiocese of San Antonio might have sued to enforce the statute. Instead, the Church acquiesced in the government's action. On the other hand, judicial review would have been a virtual certainty had the administration implemented the measure, for every taxpayer in the United States would have had standing to challenge this expenditure of federal funds on the ground that it violated the Establishment Clause of the First Amendment.[87] By taking the course that he did, the president thus greatly reduced the prospects that judicial review would occur.

Closing American Consulates Abroad

The fourth law that President Carter refused to honor on constitutional grounds prohibited him from proceeding with a plan to close ten U.S. consulates and directed that if any of the ten had been closed, they were to be reopened as soon as possible.[88] In a signing statement issued in August 1979, Carter declared that because the statute interfered with the president's "right to decide when and where an Ambassador or Consul should be appointed," he would treat it "as a recommendation and not a requirement."[89] In early 1980, the administration closed seven of the ten protected consulates.[90] In 1876, President Grant had objected to a similar law directing that he close certain diplomatic offices abroad, but unlike Carter, Grant immediately complied with the provision.[91]

There was probably no one who had standing to challenge Carter's defiance of this statute. If the closing of the U.S. consulate in Goteborg, Sweden, was typical, the American personnel who worked in the closed consulates were all transferred to other posts. The only people who suffered any cognizable injury were foreign nationals who had served as chauffeurs, secretaries, and the like.[92] These individuals probably lacked standing to sue because the law requiring that consulates be kept open was surely not designed to protect their interests; they would therefore be attempting to assert the legal rights of others rather than their own legal rights. Yet if Carter had instead honored the statute, it is also unlikely that anyone could have claimed an injury that would have given them standing to challenge the requirement that the offices remain open. In short, this was perhaps another case where there was no way to obtain judicial review of the disputed law regardless of how the president had responded to it.

The Advisory Council on Historic Preservation

The final instance in which the Carter administration refused to implement an allegedly unconstitutional law involved the Advisory Council on Historic Preservation. In a December 1980 signing statement, Carter said that because some of the council's members were not appointed in a manner consistent with the Appointments Clause, they "should participate only in the Council's advisory activities."[93] The president was evidently troubled by the fact that though he could appoint most of the council members, a few seats were reserved for individuals who did not acquire their positions in accordance with Article II.[94] The council honored Carter's objection by treating the persons in question as ex officio members.[95]

In theory, the president's action was not insulated from judicial review. The ex officio members might have sued the council, claiming that the statute gave them a right to vote, forcing the council to defend its action on the ground that the law was unconstitutional. As a practical matter, however, these members probably had no incentive to sue, for the expense would have far outweighed any apparent benefit they might have derived from being voting members of the council. By contrast, Carter could have ensured a judicial resolution of the issue if he had complied with the law and then ordered the attorney general to bring quo warranto proceedings against the disputed members, asking the court to hold that the manner in which they were selected violated the Appointments Clause.

It is difficult to explain why Jimmy Carter disregarded five statutes to whose constitutionality he had objected in signing statements. His willingness to do so may have been influenced by his prior experience as governor of Georgia, the first state to give its chief executive an item veto. On the other hand, after he had been in the White House for a time, Carter began to doubt the wisdom of giving the U.S. president an item veto.[96] It is also interesting that all of the earlier instances where presidents had signed but then refused to comply with a law on constitutional grounds arose in settings where the opposition party controlled at least one house of Congress, limiting the chief executive's ability to cure the bill's defect during the lawmaking process. In Carter's case, this was not so, for the Democrats controlled both the House and the Senate all four years that he was in office.[97]

SUMMARY: THE IMPACT OF DEFIANCE ON JUDICIAL REVIEW

Of the twelve incidents of executive noncompliance examined here, in only two—involving Buchanan and Taft—could it be said that such presidential action was necessary to secure judicial review of the statute in question. Review occurred in neither cases, however, partly because the White House took no steps to facilitate it.

In three instances—one involving Gerald Ford and two involving Jimmy Carter—judicial review was possible whether or not the president honored the law. Yet in each of these cases, the president's act of defiance severely reduced the chances that judicial review would occur.

In the seven remaining cases, the executive's refusal to execute an allegedly unconstitutional law was insulated from judicial review, with the result that the president's action amounted to an absolute veto. In two of these cases—involving Wilson and Carter—no one would have had standing to test the law's validity regardless of how the executive had responded. In the other five cases, however, by refusing to carry out the disputed statute, Presidents Arthur, Eisenhower, Ford, and Carter twice foreclosed judicial review that might otherwise have occurred.

FIVE APOCRYPHAL CASES OF PRESIDENTIAL DEFIANCE

There are a number of incidents—a few of them quite well known—that are sometimes cited as cases where a president refused to honor a law whose constitutionality he had challenged in a signing statement. Lest the reader think this account of presidential defiance is incomplete, we will note these instances briefly and explain why they are spurious.

James Monroe: The Reassignment of Army Officers

In March 1821, President Monroe approved a law that reduced the size of the army and specified how the president was to go about selecting officers for the newly reorganized regiments.[98] In mid-April, after his implementation of the act drew criticism, Monroe sent Congress a detailed and lengthy message defending his construction of the statute.[99] He noted that with respect to the naming of officers, "Congress could not under the Constitution restrain the free selection of the President from the whole body of his fellow-citizens. . . . *If the law imposed such restraint, it would in that case be void. But, according to my judgment, the law imposed none.*"[100] As the emphasized sentence indicates, the president did not claim that the act was unconstitutional. Instead, both he and the secretary of war believed his actions were "strictly conformable to law."[101] While Congress did not agree with Monroe's reading of the statute,[102] this was not a case—as some have argued[103]—where the president claimed that a law was unconstitutional and therefore refused to comply with it. Instead, Monroe appears to have implemented the statute in good faith, even though some members of Congress disagreed with his interpretation of it.

Abraham Lincoln: The Rush-Bagot Agreement

President Lincoln is alleged to have "ignored Congressional directions to terminate the Rush-Bagot Agreement disarming the Great Lakes."[104] Yet no such directions existed. After Secretary of State William H. Seward had initially notified Great Britain that the 1817 Rush-Bagot treaty would be terminated, Congress passed a joint resolution that "adopted and ratified" the termination notice "as if the same had been authorized by congress."[105] However, because Congress merely "authorized" rather than directed termination of the treaty, Seward's later withdrawal of the termination notice did not amount to a refusal to comply with the joint resolution.[106]

Ulysses Grant: The River and Harbor Bill

In 1876, President Grant signed a river and harbor appropriations bill but objected that many of the items were "for works of purely private or local interest, in no sense national" and stated that "during my term of office no public money shall be expended upon them."[107] Grant made good on this promise. His administration spent nothing on more than half the 146 projects funded by the act; many others received only partial funding.[108] While for some earlier presidents an objection to funding "local" projects would have reflected constitutional scruples, this was not so with Grant. He had previously and without objection signed two river and harbor bills that funded many of the same projects he now refused to undertake.[109] The problem in 1876 was that the country was in a depression and tax revenues were down. Grant's signing statement gave as the sole reason for his action that "[t]here is very great necessity for economy of expenditures at this time."[110] The president's objection to this bill was thus fiscal rather than constitutional.

Harry Truman: The Size of the Air Force

In 1949, Congress appropriated funds to increase the size of the air force to fifty-eight groups.[111] President Truman, believing that forty-eight groups were sufficient, impounded the extra funds. Though it has been said that Truman objected to the law partly because it impaired his "authority as Commander-in-Chief,"[112] his opposition rested solely on policy grounds.[113] In directing the secretary of defense not to spend the funds, Truman noted that the order was issued pursuant to "the authority vested in me as President of the United States and Commander in Chief of the Armed Forces," but he nowhere claimed that the law in any manner interfered with this authority.[114]

John Kennedy: The RS-70 Bomber

President Kennedy refused to spend funds that Congress appropriated in 1962 to develop the RS-70 weapons system. This action was not based on constitutional grounds, nor did it amount to a refusal to carry out the law. When the bill was before Congress, Kennedy opposed a provision that would have ''directed'' the administration to spend at least $491 million on the program, stating that this would impair his constitutional authority as commander in chief.[115] Congress responded by changing the language from ''directed'' to ''authorized'' before the bill became law.[116] Kennedy's only remaining objection to the measure rested solely on policy grounds.[117] Because Congress had expressly modified the wording of the statute to make it permissive rather than mandatory, Kennedy's failure to spend all of the funds was thus not a refusal to comply with the law.

8

Laws Enacted During a Prior Administration

Presidents have at times refused to comply with laws that were adopted during an earlier administration on the ground that the laws were unconstitutional (see Table 8.1). In such cases, the President had no opportunity to veto the measure or to take issue with parts of it in a signing statement. Before we look at these incidents, it is important to note that even in this setting, a president has other ways of dealing with the situation short of refusing to comply with the law.

ALTERNATIVES TO NONCOMPLIANCE

One alternative available to a president is to urge Congress to amend or repeal the offending provision. For example, the Tenure of Office Act, which passed in 1867 over Andrew Johnson's veto, was finally repealed twenty years later after Presidents Grant, Hayes, and Cleveland each pressed Congress to take this step.[1] Dwight Eisenhower secured the repeal of a committee approval requirement adopted during the Truman years, following repeated messages to Congress charging that the provision was unconstitutional.[2]

Another presidential option, albeit one that has generated controversy, is for the White House to refuse to defend an allegedly unconstitutional law when it is challenged in court, perhaps even joining in the attack on the measure.[3] During the Kennedy administration, the United States intervened in a suit attacking the 1946 Hill-Burton Act to the extent that it allowed the construction of racially segregated hospitals; throughout the proceeding, the government joined plaintiffs in urging that the law was unconstitutional.[4] Under President Carter, the Justice Department refused to defend the validity of a statute, first adopted in 1905,

Table 8.1
Presidential Noncompliance with Laws Enacted During a Prior Administration (1789–1981)

President	Statute	Year Defied	Nature of Objection
Cleveland	Act of Jan. 16, 1883, ch. 27, § 3, 22 Stat. 403, 404	1886	Chief Examiner of Civil Service Commission is an officer of the U.S. and cannot be chosen by Commission but must be appointed in accord with Article II.
Wilson	Act of July 12, 1876, ch. 179, § 6, 19 Stat. 78, 80	1920	Congress may not limit President's power to remove postmasters by requiring that removal may occur only with advice and consent of the Senate.
F. Roosevelt	Fed'l Trade Comm'n Act, ch. 311, §1, 38 Stat. 717, 718 (1914)	1933	Congress may not limit President's power to remove Federal Trade Commissioners by requiring that removal may occur only for cause.
L. Johnson	Act of Aug. 4, 1954, ch. 566, § 2, 68 Stat. 666	1967-1968	Congressional committees cannot be given the power to approve or veto public works projects undertaken by the executive branch pursuant to an act of Congress.
Ford	War Powers Resolution, Pub. L. No. 93-148, 87 Stat. 555 (1973)	1974-1976	President cannot be compelled to notify or receive approval of Congress in order to make use of armed forces.
Carter	War Powers Resolution, Pub. L. No. 93-148, 87 Stat 555 (1973)	1978-1980	President cannot be compelled to notify or receive approval of Congress in order to make use of armed forces.
Carter	Act of Aug. 21, 1974, Pub. L. No. 93-380, § 509, 88 Stat. 484, 566-88	1980	Congress may not reserve for itself a two-House legislative veto over regulations issued by Department of Health, Education, and Welfare.

that required the secretary of the army to sell firearms at cost to members of the National Rifle Association. After the federal district court held the law unconstitutional, the Justice Department decided not to appeal the decision.[5]

Finally, the president may have been given statutory discretion not to employ the disputed provision, in which case the executive can refrain from acting without being guilty of defying the law. Lyndon Johnson chose this avenue to avoid congressional committee veto and approval requirements contained in a number of statutes that were enacted before he entered the White House. Johnson, claiming that such provisions were unconstitutional,[6] initially challenged them by exercising the veto,[7] by objecting in signing statements,[8] and by submitting legislation for their repeal.[9] In mid-1966, he announced that his administration would no longer pursue public works projects under statutes that contained congressional committee veto or approval requirements.[10] Four of these laws were already on the books when Johnson took office; however, each of them was so worded as to authorize but not direct that the projects be pursued, and each specified that no funds would be appropriated until after a project had been cleared by the respective congressional committees.[11] Congress's use of permissive authorization language, together with its failure to appropriate funds, allowed Johnson not to pursue the projects without defying the law. Instead, he exercised discretion that Congress had given the president by statute.

Not all presidents chose to pursue these alternatives to noncompliance, or if they did, they were sometimes coupled with a refusal to comply with the law. We turn now to a consideration of the cases in which a president, for constitutional reasons, refused to honor a statute that was enacted before he entered the White House. In addition to the incidents discussed below, one case discussed in the last chapter might have been placed here instead, that is, Jimmy Carter's refusal to enforce the ban against editorializing by public broadcasters. The ban was first imposed by the Public Broadcasting Act of 1967, well before Carter took office. When the act was amended in 1978, Carter objected that Congress had not deleted the ban. In one sense, Carter was challenging a law from a prior administration. Yet because he used a signing statement to object to Congress's decision to continue the ban, the case has been treated as one in which a president objected to a law enacted during his administration.

GROVER CLEVELAND: THE CIVIL SERVICE CHIEF EXAMINER

In 1886, Grover Cleveland confronted the same issue that President Arthur had faced a number of years earlier concerning the status of the chief examiner of the Civil Service Commission. Cleveland's attorney general reached the same conclusion that Arthur's had, namely, that the chief examiner was an "officer" of the United States who could not constitutionally be appointed by the Commission itself,[12] as allowed by an 1883 statute.[13] Like his predecessor, Cleveland submitted his own nominee. The Senate again acquiesced in this defiance of the statutory scheme, this time confirming the appointment without reservation.[14] As in President Arthur's case, the practical effect of the executive's action was to foreclose any possibility of judicial review. Cleveland could have ensured a judicial determination of the constitutional issue if he had instead directed the attorney general to file a quo warranto proceeding against whomever the commission appointed to the position.

WOODROW WILSON: REMOVING A POSTMASTER

On February 2, 1920, President Wilson fired Frank Myers from his position as postmaster in Portland, Oregon, before Myers's four-year term had expired.[15] Wilson's action ignored an 1876 statute providing that such postmasters could be removed by the president only "with the advice and consent of the Senate."[16] When he fired Myers, Wilson never notified the Senate much less sought its consent.[17] Though the president did not specify that his defiance of the statute was based on constitutional grounds, it seems likely that it was. Decades earlier, Wilson had said of the heads of departments: "Once installed, their hold upon their offices does not depend upon the will of Congress."[18] Moreover, many of his predecessors, including Andrew Johnson, had opposed attempts by Congress to restrict the president's removal power.[19] Finally, not long after he dismissed Myers, Wilson vetoed a bill making certain federal officers removable only upon a concurrent resolution of the House and Senate; in his veto message, Wilson asserted that "Congress is without constitutional power to limit the appointing power and its incident, the power of removal derived from the Constitution."[20] For these reasons, the case is treated as one in which the president refused to comply with a law because he believed it to be unconstitutional.

As was true of Andrew Johnson's violation of the Tenure of Office Act, no one would have had standing to challenge the validity of the law unless Wilson had defied the measure. The difference was that in this instance, judicial review occurred, though not due to any efforts on the part of the administration. A month after Wilson left office, Myers sued in the Court of Claims for the unpaid balance of his salary. The Department of Justice defended the case by challenging the validity of the 1876 act. The Court of Claims ruled against Myers under the doctrine of laches,[21] but the Supreme Court affirmed on the ground that the statute was unconstitutional. In an opinion by Chief Justice William Howard Taft, the Court finally resolved the issue that had triggered the Johnson impeachment, holding that Congress may not reserve for itself a role in the removal of federal officers.[22]

FRANKLIN ROOSEVELT: REMOVING A TRADE COMMISSIONER

The president's view as to the scope of his removal powers was the basis for another act of executive defiance, this time involving Franklin Roosevelt's refusal to honor a 1914 law that allowed the president to remove Federal Trade Commission (FTC) commissioners only "for inefficiency, neglect of duty, or malfeasance in office."[23] In 1933, Roosevelt dismissed FTC Commissioner William Humphrey who had been appointed by President Herbert Hoover. Roosevelt noted that his action did not reflect upon Humphrey or the quality of his work and that the removal stemmed solely from the president's desire to fill the position with someone who was more supportive of the administration's policies.[24]

Humphrey challenged his dismissal in the Court of Claims, which promptly certified the matter to the Supreme Court. There, the Justice Department urged that Congress's restriction on the president's removal power was unconstitutional. The Court upheld the act, distinguishing *Myers* on the basis that the office there was purely executive, whereas FTC commissioners perform quasi-legislative and quasi-judicial functions.[25] As in *Myers*, this judicial resolution of the constitutional dispute between Congress and the president could not have occurred had the president complied with the statute. Though the Roosevelt administration took no apparent steps to facilitate or encourage judicial review, the fact that these were Depression years and that roughly $50,000 was at stake made it virtually certain that a lawsuit would be filed on Humphrey's behalf.

LYNDON JOHNSON: IMPOUNDING WATERSHED FUNDS

After President Johnson announced in 1966 that he would no longer undertake public works projects that were subject to veto or approval by congressional committees,[26] his administration nevertheless submitted proposals to Congress under the Watershed Protection and Flood Prevention Act of 1954, a law that contained a committee approval requirement.[27] Ninety-six of these projects were thereafter approved by the Agriculture Committees of the House and the Senate, but the president refused to proceed with them until Congress amended the statute to delete the committee approval requirement.[28] Because the effect of the committees' approval was to make funds available for the approved projects, Johnson's failure to implement the projects was an impoundment of appropriated funds and a defiance of the law.

The president's action was not shielded from judicial review. Any of the local governmental or nonprofit organizations whose proposals had been approved might have sued the secretary of agriculture to compel release of the funds. The secretary might then have raised the constitutional issue as a defense, arguing that because the appropriation was in effect made by two congressional committees, rather than by the full Congress, no funds were legally available for the projects.[29] Yet it does not appear that any such suits were filed or that the administration did anything to encourage them. The secretary could also have initiated judicial review on his own by filing a declaratory judgment action against any of the local applicants, asking the court to determine whether the purported appropriation was valid.[30] It was not even necessary for the president to defy the law in order to secure judicial review. The administration could have urged applicants whose proposals were *not* approved by the committees[31] to bring suit against the secretary of agriculture to compel release of the funds on the theory that the approval requirement was unconstitutional. Yet despite all of these various possibilities, no judicial review occurred. The funds in question were finally released by President Nixon.[32]

GERALD FORD AND JIMMY CARTER: THE WAR POWERS RESOLUTION

Perhaps the best-known examples of executive defiance of an allegedly unconstitutional law involve the War Powers Resolution, enacted over Richard Nixon's veto in 1973.[33] Nixon's successors have uniformly adhered to his view that the resolution's consultation, notification, and termination provisions infringe on the president's authority as commander in chief to use the armed forces as he wishes. Chief executives have sometimes complied with section 3 of the resolution by consulting with Congress before armed forces are introduced into hostile situations.[34] However, the consultation and notification requirements have frequently been ignored.

Presidents Ford and Carter sometimes refused to notify Congress under section 4(a)(1) when introducing troops into hostilities, thereby avoiding section 5's command that the forces be withdrawn within sixty days unless Congress declared war or authorized a longer engagement.[35] Ford and Carter either gave no formal notice to Congress, failed to specify that notice was being given under section 4(a)(1), or gave a section 4(a)(1) notice only after the incident was over.[36] Ronald Reagan later exhibited a similar disdain for the War Powers Resolution in sending combat forces into Lebanon, Grenada, Central America, Libya, and the Persian Gulf.[37] Presidents Bush and Clinton ignored the resolution in other settings.[38]

It has been argued that the federal courts may entertain challenges to a president's failure to comply with the War Powers Resolution.[39] In the Ford and Carter cases, however, the uses of force were so brief that if any suits had been filed challenging the presidents' failure to start the sixty-day clock, they might well have been dismissed as moot.[40] To date, all such cases have been dismissed on grounds of being nonjusticiable or under the doctrine of remedial discretion.[41] Judicial review of the War Powers Resolution would be even less likely to occur if a president were to comply with its consulting and notification provisions, for it is difficult to conceive of anyone who would then have standing to challenge the resolution's validity.

JIMMY CARTER: ISSUING VETOED REGULATIONS

When Gerald Ford signed a 1974 omnibus education bill, he objected to several of its provisions that subjected decisions of the Department of Health,

Education, and Welfare to "various forms of Congressional review and possible veto."[42] One of the provisions allowed Congress, by concurrent resolution, to block final regulations issued by HEW.[43] Congress never exercised this two-house legislative veto during Ford's term in office. In 1980, however, the last year of Carter's presidency, Congress passed four concurrent resolutions disapproving regulations issued by the Department of Education, HEW's successor.[44] On June 5, 1980, the attorney general advised the secretary of education that because the legislative veto provision was unconstitutional, she was "entitled to implement the regulations in question in spite of Congress' disapproval."[45] The secretary followed this advice and placed all of the regulations into effect.[46]

The attorney general justified his recommendation that the secretary defy the law partly on the ground that to honor the concurrent resolutions "might well foreclose effective judicial challenge to their constitutionality."[47] However, there was no assurance that anyone harmed by the regulations in question would sue to have them invalidated. Had the secretary complied with the law by withholding the regulations, those who would have benefited from them could have sued to have the legislative veto declared unconstitutional, thereby freeing the department to implement the regulations. The secretary might even have encouraged the filing of such a lawsuit. Thus, while this was not a case where the executive's defiance of the law precluded judicial review, neither was it one where such action was necessary in order to make a legal challenge possible.

SUMMARY

As Table 8.1 shows, there were seven occasions when presidents refused to comply with allegedly unconstitutional laws adopted during a prior administration. The first such instance did not occur until 1886; there, President Cleveland's defiance precluded judicial review. On four other occasions, noncompliance created the possibility of judicial review, but this occurred in only two of the cases, involving Woodrow Wilson and Franklin Roosevelt.

9

Presidential Practice: A Summary of the Historical Record

RHETORIC AND REALITY: 1789–1981

We have now reviewed all of the known instances in which American presidents, between 1789 and 1981, objected to a law on the ground that it was unconstitutional. Two important findings emerge from this study. First, throughout most of our history, the rhetoric of presidential objection to a law has seldom been accompanied by the reality of noncompliance. Second, cases of actual presidential defiance were extraordinarily rare until the last half of the twentieth century.

In the nearly 200 years covered by this study, there were roughly 145 cases in which the president claimed that a statute was unconstitutional. This figure includes the following: 27 laws that were enacted over a president's constitutionally based veto (see Table 4.1); 101 statutory provisions that were challenged in presidential signing statements (see Table 5.2); 7 laws that were passed during a prior administration and which a later president refused to honor (see Table 8.1); and 10 instances where presidents objected to the validity of a previously enacted law by seeking its repeal or refusing to defend it in court (see chapter 8). In only 20 of these 145 cases did the president then refuse to honor or comply with the law. These 20 cases are summarized in Table 9.1.

The first incident of presidential defiance did not occur until 1860—more than seventy years after the Constitution was ratified—when James Buchanan ignored a law requiring that the Washington Aqueduct be built under the supervision of Captain Meigs. Though Buchanan was the first president to defy a

Table 9.1
Incidents Where Presidents Defied an Allegedly Unconstitutional Law (1789–1981)

PRESIDENT	MANNER OF OBJECTION	DATE OF DEFIANCE	NATURE AND DATE OF STATUTE DEFIED	NECESSARY TO, OR PRECLUDE, REVIEW?
Buchanan	Signing Statement	1860	Construction of Washington Aqueduct (1860)	Necessary but no review occurred
A. Johnson	Veto	1868	Tenure of Office Act (1867)	Necessary but no review occurred
Arthur	Signing Statement	1883	Appointing Chief Examiner of Civil Service (1883)	Unnecessary, and precluded review
Cleveland	Prior Law	1886	Appointing Chief Examiner of Civil Service (1883)	Unnecessary, and precluded review
Taft	Signing Statement	1913	Form of Federal Budget (1912)	Neccesary but no review occurred
Wilson	Prior Law	1920	Removal of Postmasters (1876)	Neccesary, and review occurred
Wilson	Signing Statement	1920	Termination of Treaties (1920)	Review precluded in any event
F. Roosevelt	Prior Law	1933	Removal of FTC Commissioners (1914)	Neccesary, and review occurred
Eisenhower	Signing Statement	1959	Entering Executive Agreements (1958)	Unnecessary, and precluded review
L. Johnson	Prior Law	1967-68	Committee Approval of Watershed Projects (1954)	Unnecessary but did not preclude review; no review occurred

Ford	Signing Statement	1974	Appointing CFTC Commissioners (1974)	Unnecessary, and precluded review
Ford	Signing Statement	1975	Appointing Japan- U.S. Friendship Commission (1975)	Unnecessary but did not preclude review; no review occurred
Ford	Prior Law	1974-76	War Powers Resolution (1973)	Necessary but no review occurred
Carter	Signing Statement	1977	Implementation of Pardon (1977)	Unnecessary, and precluded review
Carter	Signing Statement	1978	Editorial Ban on Public Broadcasters (1978)	Unnecessary, and precluded review
Carter	Signing Statement	1978	Restoration of San Antonio Missions (1978)	Unnecessary but did not preclude review; no review occurred
Carter	Prior Law	1978-80	War Powers Resolution (1973)	Necessary but no review occurred
Carter	Signing Statement	1980	Closing Consulates Abroad (1979)	Review precluded in any event
Carter	Prior Law	1980	Two-House Veto of HEW Regulations (1974)	Unnecessary but did not preclude review; no review occurred
Carter	Signing Statement	1980	Appointing Historic Preservation Council (1980)	Unnecessary but did not preclude review; no review occurred

statute on constitutional grounds, he was not the first to claim that an enacted law was unconstitutional. Presidents Jackson, Tyler, and Pierce had all preceded Buchanan in this regard. However, Jackson and Tyler had no occasion to ignore the laws in question and thus did not have to choose between compliance and defiance. President Pierce did confront that choice as to five river and harbor appropriation bills that were passed over his veto in 1856. In contrast to Buchanan, he implemented the measures despite his constitutional objections. If one puts aside the questionable case of Andrew Johnson's failure to honor the Tenure of Office Act, the second case of presidential defiance did not occur until 1883, nearly a century after the adoption of the Constitution, when President Arthur insisted upon appointing the chief examiner of the Civil Service Commission.

Thereafter, from the late nineteenth through the mid-twentieth century, instances of executive defiance of allegedly unconstitutional laws continued to be rare. As of 1960, presidents had ignored such laws on only nine occasions. Though it has been said that "every President in this century has used the power of presidential review to refuse to enforce statutes,"[1] Presidents McKinley, Theodore Roosevelt, Harding, Coolidge, Hoover, Truman, Kennedy, and Nixon—as best we can tell—never ignored a law on constitutional grounds. It was not until the mid-1970s that presidential defiance of allegedly unconstitutional laws began to reach significant proportions. Of the twenty such incidents that occurred between 1789 and 1981, ten occurred after 1973. President Carter alone was responsible for seven of them, representing more than a third of the total.

These findings are significant for several reasons. First, as we noted earlier, when the Court interprets the Constitution it sometimes seeks to discern original intent by looking to the actual practices of the government in the years shortly after the Constitution was adopted.[2] These practices may shed light on the Founders' intent, for many who played roles in the drafting and ratification of the Constitution held office under the federal government during its formative years. "The relevancy of prior [practices] is limited largely to the insight they afford in correctly ascertaining the draftsmen's intent. Obviously, therefore, the precedential value of these cases tends to increase in proportion to their proximity to the Convention in 1787."[3] As we have seen, there were no incidents of presidential noncompliance with allegedly unconstitutional laws until more than seven decades after the adoption of the Constitution. Thus, the historical record does not support an originalist argument for presidential defiance based on early governmental practices.

Second, the historical record precludes any claim that the authority to disregard unconstitutional laws now belongs to the president by a process of prescription. Though Justice Frankfurter once suggested that "a systematic, unbroken, executive practice, long pursued to the knowledge of Congress and never before questioned . . . may be treated as a gloss on 'executive Power' vested in the President,"[4] the modern Court has seemingly rejected the Madisonian notion that the boundaries separating the branches may be altered in this fashion. In *Immigration and Naturalization Service v. Chadha*, the justices struck down the legislative veto as being inconsistent with the text of the Constitution and the intent of the Founders, despite the fact that for some fifty years the device had been included in hundreds of laws, most of which were approved by the president.[5] In 1992, in *New York v. United States*, the Court flatly declared that "[t]he Constitution's division of power among the three Branches is violated where one Branch invades the territory of another, whether or not the encroached-upon Branch approves the encroachment."[6]

Yet even if the prescriptive process has continuing validity with respect to separation of powers,[7] the known instances of executive defiance of allegedly unconstitutional laws have simply been too few and far between to satisfy the requirement of "a systematic, unbroken, executive practice." The desultory record of presidential noncompliance, involving twenty incidents spread over a period of almost 200 years, can hardly suffice to alter the constitutional framework by giving the president what amounts to an absolute item veto.

The second half of Frankfurter's equation is not satisfied either, for it cannot fairly be said that Congress has acquiesced in these sporadic acts of presidential noncompliance. As we saw in chapter 4, when Andrew Johnson defied the Tenure of Office Act, he was immediately impeached. Woodrow Wilson's refusal to comply with a statute requiring the termination of certain treaties might have led to his impeachment had Wilson not been on the eve of leaving office.[8] Lyndon Johnson's failure to implement public works projects that were subject to committee approval triggered congressional hearings,[9] as did Gerald Ford's and Jimmy Carter's disregard of the War Powers Resolution.[10] When Carter refused to honor the legislative veto of regulations issued by the Department of Education, a Senate subcommittee demanded that the attorney general defend "the Justice Department's assertion that it can deny the validity of Acts of Congress."[11]

The historical record thus does not support a claim that the president has acquired, by prescription, the power to disregard laws that he believes to be unconstitutional. Those who contend otherwise often fail to distinguish between presidential rhetoric and presidential practice.[12] For example, during the Clinton administration, the attorney general's Office of Legal Counsel (OLC) took the position that "there are circumstances in which the President may appropriately decline to enforce a statute that he views as unconstitutional," claiming that "consistent and substantial executive practice" supported this position.[13] As evidence, OLC cited a dozen presidential messages, most of them signing statements, in which the White House had objected to the constitutionality of a law.[14] Yet OLC failed to indicate whether or not the executive subsequently refused to honor the statute. In fact, of the twelve incidents cited, only two—involving Woodrow Wilson and Lyndon Johnson—appear to have been cases where the president actually refused to enforce the law.

POSTSCRIPT: CONTINUED DEFIANCE AND ESCALATING RHETORIC

In the period between 1981 and 1996, presidents objected to the constitutionality of laws at a rate that equaled or exceeded that of their predecessors. As Table 5.1 shows, during the Reagan and Bush years, the use of constitutionally based signing statements escalated dramatically, reaching an average of 29 such statements a year, as compared to a previous high of 7.5 a year. Between them, Reagan and Bush assailed the validity of more than 200 statutes. In Clinton's first term, the frequency of such challenges dropped to the level that prevailed under Carter—a level that was still double that of any president before Carter.

This study has not attempted to go beyond the rhetoric to determine the precise extent to which Presidents Reagan, Bush, and Clinton actually defied the laws whose validity they questioned. However, it is clear that they at times did so. The Reagan administration, which viewed the constitutionally based signing statement as a *de facto* item veto rather than as a mere rhetorical device, claimed to have made a practice of ignoring allegedly unconstitutional statutes. According to Douglas Kmiec, the Reagan administration's principal spokesperson on this issue, "[t]he approval of legislation with constitutional reservations necessarily means that executive action will not be immediately taken to enforce the suspect provisions. If such non-enforcement is challenged, whether the president's judgment is ultimately vindicated . . . will depend on the considered judgment of the Judiciary."[15] This strongly suggests that the administration disregarded a good many of the eighty-seven laws that Reagan attacked in signing statements.

Among the laws that President Reagan defied was the 1984 Competition in Contracting Act.[16] In a signing statement, Reagan charged that the act gave the comptroller general, an officer of Congress, functions that could be performed only by executive branch officials.[17] Reagan specifically objected to an automatic stay provision that barred the award of government contracts while the comptroller general investigated complaints that an agency had not followed the act's competitive bidding procedures. At the attorney general's direction, federal agencies disregarded the stay requirement.[18] A series of lawsuits followed in which the federal courts uniformly rejected Reagan's claim that the law was unconstitutional.[19] The Bush administration later ignored the fee-recovery provision of the same act, claiming that it, too, was unconstitutional.[20]

Reagan was the first president in over a century, and only the second in history, to defy a statute that was enacted over his veto. The Comprehensive Anti-Apartheid Act was adopted in 1986 over Reagan's objection that it would "infringe on the President's constitutional prerogative to articulate the foreign policy of the United States."[21] From 1986 until 1991, when the sanctions were finally lifted, the Reagan and the Bush administrations exploited loopholes in the law and quietly permitted U.S. companies to trade with South Africa in violation of the act's express prohibitions.[22]

In addition, Reagan and Bush refused to honor a series of laws that barred the government from enforcing nondisclosure agreements with federal employees who had access to classified material,[23] claiming that the provisions impaired the president's duty to protect national security.[24] President Bush refused to honor a provision of the Foreign Relations Authorization Act that barred the government from sending a delegation to a negotiating session unless it included members of the Commission on Security and Cooperation in Europe;[25] Bush contended in a signing statement that the provision encroached on his appointment power and on his power to conduct foreign relations.[26] Like their immediate predecessors, Reagan and Bush refused to comply with the 1973 War Powers Resolution on the ground that it was unconstitutional.[27]

The Clinton administration refused to honor a provision in a 1994 law requiring that the executive branch have all of its printing done by the Government Printing Office (GPO) unless the GPO authorized the work to be done elsewhere.[28] In signing this law, Clinton stated that "[t]he Act raises serious constitutional concerns," and said that he would construe it narrowly to exclude certain categories of work.[29] After the comptroller general rejected the president's reading of the statute,[30] the Department of Justice declared that "the GPO's extensive control over executive branch printing is unconstitutional under the doctrine of separation of powers."[31] The department literally invited executive agencies to ignore the provision by advising them that there was "little or no risk of liability or sanction to contracting officers who act consistently with this opinion."[32] Some executive agencies—including the Department of Commerce and the Bureau of the Census—did just that by arranging for private companies to print and copyright some of the agencies' major publications rather than going through the GPO.[33]

The Clinton administration also refused on constitutional grounds to enforce part of the Telecommunications Act of 1996.[34] In a signing statement, Clinton objected to a section of the act that broadened the federal ban against transmitting abortion-related speech to include transmittals by interactive computer services. Backed by advice from the Justice Department, Clinton announced that these federal criminal code provisions were "unconstitutional and will not be enforced because they violate the First Amendment."[35]

In addition to an increased use of constitutionally based signing statements and continuing incidents of noncompliance, presidential rhetoric grew bolder in the mid-1980s. In 1980, when Congress challenged Jimmy Carter's refusal to honor a series of two-house vetoes of Department of Education regulations, the Justice Department responded in a conciliatory vein. It acknowledged that "if executive officers were to adopt a policy of ignoring or attacking Acts of Congress whenever they believed them to be in conflict with the provisions of the Constitution, their conduct in office could jeopardize the equilibrium established within our constitutional system."[36] The attorney general took the position "that the Executive can rarely defy an Act of Congress," and suggested that this is proper only if a law is "transparently inconsistent with the Constitution."[37]

While the Carter administration seems to have ignored this standard in refusing to comply with a number of allegedly unconstitutional laws, its rhetorical claims were nevertheless modest.

Five years later, when Congress inquired into the Reagan administration's refusal to comply with the Competition in Contracting Act, the attorney general made the sweeping claim that it is "the duty of the President to uphold the Constitution in the context of the enforcement of Acts of Congress,"[38] and declared that the president may ignore any law that he believes is contrary to the Constitution. According to the Justice Department, "The requirements of the Constitution prevail over any statute adopted by Congress. Therefore, in the case of a conflict between the Constitution and a statute, the President's duty faithfully to execute the laws requires him not to observe a statute that is in conflict with the Constitution, the fundamental law of the land."[39] While the attorney general suggested that the case for defiance would be strengthened if a law encroached on the presidency or if noncompliance might facilitate judicial review, neither of these was a prerequisite to the executive's claimed right to ignore an allegedly unconstitutional law.[40] President Reagan's counsel, Fred Fielding, was equally bold. "There are times," he said, "when the Administration has been accused of ignoring the law. But remember that the President is sworn to uphold both the Constitution and the laws. We seek to resolve the conflicts. Strong presidents especially are mindful of their responsibility to those who come after them, and seek to assure that they do not erode any executive prerogative."[41]

The Bush administration also took an expansive view of the president's authority to ignore unconstitutional laws. Bush's attorney general asserted that the president may "use signing statements to say that agencies should refuse to enforce part of a law because it is unconstitutional. . . . If the President is confronted with a circumstance where the Constitution says one thing and a statute says another, the President . . . has to choose the supreme law of the land. Particularly where a law encroaches on executive power, the only effective way of challenging the law is by declining to enforce it. Otherwise, the President would be at the mercy of Congress."[42]

During Clinton's first term, presidential rhetoric became more subdued. While the Office of Legal Counsel advised the White House that "there are circumstances in which the President may appropriately decline to enforce a statute that he views as unconstitutional,"[43] the scope of this authority was described in considerably narrower terms than was claimed by the previous two administrations. OLC noted that since "the President's obligation to act in accord with the Constitution appears to be in tension with his duty to execute laws enacted by Congress," he "should proceed with caution."[44] It urged the president to "give deference to the fact that Congress passed the statute and that Congress believed it was upholding its obligation to enact constitutional legislation."[45] The president was advised to comply with a law, "notwithstanding his own beliefs about the constitutional issue," if it seemed likely the Supreme Court would uphold the measure.[46] OLC recommended that the President take into account "the likelihood that compliance or non-compliance will permit judicial resolution of the issue. That is, the President may base his decision to comply (or decline to comply) in part on a desire to afford the Supreme Court an opportunity to review the constitutional judgment of the legislative branch."[47] These are important qualifications. If followed, they would significantly restrict the circumstances under which presidents fail to enforce laws because they think them unconstitutional.

A *DE FACTO* ITEM VETO OR A SUSPENDING POWER?

Since the mid-1970s, there has been a dramatic rise both in the use of constitutionally based signing statements and in the instances where presidents then defied the law to which they objected. These developments have sometimes been accompanied by broad claims that the president now has the prerogative to ignore any part of a law that he believes to be invalid. It is perhaps no coincidence that these events have coincided with White House efforts to obtain an item veto for the president. Yet, while executive defiance of an allegedly unconstitutional statute in some ways constitutes a *de facto* item veto, it is more accurately viewed as a revival of the once discredited royal suspending power.

Presidents Ford, Carter, Reagan, Bush, and Clinton, each of whom made frequent use of signing statements to attack the constitutionality of bills they signed into law, favored granting the president the authority to veto parts of a bill. Planks supporting the line-item veto were included in the 1984 and 1988 Republican Party platforms, and both Reagan and Bush both lobbied for a constitutional amendment to this effect.[48] Reagan and Bush also explored the possibility that the president already possessed an inherent item veto authority, but they abandoned this position after the Office of Legal Counsel twice rejected the contention.[49] Clinton, though favoring a line-item veto,[50] did not campaign on a platform that included such a plank. Instead, during his first term, the item veto was a Republican priority and constituted the first promise in the House GOP's 1994 "Contract with America."[51] That the item veto was a lower priority for Clinton than it was for Reagan and Bush may account for Clinton's having made much less use of constitutionally based signing statements than did either of his immediate Republican predecessors.

It has been suggested that the surge in constitutionally based signing statements during the Reagan and Bush years was part of an "underhanded quest for a de facto item veto."[52] There is some evidence to support this charge. Until 1984, when he and his party first urged giving the president an item veto,[53] Reagan averaged fewer than six constitutionally based signing statements a year; thereafter, his average jumped to fourteen a year.[54] George Bush, who continued the campaign for an item veto, averaged twenty-nine such statements a year—more than double Reagan's rate. Like water slowly carving a channel into rock, the steady flow of White House statements challenging the validity of parts of laws may gradually alter the constitutional landscape. Indeed, the phenomenon illustrates Professor Daniel Franklin's observation that "the rhetoric of the presidency has been used to assert the president's own interpretation of his administrative and emergency powers under the Constitution. . . . This kind of presidential rhetoric provides a justification for and lays the groundwork for future executive actions deemed proper pursuant to the president's own interpretation of the Constitution."[55] As the public becomes accustomed to hearing White House objections to particular statutory provisions, presidential defiance of those laws may in the end pass unnoticed.

The link between signing statements and the item veto was expressly noted by the Justice Department in defending President Reagan's defiance of the Competition in Contracting Act, which Reagan had challenged in a signing statement.[56] The attorney general explained that though the president's "veto power is usually adequate to express and implement his judgment that an Act of Congress is unconstitutional," at times "the exercise by the President of his veto power may not be feasible."[57] Another Justice Department official said that nonenforcement of parts of a law was a means of dealing with bills that Congress "has made effectively veto-proof."[58] David Stockman, whose Office of Management and Budget issued the final directive to ignore the Competition in Contracting Act, told a House subcommittee: "We would not be here today if we had a line item veto, because these two provisions would have been stricken from the act when we signed it."[59]

In chapter 2, we saw that modern presidents have defended their right to ignore "unconstitutional" laws on the ground that it compensates for congressional practices that have allegedly undermined the efficacy of the veto power. Yet those practices, involving the use of riders and omnibus bills, were well known to the Founders and endorsed by them. Moroever, even if there were merit to this charge that Congress's use of riders and omnibus bills has upset the scheme envisioned by the Founders, the White House has not limited its defiance to situations where tacking or bundling is present. Of the twenty laws with which presidents refused to comply due to constitutional objections, four were omnibus bills and three involved riders. In the other thirteen cases—representing 65 percent of the total—the law posed neither of the evils that supposedly justifies presidential noncompliance.[60]

The issuance of constitutionally based signing statements thus sets the stage for what amounts to a *de facto* item veto. The president is assisted in this undertaking by the Justice Department's Office of Legal Counsel, which reviews all enrolled bills for possible constitutional defects.[61] Douglas Kmiec headed OLC during the Reagan years. In 1993, at the close of the Reagan-Bush era, he noted that "[i]n modern practice, presidents, aided and abetted by OLC itself, have exercised a de facto item veto, at least in those limited circumstances where provisions of enrolled bills are manifestly unconstitutional or they encroach upon executive power."[62]

Yet this *de facto* item veto, through which the executive has staked out the authority to ignore allegedly unconstitutional statutory provisions, is much more versatile and powerful than the line-item veto granted the president by statute in 1996 and than the item veto that would be conferred by a constitutional amendment. The 1996 Line Item Veto Act, even if it is found to be constitutional, merely allows the president to cancel or rescind certain fiscal items in bills the president has signed into law. Items that can be canceled are limited to new appropriations, new spending programs, and tax breaks for small numbers of beneficiaries. Moreover, this veto is qualified rather than absolute, for Congress may override the president's action by a two-thirds vote of each house.[63] Most proposals to confer an item veto by constitutional amendment would likewise confine the item veto to fiscal items and virtually all of them would give Congress the right to override a presidential veto.[64]

The *de facto* item veto that presidents exercise when they refuse to comply with an allegedly unconstitutional law is far more versatile. It may be used against any type of statutory provision, not just taxing and spending items. Thus, of the twenty cases where presidents employed the *de facto* item veto between 1789 and 1981, only four involved fiscal provisions that could have been blocked under a statutory or constitutional item veto provision.[65]

The president's *de facto* item veto is also more potent than other versions of the item veto for it is absolute rather than qualified. When the executive refuses to comply with a statutory provision on the ground that it is unconstitutional, Congress has no opportunity to override that decision. In other words, the president exercises a "power of 'constitutional excision' " which "effectively vetoes legislation without giving Congress an opportunity to override that veto."[66] Though the president's determination that a provision is unconstitutional may be overturned by the courts, this does not guarantee that the measure will then be enforced, for the Reagan administration at times refused to comply with the rulings of lower federal courts in such cases.[67]

The president's *de facto* item veto might in one respect seem less effective than a typical item veto. The veto conferred by the 1996 Line Item Veto Act, like that which would be granted by a constitutional amendment, may be exercised for any reason the president wishes. The *de facto* item veto, however, must be based on the alleged unconstitutionality of the provision in question and cannot rest solely on policy grounds. Yet this apparent drawback is more illusory than real. With a little imagination, almost any policy disagreement can be couched in constitutional terms. Lyndon Johnson demonstrated the point when he objected to a law that barred the Defense Department from closing the Naval Academy's dairy farm in Annapolis. The president charged that Congress's attempt to withdraw the "Department's authority over 380 cows" was objectionable because it presented "questions concerning the constitutional separation of powers."[68] If this dispute could be cloaked in constitutional garb, it is difficult to imagine a disagreement between Congress and the president that could not likewise be transformed into a constitutional issue.

For these purposes, presidents need not depend on their own creativity in identifying constitutional defects in a law. There is, of course, nothing that prevents a president from raising such issues on his own, even if he has no legal training. One suspects this to have been the case with Johnson's concern for the dairy cows in Annapolis. However, presidents may seek input from more informed sources, including White House counsel and the Justice Department.[69]

The principal source of advice in these matters is the Justice Department's Office of Legal Counsel, which reviews all enrolled bills for possible constitutional defects before the president signs them.[70] OLC's scrutiny is not always neutral, for the office serves in part as an advocate for the president's policies.[71] According to Douglas Kmiec, head of OLC during the Reagan years, the office "was asked to include draft signing statements for the president that would be consistent with administration policy. This we did."[72] Another member of OLC during those years admitted that there was no "simple answer" to the question of "to what extent OLC's decisions reflect Administration policy considerations." The OLC "strongly resisted the temptation to allow political pressures to affect its ability to render the best possible legal advice," he said, yet "good lawyers know or soon learn . . . that sophisticated clients will not continue to seek advice from an attorney whose loyalty is questionable or who fails to employ legal skills creatively to address the client's legal problems."[73]

The more than 200 constitutionally based statements issued by Presidents Reagan and Bush indicate just how creative and accommodating the Justice Department can be. OLC lawyers often made it possible for the president to challenge the validity of multiple provisions of a bill.[74] The record may be held by President Bush who, in a November 1989 signing statement, found ten constitutional defects in a bill he signed into law.[75] While the White House will not necessarily defy every statute to which it has objected, a resourceful Justice Department can maximize the President's options in terms of which provisions of law he may choose to ignore.

Although a president's refusal to honor an allegedly unconstitutional statutory provision operates as a *de facto* item veto, it differs from the typical item veto in several important respects, some of which have already been noted. First, the *de facto* item veto is absolute, for Congress cannot vote to override the president's action. Second, the *de facto* item veto may be applied to any type of statutory provision, not just to fiscal items; the only limitation is that the basis for objection must be expressed in constitutional terms. Third, this *de facto* item veto—unlike any other veto—may be applied to laws that were enacted during a prior administration. Finally, the president or his successors may at any time reverse course and decide to honor the contested provision; by contrast, once a bill has been successfully vetoed, it is dead and can never be revived.

In each of these respects, the president's refusal to comply with allegedly unconstitutional legislation much more closely resembles a suspending power than it does an item veto. Under the royal prerogative of suspending the laws, the Crown could similarly refuse to honor all or parts of a law, on either a permanent or temporary basis, without danger of Parliament's overriding its action.[76] The only real difference between the royal suspending power and the president's *de facto* item veto is historical: While the former was abolished in England in 1689 and rejected by the framers of our Constitution, the latter is very much alive and well in the United States today.

10

Limiting Presidential Defiance

THE FEDERAL COURTS AND PRESIDENTIAL DEFIANCE

The text of the Constitution and the debates that accompanied its adoption reveal, as we saw in chapter 2, that the Founders did not intend to give the president a power to suspend laws that he thinks are unconstitutional. Moreover, as we sought to demonstrate in chapters 3 through 9, the history of presidential practice in the years since the adoption of the Constitution has not altered the framework created in 1787. Only by adopting a wholly nonoriginalist approach to constitutional interpretation—one that does not purport to anchor its reading of the text in the understanding of those who created it—could the claimed presidential prerogative to ignore "unconstitutional" laws be accepted as legitimate.

The Supreme Court has not directly addressed the issue of whether the president may refuse to comply with a law that he believes is unconstitutional. In 1838, in *Kendall v. United States ex rel Stokes*, the Court held that the president does not possess a general "dispensing power" that allows him to ignore the law, but the executive's refusal to honor the statute in that case did not rest on constitutional grounds.[1] Similarly, in *United States v. Smith*, the U.S. Circuit Court in 1806 ruled that the Constitution "imparts no dispensing power to the president," but again there was no claim that the law in question was invalid.[2] Of the twenty instances between 1789 and 1981 in which presidents refused to comply with a law due to its alleged unconstitutionality, only two culminated in judicial review. However, in neither case did the Supreme Court discuss the president's failure to honor the law; instead, the Court simply ruled on the validity of the statute in question.[3] To be sure, the federal courts have recognized the legitimacy of prosecutorial discretion, but this doctrine rests on a range of policy considerations that do not include a right to simply ignore "unconstitutional" laws.[4]

Though the Supreme Court has not spoken to the question of the president's authority to disregard allegedly unconstitutional laws, it has held that executive branch agencies lack the inherent authority to pass on the constitutionality of statutes they are charged with enforcing.[5] In *Weinberger v. Salfi*,[6] the Court determined that the secretary of health, education and welfare lacked authority to rule on the validity of the Social Security Act, since that "is a matter of constitutional law concededly beyond his competence to decide."[7] The Court's opinion in *Salfi* was written by Justice William Rehnquist who had taken a similar position in a 1969 memorandum written while he was an assistant attorney general with the Office of Legal Counsel:

> It is in our view extremely difficult to formulate a constitutional theory to justify a refusal by the President to comply with a Congressional directive to spend. . . . [T]he execution of any law is, by definition, an executive function, and it seems an anomalous proposition that because the Executive branch is bound to execute the laws, it is free to decline to execute them.[8]

Executive agencies may rule on the constitutionality of a law only if Congress has clearly authorized them to do so.[9] In such cases, Congress may be deemed to have assigned adjudicatory authority to the executive branch. Alternatively, one might view the situation as one in which Congress has allowed the executive, under narrowly defined conditions, to suspend the law. This is consistent with the principle of the English Bill of Rights, which barred the Crown from suspending the laws "without consent of Parliament."[10] However, because of the discredited status of the suspending power, federal courts are reluctant to find such a congressional authorization, especially "when the constitutional claim asks the agency to act contrary to its statutory charter . . . or when the consequence of committing the issue to the agency would be to deny judicial review of the constitutional claim."[11] In the absence of an unmistakable grant of such authority from Congress, executive agencies may not decline to honor a law on the ground that they believe it to be invalid.

On two occasions, Justice Antonin Scalia has suggested—once for himself and once for three other members of the Court—that the president may ignore an allegedly unconstitutional law. Yet in neither case was this issue before the Court, nor did Scalia seek to reconcile this position with either the text of the Constitution or with the original understanding. In *Morrison v. Olson*, he asserted in a dissenting opinion that "the Executive can decline to prosecute under unconstitutional statutes."[12] The sole authority cited for this proposition was *United States v. Lovett*,[13] a case in which Franklin Roosevelt *complied* with a law even though he believed it to be unconstitutional.[14] While the *Lovett* Court agreed with Roosevelt's assessment of the statute, its opinion in no way suggested that the president might have refused to honor the law. Justice Scalia repeated the same view in *Freytag v. Commissioner*, where he suggested in a concurring opinion that if Congress were to pass laws invading the executive domain, the president would have the power ''even to disregard them when they are unconstitutional.''[15] This time, his authority consisted of a citation to Frank Easterbrook's article setting forth a logical argument for ''presidential review.''[16] While Justices O'Connor, Kennedy, and Souter joined Scalia's *Freytag* concurrence, his statement concerning the president's authority to disregard the laws was a gratuitous aside in a case dealing with whether the Appointments Clause barred the chief judge of the Tax Court from naming special trial judges for certain tax proceedings. The case in no way involved an executive failure to comply with the law. Justice Scalia's use of *Morrison* and *Freytag* as vehicles to advance the principle of presidential review is perhaps explained by the fact that he headed the Office of Legal Counsel from 1974 to 1977 during the Ford administration. Yet his position is a surprising one for a Justice who has long endorsed originalism as the preferred method of constitutional interpretation.[17]

A majority of the Supreme Court has not accepted Scalia's position. If and when the matter is squarely presented to the Court, it will have a chance to consider the issue with the benefit of full briefing, oral argument, and deliberation. The Justices—including Justice Scalia—will hopefully realize that a presidential power to disregard ''unconstitutional'' laws is fundamentally at odds with the system of government created by the Founders. This is the conclusion reached by the lower federal courts that have directly confronted and considered the issue. The U.S. Court of Appeals for the Ninth Circuit, in ruling on a challenge to President Reagan's refusal to comply with the Competition in Contracting Act, rejected as ''utterly at odds with the texture and plain language of the Constitution'' the claim that ''the President's duty to uphold the Constitution and faithfully execute the laws empowers the President to *interpret* the Constitution and *disregard* laws he deems unconstitutional.''[18] Similarly, the Court of Appeals for the Third Circuit, in another case involving the same act, stated that ''this claim of right for the President to declare statutes unconstitutional and to declare his refusal to exercise them, as distinguished from his undisputed right to veto, criticize, or even refuse to defend in court, statutes which he regards as unconstitutional, is dubious at best.''[19]

A LIMITED RIGHT OF EXECUTIVE DEFIANCE?

If the Constitution, construed in light of the original understanding, did not give the president power to suspend the laws whenever he believes them to be unconstitutional, and if the record of presidential practice is not sufficient to alter the original framework, is the executive ever justified in refusing to comply with an allegedly unconstitutional law? One can make a strong argument that a president may never refuse to enforce a law on the ground that he believes it to be unconstitutional.[20] As we saw in chapter 2, the Constitution provided the president with other means of dealing with this situation short of refusing to honor the law, most notably the qualified veto. At the same time, the Founders realized that unconstitutional laws might be enacted, either because a presidential veto was overridden or for other reasons. With this possibility in mind, they provided for judicial review as a check against such a malfunctioning of the lawmaking process. Consistent with this scheme, a president might therefore be justified in disregarding an allegedly unconstitutional law where this is the only means of creating a "case or controversy" through which judicial review of that law may occur.[21] Otherwise, Congress could ignore the Constitution with impunity, a danger that the Founders feared and expressly sought to avoid.[22] This possible exception to the rule against executive defiance of the law may come into play, however, only if there is no other avenue for securing judicial review. It is not enough, as some have urged, that the president desires to bring about a test case.[23] The situation must be one in which judicial review could not take place without executive noncompliance.

Presidential defiance under these narrow circumstances would serve as a safeguard against legislative tyranny without raising the specter of executive autocracy. In contrast to the royal suspending power, a president's refusal to execute the law would be subject to immediate judicial review. If the courts upheld the statute, the president would be obliged to honor it without regard to his own belief as to its validity.[24] On the other hand, if a federal court were to hold the law unconstitutional, the judiciary rather than the executive would become responsible for the statute's nonenforcement. The president would then be justified in disregarding the law until the decision was reversed on appeal or a contrary ruling was handed down by a higher court. In either case, any suspension of the law by the president would be of only temporary duration.

FOUR PRINCIPLES LIMITING PRESIDENTIAL DEFIANCE

If the Supreme Court were to recognize that the executive possesses a limited right of noncompliance with the law, four principles would have to be satisfied for the right to be properly invoked. Even in the absence of judicial recognition, these principles might operate as guides to the president. While the notion that the executive would place limitations on its own actions may appear naïve, during Bill Clinton's first term, the Office of Legal Counsel suggested guidelines that were intended to narrow the "circumstances in which the President may appropriately decline to enforce a statute that he views as unconstitutional."[25] While those guidelines were considerably less stringent than those proposed here, they nonetheless reflect a salutary attempt at self-restraint on the executive's part.

The four proposed conditions for presidential defiance of the law are as follows. First, the situation must be such that defiance is the only way to bring the issue of the law's validity before the courts. Second, the unconstitutionality of the law must be clearly indicated by the text of the Constitution, the intent of the Founders, or prior rulings of the Supreme Court. Third, the White House must have exhausted all available avenues for redressing the matter through the lawmaking process. Fourth, if the executive does defy the law, it must take all possible steps to ensure that judicial review actually occurs. Without these limitations, the narrow privilege of noncompliance could easily become a modern equivalent of the suspending power. Each of these four principles will be considered in turn.

Defiance as the Sole Route to Judicial Review

The president is justified in refusing to comply with a law that he believes is unconstitutional only if judicial review of the measure would otherwise be impossible. Except in the rare instances where this requirement is satisfied, the executive must honor the law. It is up to those who are harmed by the statute to challenge its validity in court, either by filing suit or by raising the constitutional issue defensively. The administration might encourage such challenges by advising potential litigants of their right to sue and the grounds for doing so. Once the matter is in court, the executive might decline to defend the law or join in seeking to have it held unconstitutional.[26] The president may not have to depend on others to initiate the challenge. In the case of an allegedly invalid appointment procedure, for example, the executive might honor the statute but bring a quo warranto proceeding to test the officeholder's right to the position.[27] In other instances, the executive may be able to seek a declaratory judgment that a law with which it has complied is unconstitutional.

Defiance is appropriate only where it is truly an avenue of last resort.[28] Presidents may readily claim that noncompliance is necessary to facilitate judicial review, but such assertions must be closely scrutinized. The Carter administration, in refusing to honor legislative vetoes of Department of Education regulations, stated that without such defiance a court challenge to the veto provision might be foreclosed.[29] In fact, those who would have benefited from the vetoed programs could have sued to compel the department to implement the regulations. Similarly, the Reagan administration sought to justify its defiance of the Competition in Contracting Act on the basis that judicial review was otherwise unlikely to occur.[30] As numerous critics pointed out, however, this assertion was utterly without merit.[31] During the Clinton administration, the Office of Legal Counsel suggested that the president may consider whether compliance with the law would preclude judicial review, but the OLC did not insist that this be an absolute precondition for noncompliance.[32]

Even where noncompliance is indispensable to securing judicial review, the scope of defiance should be no broader than necessary to attain this goal.[33] Thus, for example, even if it had been true that the Competition in Contracting Act could not be challenged in court unless the Reagan administration ignored the statute, this could have been done in a few selected instances to produce a test case rather than on an across-the-board basis affecting virtually all government contracts.[34] The Bush administration may have adhered to this principle in testing a different section of the Competition in Contracting Act, that is, the fee-recovery provision.[35] Instead of paying the statutorily mandated fees to two disappointed bidders, the Justice Department sued the bidders seeking a declaratory judgment that the fee provision was unconstitutional. Even if the executive's defiance was confined to these two cases, however, noncompliance was nonetheless improper because Congress was at the time considering a curative amendment to the act.[36] Under our third limiting principle, discussed later, the administration thus failed to exhaust all available legislative avenues of redress.

A Clearly Unconstitutional Law

The executive may refuse to comply with a law only if it is patently unconstitutional. When a president opts to veto a bill, he acts in a legislative capacity.[37] Like any member of Congress, he may cast his vote against the measure because of mere doubts as to its validity.[38] However, when the president refuses to enforce a statute on the ground that it is unconstitutional, he is no longer functioning as a lawmaker. There is no independent basis in the executive power for refusing to carry out such a law. The president's only legitimate basis for noncompliance is that it is necessary for judicial review. Just as "the judiciary has always given to congressional enactments a presumption of validity,"[39] so should the executive.[40] Unless the grounds for believing a statute to be invalid are very strong, the president should execute the measure even though nonfrivolous arguments can be marshalled against it.

Without such a presumption in favor of compliance, the White House—assisted by creative minds in the Justice Department—could refuse to honor an endless array of laws even though there is little or no chance of them later being overturned by the courts. The requirement that a law be clearly unconstitutional, based on the text of the Constitution, the Founders' intent, or Supreme Court precedent, amounts to a rejection in this specific context of the position that a president has total autonomy to interpret the Constitution as he chooses.[41]

Counsel for various presidents, including Andrew Johnson, Woodrow Wilson, Jimmy Carter, Ronald Reagan, and Bill Clinton, have taken the position that the executive may ignore a law that is patently or clearly unconstitutional.[42] This view has also found support in academic circles.[43] The trick is figuring out a way to make the condition a meaningful one. One might insist that the White House publicly explain the legal basis for its view that a law is invalid, on the theory that this will dissuade the executive from relying on tenuous constitutional objections. During the Clinton years, the Office of Legal Counsel recommended that the president disregard a law only when "it is probable that the Court would agree with him" that it is invalid.[44] Under this fairly strict test for "clearly unconstitutional," a requirement that the White House justify its decision based on Supreme Court precedent might serve to limit the instances of noncompliance. By contrast, if it were merely necessary to advance a legal theory by which the law might be found unconstitutional, the requirement would likely be reduced to a mere formality for, as Arthur S. Miller observed, "Government lawyers always can be found . . . to create a counterpane of putative legality over any action the President desires."[45] The Justice Department, for example, assured Congress that the Competition in Contracting Act was "in clear contravention of the Constitution,"[46] yet the act was subsequently upheld by every federal court to rule on the question.[47] The solicitor general might be a more trustworthy source of such legal opinions than the attorney general, for that office has, at least until recently, enjoyed a better reputation for independence from the White House.[48]

Yet it would be naïve to expect that this requirement will, by itself, significantly curtail the executive's ability to ignore allegedly unconstitutional statutes. The distinction between laws that are clearly invalid and those that are only arguably so is likely to reflect one's convictions as much as one's ability to decipher the Constitution. To be sure, the distinction may sometimes be apparent. After the decision in *INS v. Chadha*,[49] most lawyers would agree that a statute containing a one-or two-house legislative veto is clearly unconstitutional.[50] And most lawyers would also probably agree that a law barring the president from closing the navy's dairy farm in Annapolis was not patently unconstitutional, despite Lyndon Johnson's claim to the contrary.[51] To suggest as some have that the executive may automatically disregard any statute that is "plainly unconstitutional"[52] would effectively give the president a *carte blanche* to defy the law. The requirement that a law be clearly invalid must be viewed as only one of several conditions, all of which must be met before the executive may disregard an act of Congress.

Exhausting Legislative Avenues of Redress

Before a president may take the extreme step of refusing to execute a statute on the ground that it is unconstitutional, all other available means for redressing the situation through the lawmaking process must have been exhausted. This requirement follows from the fact that the sole justification for defiance of the law is as an adjunct to judicial review. It has often been recognized that federal courts must decide constitutional issues only as a matter of last resort.[53] Unless the executive is governed by a similar principle, the judiciary might be placed in the position of having to review statutes whose constitutional defects could easily have been redressed by other means.

The White House may be able to prevent an unconstitutional provision from being enacted into law by using its influence to have a bill amended or defeated in Congress. The Office of Legal Counsel thus advised the Clinton White House that "[w]hen bills are under consideration by Congress, the executive branch should promptly identify unconstitutional provisions and communicate its concerns to Congress so that the provisions can be corrected."[54] If these efforts are unavailing and the president believes that the bill is unconstitutional, he has the option, if not the duty, to veto the measure. While the White House in recent years has claimed that the veto is often impractical,[55] such policy-based concerns should not suffice to outweigh a genuine and well-founded constitutional objection.[56] Even in the worst case scenario, when the offending provision is part of an omnibus bill or is tacked as a rider to an urgent end-of-the-session appropriations package, a president committed to the Constitution might still employ the negative and, at the same time, submit a new bill that meets his concerns; if necessary, he might call a special session of Congress to consider the substitute measure.

These efforts may, of course, fail. Nor are the options of working with Congress or employing the veto available to a President if the law in question was passed during a previous administration. In this event, the avenues for legislative redress narrow. The executive may, however, urge Congress to amend or repeal the allegedly invalid statute, an approach that has sometimes met with success.[57] If no response is immediately forthcoming, the president may have to repeat the request before he can be deemed to have exhausted this option. Where compliance with the allegedly unconstitutional law does not cause serious harm, the requisite exhaustion period may stretch over many years. It took decades of presidential requests before the Tenure of Office Act was finally repealed.[58] Lyndon Johnson sought the repeal of various committee approval requirements for three years before deciding not to pursue any further projects under the offending laws.[59]

Ensuring That Judicial Review Occurs

In cases where all three of the conditions previously discussed have been met, a president is still not justified in refusing to honor an allegedly unconstitutional law unless he takes all steps necessary to secure a judicial ruling as to the law's validity. In the eyes of at least some members of Congress, it was here that Andrew Johnson fell short in his defiance of the 1867 Tenure of Office Act. While executive defiance was necessary to bring about a test case, Johnson's attorneys failed to pursue any of several available routes for obtaining judicial review.[60]

In order to satisfy this requirement, it may be possible for the executive to initiate a suit that will raise the constitutional issue. This could occur if a lower level federal official refused to carry out the president's order to disregard the law. Thus, with respect to the Tenure of Office Act, Andrew Johnson's attorney general might have instituted quo warranto proceedings against Secretary of War Stanton after he refused to surrender the office.[61] In the Competition in Contracting Act setting, either the Justice Department or the Office of Management and Budget, each of which had ordered federal agencies to ignore the act's stay provisions, might have sued a government department that refused to defy the law.

If the executive branch is not in a position to trigger judicial review, the president must make every effort to ensure that other persons with standing to sue, or who are in a position to raise the constitutional issue, in fact do so. In the Tenure of Office Act case, the attorney whom Andrew Johnson hired to represent General Thomas could have challenged the act's validity either by raising the issue as a defense to the pending criminal action or by seeking a writ of habeas corpus.[62] Neither of these avenues was pursued. It may also be necessary for the executive to notify adversely affected individuals that they can sue to enforce their rights under the statute the president has defied.

It is possible that despite the executive's good faith efforts to bring about judicial review, no one with standing to sue in fact does so. Is the president then free to continue defying the law indefinitely? One might argue that the fact no one has sued means that any injury caused by the noncompliance is de minimis and hence of no constitutional concern.[63] Yet there may be good reasons why a genuinely aggrieved individual has not sued, including the cost of litigation or secondary consequences such as the loss of privacy. While the issue is a debatable one, the burden should remain on the executive to ensure that a test case is filed. If none is instituted within a reasonable time, presidential defiance of the law should cease. Were the rule otherwise, the White House might not take seriously its duty to ensure that judicial review occurs, thereby giving itself the final word as to whether or not an act of Congress will be enforced.

THE FOUR PRINCIPLES AND PRESIDENTIAL PRACTICE

Under the conditions just outlined, a president may refuse to honor an allegedly unconstitutional law if such defiance is necessary to securing judicial review. Even then, defiance is unwarranted unless the law is clearly unconstitutional, and the executive has exhausted its avenues of redress through the lawmaking process, and all feasible steps are taken to bring about judicial review. Measured against these standards, none of the twenty cases of presidential defiance that occurred between 1789 and 1981 was proper.

As Table 9.1 indicates, in eleven of the twenty instances of presidential defiance, it was not necessary for the executive to defy the law in order to permit judicial review. Indeed, in six of these eleven cases—involving Presidents Arthur, Cleveland, Eisenhower, Ford, and two laws ignored by Carter—noncompliance had the effect of preventing judicial review that might otherwise have occurred.

In addition, there were two instances in which judicial review was effectively precluded regardless of what action the executive took. In these two cases—involving Wilson's failure to send treaty termination notices,[64] and Carter's closure of the American consulates[65]—presidential defiance was unwarranted under our first principle, since it did not facilitate judicial review. It may seem unfair to require compliance with the law in such instances where the president's objection is that Congress had encroached on the executive domain. Yet in each of these cases, the president signed the bill instead of using the veto power that the Founders gave him for the purpose of defending against such laws. Moreover, it was highly questionable whether either of these laws encroached on the executive domain. The issue of which branch has the authority to terminate treaties remains an open one even today.[66] The question of who possesses the authority to close American consulates is equally unclear, even though the issue was raised by President Grant a century before Carter did so.[67] Nevertheless, had Wilson and Carter truly believed that Congress was usurping powers that clearly belonged to the president, they had ample means of protecting the executive branch through exercise of the veto.

Of the twenty instances of executive defiance, this leaves seven cases in which judicial review would have been impossible without noncompliance. As indicated in Table 9.1, these involved James Buchanan's transfer of Captain Meigs; Andrew Johnson's dismissal of the Secretary of War; William Howard Taft's submission of his own budget to Congress; Woodrow Wilson's firing of a postmaster; Franklin Roosevelt's removal of a federal trade commissioner; and Gerald Ford and Jimmy Carter's refusal to honor the War Powers Resolution. Yet none of these incidents met the three other conditions that must be satisfied before a decision to defy the law may be justified.

President Buchanan's defiance of the law requiring that certain monies for building the Washington Aqueduct be spent under the personal supervision of Captain Meigs was based on Buchanan's belief that Congress had violated the Commander-in-Chief Clause by dictating which army officer was to perform a particular duty. The law was not clearly unconstitutional. The president could do whatever he wished with Captain Meigs, since Congress had left the President with the option of not spending the money. Nor did Buchanan exhaust other avenues of redress, for he signed rather than vetoed the bill containing the Meigs proviso.[68]

Andrew Johnson's refusal to honor the Tenure of Office Act likewise involved a law that was not clearly unconstitutional. The issue of whether Congress may limit the executive's ability to remove officers of the United States had been debated since the time of the first Congress. It was not resolved by the Court until more than fifty years after Andrew Johnson left the White House.[69] Johnson did meet the third principle, for he vetoed the Tenure of Office Act; after it was re-enacted over his veto, he then urged Congress to repeal the measure. However, as we saw earlier, Johnson did not satisfy the fourth requirement, for he failed to take advantage of three different avenues that could have produced a test case.[70]

Taft's defiance of the statute that prohibited him from submitting a proposed budget to Congress except in a certain form was the one case where the law in question appears to have been patently unconstitutional. The statute violated Article II, section 3, which authorizes the president to "recommend . . . such Measures as he shall judge necessary and expedient." However, noncompliance was still unwarranted, for Taft did not meet the third or fourth principles. By signing rather than vetoing the bill, he failed to exhaust all avenues of redress through the lawmaking process. Nor did he take all steps to ensure that judicial review would occur, for he failed to give prior notice to those who could be harmed by his budget recommendations and who might have sued to enjoin his submission of a separate budget.[71]

Woodrow Wilson's dismissal of a postmaster without consent of the Senate was one of only two cases of presidential defiance that resulted in judicial review. Though the Court in *Myers v. United States* agreed that this restriction on the president's removal power was unconstitutional, Wilson's action was improper because the law in question was not clearly invalid. As previously noted in connection with Andrew Johnson, the issue was one that had been debated since the adoption of the Constitution. That the statute was not patently unconstitutional is evident from the fact that Justices Oliver Wendell Holmes, Louis D. Brandeis, and James C. McReynolds each dissented from the Court decision invalidating the measure.[72] Moreover, with respect to our third principle, it does not appear that Wilson took any steps to have the law, which was enacted long before he took office, repealed or amended by Congress.

For similar reasons, Franklin Roosevelt's defiance of a law that allowed the president to remove federal trade commissioners only for cause was unwarranted. The earlier decision in *Myers*, barring the Senate from directly participating in the removal process, did not clearly invalidate statutory limitations on the grounds on which the president could remove an officer. Indeed, while this was the only other case where the executive's defiance of the law led to judicial review, the Court held unanimously in *Humphrey's Executor v. United States* that the statute in question was constitutional.[73] In addition to not satisfying the second principle, Roosevelt probably failed to meet the third condition for there is no evidence that he sought to have this law, which had been on the books since 1914, amended or repealed before he decided to defy it.

Presidents Ford and Carter both refused to comply with the notification provisions of the 1973 War Powers Resolution. While judicial review would have been impossible had they honored the resolution, it is a close question whether noncompliance did much if anything to enhance the prospects for review. The uses to which they put the armed forces were so brief that any judicial challenge might have become moot before a court could rule on the resolution's validity. Yet even assuming that our first principle was satisfied here—that defiance was necessary to allow for judicial review—the second principle was not met. Despite the contention of President Nixon and his successors, the War Powers Resolution is not clearly unconstitutional. The executive's claim that the power to employ the armed forces in hostilities without the approval of Congress flies in the face of Article 1, section 8, which provides that "Congress shall have Power . . . To declare War."[74]

In sum, none of the twenty incidents in which presidents refused to honor an allegedly unconstitutional law during the period from 1789 to 1981 can be defended under the exception for facilitating judicial review. Even in the two instances where judicial review occurred, the executive's conduct was unjustified due to the fact that the law was not patently unconstitutional. In eighteen of the twenty cases, no review occurred, often because the executive's action foreclosed any possible court challenge to the law in question. On each of these eighteen occasions, the president suspended a provision of law under circumstances where his act of defiance could not be overturned either by Congress or by the courts.

TWO REJECTED GROUNDS FOR PRESIDENTIAL DEFIANCE

The proposal advanced here rejects two grounds that are sometimes urged as being sufficient to warrant presidential noncompliance with the law. The first involves statutes that allegedly invade the executive domain.[75] In defending its defiance of the Competition in Contracting Act, the Reagan administration took this position, arguing that the president ''has a constitutional duty to protect the Presidency from encroachment by other branches.''[76] The Bush and Clinton administrations adopted a similar stance.[77] While a president's refusal to comply with such laws would be warranted if all four of our requirements were met, the fact that a law is perceived as infringing upon executive power cannot be sufficient by itself. If it were, the primary reason for giving the president a veto power would be rendered superfluous.[78] One might respond that the veto would still be useful when a statute as a whole violates rights of the executive and that selective defiance would be employed in cases involving omnibus bills and legislative riders. Yet proponents of the view that presidents may ignore laws that invade the executive domain do not restrict the power to these two situations. Moreover, the encroachment rationale would open the door wide to defiance of the law, for between 1789 and 1981 more than 80 percent of the constitutional objections asserted in signing statements charged that there had been an impairment of executive power.[79] Finally, as Professor Sanford Levinson has observed, it is here that we should ''be least willing to trust independent presidential decisionmaking, since there is no reason at all to view the President as a genuinely disinterested party.''[80]

A second suggested criterion that this proposal does not adopt is one that would allow the president to disregard a law whenever it is perceived as violating basic individual rights.[81] Though intuitively appealing, the argument for executive defiance is at its weakest in this class of cases, for judicial review is virtually always available when such statutes are enforced. The individuals whose rights are allegedly violated through executive compliance will have standing to challenge the law's validity in court. Even if, as some have hypothesized, Congress were to bar the federal judiciary from hearing such challenges,[82] the courts would most likely hold that the attempted restriction on their jurisdiction was itself unconstitutional.[83] On the other hand, presidential *non-*

compliance in this setting will often be immune from judicial scrutiny, as the Carter administration found when it declined on First Amendment grounds to enforce a ban against editorializing by public radio stations.[84] The same was true of President Carter's refusal on Establishment Clause grounds to restore the San Antonio Missions,[85] and of his refusal on due process and bill of attainder grounds to honor a prohibition against using funds to implement his pardon of Vietnam-era draft resisters.[86] Unless the four conditions previously outlined are met, the executive should comply with the law while taking steps to ensure that those whose rights may be infringed can promptly challenge the measure in court. This was the path followed by Franklin Roosevelt in response to a law that banned the federal government from continuing to employ three individuals.[87] In the unusual case where enforcement of such a statute might cause irreparable injury, those threatened with harm should be able to obtain immediate injunctive relief from the federal courts.

CONCLUSION

In recent years, American presidents have asserted that they now possess the authority to disregard laws that they believe to be unconstitutional. Through these claims, the White House has sought to resurrect the suspending power, a royal prerogative that was abolished in England by the Bill of Rights of 1689 after centuries of struggle between Parliament and the Crown.

Though the Constitution does not expressly deny this power to the president of the United States, it is absolutely clear that the Founders did not intend to confer such authority on the executive. The convention's decision to give the president only a qualified rather than an absolute veto, the assumption implicit in Article I, section 9 that the suspending power belongs to Congress, the president's duty to "take Care that the Laws be faithfully executed," the framers' understanding of the "executive power," the express grant of the pardon power, the absence of pressure to include a ban against the suspending power in the Bill of Rights, and the complete silence of the Anti-Federalists all support the conclusion that the Constitution did not give the American chief executive a power to suspend the laws.

For nearly three-quarters of a century, presidents respected this original understanding. Even when the executive thought that a particular statute was unconstitutional, it performed its duty to faithfully execute the law. From the mid-nineteenth century onward, the White House occasionally refused to comply with an "unconstitutional" law, but as late as 1971, there had been only ten instances of such noncompliance. Since the mid-1970s, however, the rhetoric and the reality of presidential defiance have escalated dramatically. In the 185-year span that covers the administrations of George Washington through Richard Nixon, presidents objected to the constitutionality of fewer than eighty laws. Yet in the brief span from 1974 through 1996, Presidents Ford, Carter, Reagan, Bush, and Clinton challenged the validity of more than 250 statutes. Of the twenty incidents of defiance of the law that occurred between 1789 and 1981, half occurred during the last ten years of this period.

As of this writing, the Supreme Court has not recognized the claimed presidential power to ignore allegedly unconstitutional laws. If the Court remains true to the original understanding, it will reject such claims except perhaps under extraordinarily limited circumstances.

Notes

INTRODUCTION

1. Supplemental Brief for Appellants at 21, Lear Siegler, Inc. v. Ball, 863 F.2d 693 (9th Cir. 1988), *quoted in* Morton Rosenberg, *Congress's Prerogative over Agencies and Agency Decisionmakers: The Rise and Demise of the Reagan Administration's Theory of the Unitary Executive*, 57 GEO. WASH. L. REV. 627, 633 (1989).

2. Letter from Ass't Att'y Gen. Walter Dellinger to Abner J. Mikva, Counsel to the President (Nov. 2, 1994), *reprinted in* Note, *Recent Legal Opinions Concerning Presidential Powers*, 48 ARK. L. REV. 311, 318 (1995).

3. *See infra* Table 5.1.

4. Henry P. Monaghan, *The Protective Power of the Presidency*, 93 COLUM. L. REV. 1, 31 (1993) (using phrase to describe claims that the president possesses war and emergency powers with which Congress may not interfere).

5. See *id.* at 8–10.

6. See H.R. REP. NO. 138, 99th Cong., 1st Sess., at 15–16 (1985).

7. Line Item Veto Act, Pub. L. No. 104–130, 110 Stat. 1200 (1996) (codified at 2 U.S.C.A. §§ 691 et seq. (Supp. 1997)).

8. *See* ARTHUR M. SCHLESINGER, JR., THE IMPERIAL PRESIDENCY (1973); ARTHUR M. SCHLESINGER, JR., THE CYCLES OF AMERICAN HISTORY 277–301 (1986); Martin S. Flaherty, *The Most Dangerous Branch*, 105 YALE L.J. 1725, 1816–21 (1996); Henry P. Monaghan, *Stare Decisis and Constitutional Adjudication*, 88 COLUM. L. REV. 723, 736–37 (1988).

9. Marozsan v. United States, 852 F.2nd 1469, 1490 (7th Cir. 1988) (Easterbrook, Coffey & Manion, JJ., dissenting).

10. U.S. CONST. art. II, § 3.

CHAPTER 1

1. 2 WILLIAM A. STUBBS, THE CONSTITUTIONAL HISTORY OF ENGLAND, IN ITS ORIGIN AND DEVELOPMENT 515 (Oxford, Clarendon Press, 2d ed. 1877).

2. JOHN LOCKE, TWO TREATISES ON GOVERNMENT 375 (Peter Laslett ed., student ed. 1988) (3d ed. 1698).

3. HENRY J. STEPHEN, COMMENTARIES ON THE LAWS OF ENGLAND 298 (L. Crispin Warmington ed., 21st ed., 1950).

4. *See* GEORGE B. ADAMS, CONSTITUTIONAL HISTORY OF ENGLAND 234–36 (1934).

5. 2 WILLIAM S. HOLDSWORTH, A HISTORY OF ENGLISH LAW 308, 437 (4th ed. 1936).

6. 2 STUBBS, CONSTITUTIONAL HISTORY, at 389–92, 582.

7. ADAMS, CONSTITUTIONAL HISTORY, at 197–98; 2 STUBBS, CONSTITUTIONAL HISTORY, at 570–78, 585–87.

8. ADAMS, CONSTITUTIONAL HISTORY, at 206; 2 STUBBS, CONSTITUTIONAL HISTORY, at 570–90; ALBERT B. WHITE, THE MAKING OF THE ENGLISH CONSTITUTION 449–1485, at 374 (1908).

9. 2 STUBBS, CONSTITUTIONAL HISTORY, at 575.

10. 2 HOLDSWORTH, HISTORY OF ENGLISH LAW, at 437.

11. FREDERIC W. MAITLAND, THE CONSTITUTIONAL HISTORY OF ENGLAND: A COURSE OF LECTURES DELIVERED 302–03 (1926); THEODORE F. T. PLUCKNETT, TASWELL-LANGMEAD'S ENGLISH CONSTITUTIONAL HISTORY 190–91 (11th ed. 1960).

12. Carolyn A. Edie, *Tactics and Strategies: Parliament's Attack Upon the Royal Dispensing Power 1597–1689*, 29 AM. J. LEGAL HIST. 197, 198 (1985).

13. 6 WILLIAM S. HOLDSWORTH, A HISTORY OF ENGLISH LAW 217 (2d ed. 1937).

14. Edie, *Tactics and Strategies*, at 198–99; 6 HOLDSWORTH, HISTORY OF ENGLISH LAW, at 217.

15. See Edie, *Tactics and Strategies*, at 201–02, 220 n.47.

16. WILLIAM R. ANSON, THE LAW AND CUSTOM OF THE CONSTITUTION 265 (Oxford, Clarendon Press, 1886); 6 HOLDSWORTH, A HISTORY OF ENGLISH LAW, at 218.

17. Edie, *Tactics and Strategies*, at 203 (quoting EDWARD COKE, THE THIRD PART OF THE INSTITUTES OF THE LAW OF ENGLAND: CONCERNING HIGH TREASON, AND OTHER PLEASE OF THE CROWN AND CRIMINAL CAUSES 192 (London, 1680)).

18. Edie, *Tactics and Strategies*, at 223.

19. ANSON, LAW AND CUSTOM OF THE CONSTITUTION, at 265–67; MAITLAND, CONSTITUTIONAL HISTORY, at 304; STEPHEN, COMMENTARIES ON THE LAW OF ENGLAND, at 295; Edie, *Tactics and Strategies*, at 200–23.

20. Edie, *Tactics and Strategies*, at 197, 202, 210, 215, 222–23.

21. 2 STUBBS, CONSTITUTIONAL HISTORY, at 516, 574.

22. 2 HOLDSWORTH, HISTORY OF ENGLISH LAW, at 443.

23. 23 Hen. 6, ch. 9 (1444).

24. 12 Coke's Rep. 18, 77 Eng. Rep. 1300 (Ex. 1487).

25. *See* 6 HOLDSWORTH, HISTORY OF ENGLISH LAW, at 221, 224; Edie, *Tactics and Strategies*, at 201–02.

26. 1 Jam. 1, ch. 22, § 51 (1603).

27. Edie, *Tactics and Strategies*, at 210–11.

28. ANSON, LAW AND CUSTOM OF THE CONSTITUTION, at 266–67; 6 HOLDSWORTH, HISTORY OF ENGLISH LAW, at 218–20; Edie, *Tactics and Strategies*, at 199–200.

29. 14 Car. 2, ch. 7, § 10 (1662); 14 Car. 2, ch. 18, § 11 (1662).

30. Edie, *Tactics and Strategies*, at 218, 220 n.48.

31. Edie, *Tactics and Strategies*, at 218–20. The use of nuisance clauses to restrict the prerogative was later approved in Thomas v. Sorrell, 124 Eng. Rep. 1098 (K.B. 1674); *see* Edie, *Tactics and Strategies*, at 224–26.

32. JACK HARVEY & L. BATHER, THE BRITISH CONSTITUTION 193 (2d ed. 1968).

33. Edie, *Tactics and Strategies*, at 217–18.

34. Edie, *Tactics and Strategies*, at 222.

35. Edie, *Tactics and Strategies*, at 220–22; and *see* 6 HOLDSWORTH, HISTORY OF ENGLISH LAW, at 221–22; COLIN R. LOVELL, ENGLISH CONSTITUTIONAL AND LEGAL HISTORY 370–77 (1962); PLUCKNETT, TASWELL-LANGMEAD'S ENGLISH CONSTITUTIONAL HISTORY, at 426–27; JOSEPH R. TANNER, ENGLISH CONSTITUTIONAL CONFLICTS OF THE SEVENTEENTH CENTURY, 1603–1689, at 229–30 (1966).

36. LOVELL, ENGLISH CONSTITUTIONAL AND LEGAL HISTORY, at 376; PLUCKNETT, TASWELL-LANGMEAD'S ENGLISH CONSTITUTIONAL HISTORY, at 427.

37. Godden v. Hales, 2 Show. K.B. 475, 477, 89 Eng. Rep. 1050, 1051 (K.B. 1686); 6 HOLDSWORTH, HISTORY OF ENGLISH LAW, at 223–25.

38. Godden v. Hales, 2 Show. K.B. at 478, 89 Eng. Rep. at 1051.

39. PLUCKNETT, TASWELL-LANGMEAD'S ENGLISH CONSTITUTIONAL HISTORY, at 442.

40. *See* LOVELL, ENGLISH CONSTITUTIONAL AND LEGAL HISTORY, at 370–77; PLUCKNETT, TASWELL-LANGMEAD'S ENGLISH CONSTITUTIONAL HISTORY, at 422–28, 442.

41. PLUCKNETT, TASWELL-LANGMEAD'S ENGLISH CONSTITUTIONAL HISTORY, at 442–43; *see also* LOVELL, ENGLISH CONSTITUTIONAL AND LEGAL HISTORY, at 391–92, 406–07; MAITLAND, CONSTITUTIONAL HISTORY OF ENGLAND, at 305–06.

42. Trial of the Seven Bishops (K.B. 1688), *reprinted in* 12 THOMAS B. HOWELL, A COMPLETE COLLECTION OF STATE TRIALS, 183, 427 (London, T. C. Hansard, 1816).

43. LOVELL, ENGLISH CONSTITUTIONAL AND LEGAL HISTORY, at 407.

44. 1 William and Mary sess. 2 ch. 2, preamble.

45. 1 William and Mary sess. 2 ch. 2 § i 1.

46. Edie, *Tactics and Strategies*, at 234 n. 86.

47. 1 William and Mary sess. 2 ch. 2 § i 2.

48. 1 William and Mary sess. 2 ch. 2 § xii.

49. *See* ANSON, LAW AND CUSTOM OF THE CONSTITUTION, at 269–73; 6 HOLDSWORTH, HISTORY OF ENGLISH LAW, at 240–41; Edie, *Tactics and Strategies*, at 230–34.

50. *See* Case of Non Obstante, 77 Eng. Rep. 1300 (Ex. 1487); 6 HOLDSWORTH, HISTORY OF ENGLISH LAW, at 221, 224; Edie, *Tactics and Strategies*, at 201–02.

CHAPTER 2

1. *See* Martin S. Flaherty, *The Most Dangerous Branch*, 105 YALE L.J. 1725, 1801–02 (1996).

2. *See generally* MICHAEL J. GERHARDT & THOMAS D. ROWE, JR., CONSTITUTIONAL THEORY: ARGUMENTS AND PERSPECTIVES (1993); Daniel A. Farber, *The Originalism Debate: A Guide for the Perplexed*, 49 OHIO ST. L.J. 1085 (1989).

3. Michael Perry, *The Legitimacy of Particular Conceptions of Constitutional Interpretation*, 77 VA. L. REV. 669, 673 (1991); Lawrence Solum, *Originalism as Transformative Politics*, 63 TUL. L. REV. 1599, 1612 (1986).

4. Perry, *The Legitimacy of Particular Conceptions*, at 695–701.

5. *Id.* at 698.

6. *See* Farber, *The Originalism Debate*, at 1086 & n. 4, 1096; Henry P. Monaghan, *Stare Decisis and Constitutional Adjudication*, 88 COLUM L. REV. 723 (1988); Antonin Scalia, *Originalism: The Lesser Evil*, 57 U. CIN. L. REV. 849, 861–65 (1989).

7. *See* Paul Brest, *The Misconceived Quest for the Original Understanding*, 60 B. U. L. REV. 204, 229 (1980); Farber, *The Originalism Debate*, at 1105–06; Scalia, *Originalism*, at 864.

8. Abner S. Greene, *Checks and Balances in an Era of Presidential Lawmaking*, 61 U. CHI. L. REV. 123, 129–30 (1994); Michael S. Paulsen, *The Most Dangerous Branch: Executive Power to Say What the Law Is*, 83 GEO. L.J. 217, 227 n. 24 (1994).

9. JEFFREY K. TULIS, THE RHETORICAL PRESIDENCY 8 n.9 (1987).

10. Steven G. Calabresi & Saikrishna B. Prakash, *The President's Power to Execute the Laws*, 104 YALE L.J. 541, 552–53 (1994).

11. Monaghan, *Stare Decisis*, at 724–25.

12. Flaherty, *The Most Dangerous Branch*, at 1788–90.

13. Lawrence Lessig, *Fidelity and Constraint*, 65 FORDHAM L. REV. 1365, 1368–71 (1997).

14. GARRY WILLS, INVENTING AMERICA: JEFFERSON'S DECLARATION OF INDEPENDENCE 64 (Vintage Books 1979).

15. *See* BERNARD BAILYN, THE IDEOLOGICAL ORIGINS OF THE AMERICAN REVOLUTION 30–31 (1967); GRANT GILMORE, THE AGES OF AMERICAN LAW 113–14 n.4 (1977); DAVID A. LOCKMILLER, SIR WILLIAM BLACKSTONE 169–74 (1938); FORREST MCDONALD, THE AMERICAN PRESIDENCY: AN INTELLECTUAL HISTORY 27 (1994).

16. 1 WILLIAM BLACKSTONE, COMMENTARIES, ch. 2, at *178–179.

17. *See* FREDERICK J. STIMSON, THE LAW OF THE FEDERAL AND STATE CONSTITUTIONS OF THE UNITED STATES 52 (1908).

18. EDWARD C. MASON, THE VETO POWER 17–18 (Boston, Ginn 1890); Richard A. Watson, *Origins and Early Development of the Veto Power*, 17 PRESIDENTIAL STUD. Q. 401, 404 (1987).

19. ROBERT J. SPITZER, THE PRESIDENTIAL VETO: TOUCHSTONE OF THE AMERICAN PRESIDENCY 8–10 (1988); Watson, *Origins and Early Development of the Veto Power*, at 401, 404–05; *and see* MCDONALD, THE AMERICAN PRESIDENCY, at 130–35.

20. 1 MAX FARRAND, THE RECORDS OF THE FEDERAL CONVENTION OF 1787 98–103 (1966).

21. *Id.* at 292.

22. 2 *id.* at 200.

23. Robert J. Spitzer, *The President's Veto Power, in* INVENTING THE AMERICAN PRESIDENCY 154, 168 (Thomas E. Cronin ed., 1989).

24. 2 FARRAND, RECORDS OF THE FEDERAL CONVENTION 585–87 (Sept. 12, 1787).

25. *Id.* at 585; *see also id.* at 586.

26. 1 *id.* at 103–04 (emphasis in original).

27. *Id.* at 104.

28. *See* Calabresi & Prakash, *The President's Power to Execute the Laws*, at 584 n.161.

29. 2 FARRAND, RECORDS OF THE FEDERAL CONVENTION, at 586.

30. *Id.* at 587.

31. Thomas Jefferson, *Opinion on the Constitutionality of a National Bank* (Feb. 15, 1791), *in* THOMAS JEFFERSON: WRITINGS 416, 420–21 (Merrill D. Peterson ed., Library of America 1984).

32. THE FEDERALIST No. 73, at 443, 445 (Alexander Hamilton) (Clinton Rossiter ed., New American Library, 1961); *see also* SPITZER, THE PRESIDENTIAL VETO, at 17.

33. Letter from the Federal Farmer (Jan. 17, 1788), *in* 2 THE COMPLETE ANTI-FEDERALIST 314 (Herbert J. Storing ed., 1981).

34. 1 FARRAND, RECORDS OF THE FEDERAL CONVENTION, at 98.

35. *Id.* at 98.

36. *Id.* at 94, 98.

37. THE FEDERALIST No. 73, at 443, 445 (Alexander Hamilton).

38. THE FEDERALIST No. 78, at 466 (Alexander Hamilton) (emphasis added).

39. EDWARD M. BURNS, JAMES MADISON: PHILOSOPHER OF THE CONSTITUTION 161 (1973).

40. *Observations on Jefferson's Draft of a Constitution for Virginia, in* 11 PAPERS OF JAMES MADISON 281, 284–85 (Robert A. Rutland & Charles F. Hobson eds., 1977); Letter from James Madison to Mr.———(1834), *in* 4 LETTERS AND OTHER WRITINGS OF JAMES MADISON 349–50 (Philadelphia, J. B. Lippincott & Co. 1865).

41. BURNS, JAMES MADISON, at 157–61 (quoting from undated manuscript in Madison Papers).

42. 1 FARRAND, RECORDS OF THE FEDERAL CONVENTION, at 100.

43. *Observations on Jefferson's Draft of a Constitution for Virginia, in* 11 PAPERS OF JAMES MADISON, at 281, 292–93.

44. 4 FARRAND, RECORDS OF THE FEDERAL CONVENTION, at 81 n.2a.

45. 2 *id.* at 294–95, 298.

46. 3 WESTEL W. WILLOUGHBY, THE CONSTITUTIONAL LAW OF THE UNITED STATES 1503–04 (2d ed. 1929). *But see* Gary Lawson & Christopher D. Moore, *The Executive Power of Constitutional Interpretation*, 81 IOWA L. REV. 1267, 1303–13 (1996) (arguing that in addition to the vetopower, a president may refuse to enforce an unconstitutional law).

47. 2 FARRAND, RECORDS OF THE FEDERAL CONVENTION, at 341.

48. *See* Robert L. Berg, Presidential Power and the Royal Prerogative 291 (1958) (unpublished Ph.D. dissertation, University of Minnesota).

49. *See, e.g.*, U.S. CONST. art. II, § 2, cl. 1 (restricting power to grant reprieves and pardons); U.S. CONST. art. II, § 2, cl. 2 (restricting powers to make treaties and appointments).

50. 2 JONATHAN ELLIOT, DEBATES IN THE SEVERAL STATE CONVENTIONS ON THE ADOPTION OF THE FEDERAL CONSTITUTION 108–09 (Philadelphia, J. B. Lippincott & Co., 2d ed. 1881).

51. 31 Car. 2, ch. 2 (1679).

52. 1 ST. GEORGE TUCKER, BLACKSTONE'S COMMENTARIES, app. at 290–92 (photo. reprint 1965) (Philadelphia, William Young Birch & Abraham Small 1803).

53. 8 U.S. (4 Cranch) 75 (1807).

54. *Id.* at 95 (emphasis added).

55. 3 JOSEPH STORY, COMMENTARIES ON THE CONSTITUTION § 1336 (Boston, Hilliard, Gray & Co. 1833).

56. *Ex parte* Merryman, 17 Cas. 144 (C.C.D. Md. 1861) (No. 9 487).

57. CONSTITUTION OF THE UNITED STATES OF AMERICA: ANALYSIS AND INTERPRETATION, S. Doc. No. 82, 92d Cong., 2d Sess. 364–65 (1973); ALFRED H. KELLY & WINFRED A. HARBISON, THE AMERICAN CONSTITUTION: ITS ORIGINS AND DEVELOPMENT 410–14 (5th ed. 1976).

58. *See, e.g.*, Calabresi & Prakash, *The President's Power to Execute the Laws*, at 583–84 & n.161, 603; Flaherty, *The Most Dangerous Branch*, at 1793–94; William B. Gwyn, *The Indeterminacy of the Separation of Powers and the Federal Courts*, 57 GEO. WASH. L. REV. 474, 491 n.82 (1989); Lawson & Moore, *The Executive Power of Constitutional Interpretation*, at 1313; John O. McGinnis, *Models of the Opinion Function of the Attorney General: A Normative, Descriptive, and Historical Prolegomenon*, 15 CARDOZO L. REV. 375, 402 (1993); Robert J. Reinstein, *An Early View of Executive Powers and Privilege: The Trial of Smith and Ogden*, 2 HASTINGS CONST. L.Q. 309, 320–21 n.50 (1975); Morton Rosenberg, *Congress's Prerogative over Agencies and Agency Decisionmakers: The Rise and Demise of the Reagan Administration's Theory of the Unitary Executive*, 57 GEO. WASH. L. REV. 627, 690–95 (1989); Steven Ross, *Presidential Lawmaking Power: Vetoes, Line Item Vetoes, Signing Statements, Executive Orders, and Delegations of Rulemaking Authority*, 68 WASH. U. L.Q. 533, 541 (1990) (panel discussion); Peter M. Shane, *Independent Policymaking and Presidential Power: A Constitutional Analysis*, 57 GEO. WASH. L. REV. 596, 613 (1989); Charles Tiefer, *The Constitutionality of Independent Officers as Checks on Abuses of Executive Power*, 63 B.U. L. REV. 59, 90 & n.151 (1983). *But see* Susan L. Bloch, *The Early Role of the Attorney General in Our Constitutional Scheme: In the Beginning There Was Pragmatism*, 1989 DUKE L.J. 561, 635 n.232.

59. *See* 4 THE FOUNDERS' CONSTITUTION 124–26 (Philip B. Kurland & Ralph Lerner eds., 1987); Lawrence Lessig & Cass R. Sunstein, *The President and the Administration*, 94 COLUM. L. REV. 1, 61–66 (1994); Greene, *Checks and Balances*, at 145 n.75.

60. *See, e.g.*, RAOUL BERGER, EXECUTIVE PRIVILEGE: A CONSTITUTIONAL MYTH 308 (1974); William P. Barr, *Attorney General's Remarks, Benjamin N. Cardozo School of Law, November 15, 1992*, 15 CARDOZO L. REV. 31, 39 (1993); Calabresi & Prakash, *The President's Power to Execute the Laws*, at 621–22; Frank H. Easterbrook, *Presidential Review*, 40 CASE W. RES. L. REV. 905, 919–22 (1989–90); J. Gregory Sidak & Thomas A. Smith, *Four Faces of the Item Veto: A Reply to Tribe and Kurland*, 84 NW. U.L. REV. 437, 452 (1990); Edwin Meese, *On Separation of Powers: President's Right to Challenge a Law*, N.Y. TIMES, May 21, 1985, at A26 (letter to editor).

61. *See* EDWARD S. CORWIN, THE PRESIDENT: OFFICE AND POWERS 1787–1957 68–72 (5th rev. ed. 1984); 3 WILLOUGHBY, THE CONSTITUTIONAL LAW OF THE UNITED STATES, at 1502–04; Arthur S. Miller, *The President and Faithful Execution of the Laws*, 40 VAND. L. REV. 389, 397–98 (1987).

62. SYLVIA SNOWISS, JUDICIAL REVIEW AND THE LAW OF THE CONSTITUTION 40–41 (1990).

63. David A. Strauss, *Presidential Interpretation of the Constitution*, 15 CARDOZO L. REV. 113, 121–22 (1993).

64. EDWARD S. CORWIN, THE CONSTITUTION AND WHAT IT MEANS TODAY 120 (Harold W. Chase & Craig R. Ducat eds., 1974).

65. *See* Henry P. Monaghan, *The Protective Power of the Presidency*, 93 COLUM. L. REV. 1, 65–74 (1993).

66. *See generally* Thomas E. Cronin, *The President's Executive Power, in* INVENTING THE AMERICAN PRESIDENCY, *supra* note 23, at 180, 181.

67. *See* Steven G. Calabresi & Kevin H. Rhodes, *The Structural Constitution: Unitary Executive, Plural Judiciary,* 105 HARV. L. REV. 1153, 1169 nn. 75-96, 1198 n.222 (1992) (collecting authorities); Lessig & Sunstein, *The President and the Administration,* at 47–54.

68. *See* DANIEL P. FRANKLIN, EXTRAORDINARY MEASURES: THE EXERCISE OF PREROGATIVE POWERS IN THE UNITED STATES 41–69 (1991); ARTHUR M. SCHLESINGER, JR., THE IMPERIAL PRESIDENCY 7–10, 23–25; 321–24 (1973).

69. Letter from Thomas Jefferson to John B. Colvin (Sept. 20, 1810), *in* 4 THE FOUNDERS' CONSTITUTION, at 127–128. *See also* Jules Lobel, *Emergency Power and the Decline of Liberalism,* 98 YALE L.J. 1385 (1989).

70. 2 BERNARD SCHWARTZ, A COMMENTARY ON THE CONSTITUTION OF THE UNITED STATES, PART I: THE POWERS OF GOVERNMENT 56–85 (1963); Robert Scigliano, *The President's 'Prerogative Power,' in* INVENTING THE AMERICAN PRESIDENCY, *supra* note 23, at 236, 246–51.

71. *See, e.g.,* MCDONALD, THE AMERICAN PRESIDENCY, at 181, 200, 220, 237; Steven G. Calabresi, *The Vesting Clauses as Power Grants,* 88 NW. U.L. REV. 1377 (1994); Calabresi & Rhodes, *The Structural Constitution,* at 1194–99; Lawson & Moore, *The Executive Power of Constitutional Interpretation,* at 1281–82; Monaghan, *The Protective Power of the Presidency,* at 20–24; Scalia, *Originalism,* at 858–60; *and see,* Myers v. United States, 272 U.S. 52, 118–39 (1926).

72. *See* Monaghan, *The Protective Power of the Presidency,* at 20–24.

73. Calabresi, *The Vesting Clauses as Power Grants,* at 1395–1400.

74. *See* 2 ST. GEORGE TUCKER, BLACKSTONE'S COMMENTARIES, at 237–80; William B. Gwyn, *The Indeterminacy of the Separation of Powers and the Federal Courts,* 57 GEO. WASH. L. REV. 474, 480 (1989); Monaghan, *The Protective Power of the Presidency,* at 17.

75. Berg, Presidential Power and the Royal Prerogative, at 90.

76. *Draft of Virginia Constitution,* art. II, *in* 1 PAPERS OF THOMAS JEFFERSON 329, 342, 350 (Julian P. Boyd ed., 1950), *and in* JEFFERSON, WRITINGS, at 340–41.

77. *See* THE FEDERALIST NO. 73 (Alexander Hamilton); Edmund Burke's letter to the Sheriffs of Bristol (1777), *in* 2 THE FOUNDERS' CONSTITUTION, at 389. ("The king's negative to bills is one of the most indisputed of the royal prerogatives.").

78. 1 FARRAND, RECORDS OF THE FEDERAL CONVENTION, at 65.

79. *Id.* at 65–66.

80. Scalia, *Originalism,* at 859–60.

81. RICHARD M. PIOUS, THE AMERICAN PRESIDENCY 36–40 (1979); *and see* MCDONALD, THE AMERICAN PRESIDENCY, at 185; Calabresi & Prakash, *The President's Power to Execute the Laws,* at 612.

82. STIMSON, THE LAW OF THE FEDERAL AND STATE CONSTITUTIONS, at 54 (emphasis added).

83. *See, e.g.,* Calabresi & Prakash, *The President's Power to Execute the Laws,* at 583–84, 603; Monaghan, *The Protective Power of the Presidency,* at 24–38; Scigliano, *The President's 'Prerogative Power,'* at 249–50.

84. *See* Calabresi & Prakash, *The President's Power to Execute the Laws,* at 583–84 & n.161, 620–22 & n.349; *and see* Lawson & Moore, *The Executive Power of Constitutional Interpretation,* at 1280–88, 1303–13 (arguing that whatever its precise contours,

the executive power includes the power to refuse enforcement to an unconstitutional law).

85. Calabresi & Rhodes, *The Structural Constitution*, at 1197.

86. CORWIN, THE CONSTITUTION AND WHAT IT MEANS TODAY, at 120.

87. 2 SCHWARTZ, A COMMENTARY ON THE CONSTITUTION OF THE UNITED STATES, at 57.

88. *See* W. H. HUMBERT, THE PARDONING POWER OF THE PRESIDENT 25–26, 36–42 (1941).

89. *See* Proclamation of July 10, 1795, *in* 1 A COMPILATION OF THE MESSAGES AND PAPERS OF THE PRESIDENTS 173 (James D. Richardson ed., 1897, 1917) [hereinafter MESSAGES AND PAPERS] MCDONALD, THE AMERICAN PRESIDENCY, at 239–41, 305–06.

90. *See, e.g.*, MCDONALD, THE AMERICAN PRESIDENCY, at 24, 202; Calabresi & Prakash, *The President's Power to Execute the Laws*, at 641 n.444.

91. 1 WILLIAM BLACKSTONE, COMMENTARIES, ch. 7, at *259.

92. *See* United States v. Wilson, 32 U.S. (7 Pet.) 150, 159–60 (1833); *Ex parte* Wells, 59 U.S. (18 How.) 307, 311 (1855).

93. *Ex parte* Wells, 59 U.S. (18 How.) 307, 311 (1855).

94. *See generally*, 4 WILLIAM BLACKSTONE, COMMENTARIES *397–402; HUMBERT, THE PARDONING POWER, at 21–81; William F. Duker, *The President's Power to Pardon: A Constitutional History*, 18 WM. & MARY L. REV. 475 (1977); Carolyn A. Edie, *Tactics and Strategies: Parliament's Attack Upon the Royal Dispensing Power 1597–1689*, 29 AM. J. LEGAL HIST. 197, 198 (1985).

95. DEL. CONST. art. I, § 10, and art. III, § 9 (1792), *in* 2 SOURCES AND DOCUMENTS OF THE UNITED STATES CONSTITUTIONS 206, 209 (William F. Swindler ed., 1973) [hereinafter Swindler, SOURCES]; MD. DECL. OF RIGHTS § VII (1776) and MD. CONST. § XXXIII (1776), *in* 4 Swindler, SOURCES, at 373, 380 (1975); N.C. DECL. OF RIGHTS § V (1776) and N.C. CONST. § XIX (1776) *in* 7 Swindler, SOURCES, at 402, 405 (1978); HUMBERT, THE PARDONING POWER, at 13–14; Daniel T. Kobil, *The Quality of Mercy Strained: Wresting the Pardoning Power from the King*, 69 TEX. L. REV. 569, 590 (1991).

96. JAMES M. SMITH, FREEDOM'S FETTERS: THE ALIEN AND SEDITION LAWS AND AMERICAN CIVIL LIBERTIES 268–69 & n.67, 358 n.84 (1956).

97. *See* HUMBERT, THE PARDONING POWER, at 63; Duker, *The President's Power to Pardon*, at 526.

98. *See* VA. DECL. OF RIGHTS § 7 (1776), *in* 10 Swindler, SOURCES, at 49 (1979); DEL. DECL. OF RIGHTS § 7 (1776), *in* 2 Swindler, SOURCES, at 198; MD. CONST. § VII, *in* 4 Swindler, SOURCES, at 373; N.C. CONST. § V (1776), *in* 7 Swindler, SOURCES, at 402; MASS. BILL OF RIGHTS, pt. I, art. XX (1780), *in* 5 Swindler, SOURCES, at 95 (1975); N.H. CONST., pt. I, art. XXIX (1784), *in* 6 SWINDLER, SOURCES, at 347 (1976); VT. CONST. ch. I, art. XVII (1786), *in* 9 Swindler, SOURCES, at 499 (1979); PA. CONST. art. IX, § XII (1790), *in* 8 Swindler, SOURCES, at 293 (1979).

99. VA. DECL. OF RIGHTS § 7 (1776), *in* 10 SWINDLER, SOURCES, at 49.

100. STIMSON, THE LAW OF THE FEDERAL AND STATE CONSTITUTIONS, at 291–92.

101. EDWARD DUMBAULD, THE BILL OF RIGHTS AND WHAT IT MEANS TODAY 164 (1957).

102. 3 ELLIOT, DEBATES, at 657–63.

103. 4 *Id.* at 226, 242–52.

104. CONTEXTS OF THE BILL OF RIGHTS 73, 129 (Stephen L. Schechter & Richard B. Bernstein eds., 1990); Gregory A. Stiverson, *"To Maintain Inviolate Our Liberties":*

Maryland and the Bill of Rights, in THE BILL OF RIGHTS AND THE STATES: COLONIAL AND REVOLUTIONARY ORIGINS OF AMERICAN LIBERTIES 370, 391–94 (Patrick T. Conley & John P. Kaminski eds., 1992).

105. *See* DUMBAULD, THE BILL OF RIGHTS, at 21, 182–85.

106. Letter from Thomas Jefferson to William Short (Sept. 20, 1788), *in* 13 PAPERS OF THOMAS JEFFERSON 619 (Julian P. Boyd ed., 1956).

107. 3 ELLIOT, DEBATES, at 246.

108. *Id.* at 450.

109. *Id.* at 246.

110. *Id.* at 246 (emphasis in original).

111. *Id.* at 467.

112. *Id.* at 600.

113. 5 U.S. (1 Cranch) 137 (1803).

114. 3 ELLIOT, DEBATES, at 553.

115. *Id.* at 554 (emphasis added).

116. *Id.* at 661; DUMBAULD, THE BILL OF RIGHTS, at 47 n.14.

117. *See* Letter from James Madison to Thomas Mann Randolph (Jan. 13, 1789), *in* 12 PAPERS OF JAMES MADISON, at 415–17; *Id.* at 301–04; JULIUS GOEBEL, JR., HISTORY OF THE SUPREME COURT OF THE UNITED STATES: ANTECEDENTS AND BEGINNINGS TO 1801 425–26 (1971); Kenneth R. Bowling, *"A Tub to the Whale": The Adoption of the Bill of Rights, in* THE BILL OF RIGHTS AND THE STATES, at 46, 48–49.

118. DUMBAULD, THE BILL OF RIGHTS, at 23.

119. Letter from Rep. Benjamin Goodhue to Samuel Phillips (Sept. 13, 1789), *in* CREATING THE BILL OF RIGHTS: THE DOCUMENTARY RECORD FROM THE FIRST FEDERAL CONGRESS 294 (Helen E. Veit et al., eds., 1991).

120. DUMBAULD, THE BILL OF RIGHTS, at 47 & n.14; Letter from Richard Henry Lee to Patrick Henry (Sept. 14, 1789), *in* CREATING THE BILL OF RIGHTS, at 295–96; Letter from Richard Henry Lee & William Grayson to the Speaker of the Virginia House of Delegates (Sept. 28, 1789), *in* CREATING THE BILL OF RIGHTS, at 299–300 & n.1.

121. 3 ELLIOT, DEBATES, at 658.

122. *Id.* at 600.

123. Arthur Conan Doyle, *Silver Blaze, in* 1 THE COMPLETE SHERLOCK HOLMES 335, 347 (1905). *See* Monaghan, *The Protective Power of the Presidency*, at 15 & n.65.

124. *See* DREW R. MCCOY, THE LAST OF THE FATHERS: JAMES MADISON AND THE REPUBLICAN LEGACY 78 (1989). (Madison, defending a narrow reading of the General Welfare Clause, noted that had the clause been understood to confer broad powers on the national government, it would have drawn heavy fire from the Anti-Federalists; instead, the clause passed largely unnoticed.)

125. MCDONALD, THE AMERICAN PRESIDENCY, at 190–93.

126. 1 FARRAND, RECORDS OF THE FEDERAL CONVENTION, at 98.

127. *Id.* at 98.

128. 2 *id.* at 200.

129. 2 ELLIOT, DEBATES, at 446.

130. *See* MCDONALD, THE AMERICAN PRESIDENCY, at 200–201.

131. Letter from William Symmes to Capt. Peter Osgood, Jr. (Nov. 15, 1787), *in* 4 THE COMPLETE ANTI-FEDERALIST, at 60–61.

132. 2 ELLIOT, DEBATES, at 70–75.

133. 2 *id.* at 174, 179.

134. 2 *id.* at 176–78.

135. *See* Paulsen, *The Most Dangerous Branch*, at 269–70.

136. THE FEDERALIST NO. 44, at 285–86 (James Madison) (emphasis added).

137. MCDONALD, THE AMERICAN PRESIDENCY, at 193.

138. *Id.* at 183 n.3, 190–93.

139. 2 THE COMPLETE ANTI-FEDERALIST, at 115–16.

140. 3 *id.*, at 37–38 (emphasis in original).

141. 6 *id.*, at 124.

142. 5 *id.*, at 195–96 (emphasis in original).

143. *See, e.g.*, J. Gregory Sidak & Thomas A. Smith, *Why Did President Bush Repudiate the "Inherent" Line-Item Veto?*, 9 J.L. & POLITICS 39, 51 (1992).

144. *See* Lawrence Lessig, *Fidelity in Translation*, 71 TEX. L. REV. 1165 (1993); Lessig, *Fidelity and Constraint*, at 1365–1433; *see also* Flaherty, *The Most Dangerous Branch*, at 1810–16; Greene, *Checks and Balances*, at 129–30.

145. Lessig, *Fidelity and Constraint*, at 1370 (emphasis in original).

146. *See* Charles J. Cooper, *The Line-Item Veto: The Framers' Intentions, in* PORK BARRELS AND PRINCIPLES: THE POLITICS OF THE PRESIDENTIAL VETO 29, 33–34 (National Legal Center for the Public Interest ed. 1988).

147. Sidak & Smith, *Why Did President Bush Repudiate*, at 51.

148. DOUGLAS W. KMIEC, THE ATTORNEY GENERAL'S LAWYER: INSIDE THE MEESE JUSTICE DEPARTMENT 53 (1992); *see also* Douglas W. Kmiec, *Of Balkanized Empires and Cooperative Allies: A Bicentennial Essay on the Separation of Powers*, 37 CATH. U.L. REV. 73, 81 (1987).

149. Kmiec, *Of Balkanized Empires*, at 81.

150. Remarks at Princeton, N.J. (May 10, 1991), *in* 1991 PUBLIC PAPERS OF THE PRESIDENTS OF THE UNITED STATES 496, 499 (1992) [hereinafter PUB. PAPERS].

151. *Id.* at 499.

152. Barr, *Attorney General's Remarks*, at 38–39.

153. Statement of Apr. 9, 1996, *in* 32 WEEKLY COMP. PRES. DOC. 637–38 (1996).

154. 2 WILLIAM A. STUBBS, THE CONSTITUTIONAL HISTORY OF ENGLAND 570–75 (Oxford, Clarendon Press, 2d ed. 1877); Michael B. Rappaport, *The President's Veto and the Constitution*, 87 NW. U.L. REV. 735, 746–56, 762–66 (1993).

155. CATHERINE D. BOWEN, THE LION AND THE THRONE: THE LIFE AND TIMES OF SIR EDWARD COKE 33–34 (1957).

156. 2 STUBBS, THE CONSTITUTIONAL HISTORY OF ENGLAND, at 570.

157. Spitzer, *The President's Veto Power*, at 154, 159.

158. Cooper, *The Line-Item Veto*, at 34–35.

159. *Id.* at 37–38; Paul R. Q. Wolfson, Note, *Is a Presidential Item Veto Constitutional?* 96 YALE L.J. 838, 841–43 (1987); *see also* MCDONALD, THE AMERICAN PRESIDENCY, at 106.

160. *See* Wolfson, *Is a Presidential Item Veto Constitutional?* at 844.

161. *See* 1 FARRAND, RECORDS OF THE FEDERAL CONVENTION, at 233–34, 527–28, 543–47; 2 *id.* at 224, 232–34, 262–63, 273–80, 297–98, 552.

162. Fisher, *The Presidential Veto*, at 22; Cooper, *The Line-Item Veto*, at 44–45.

163. Act of Sept. 29, 1789, ch. 23, 1 Stat. 95; *see* Louis Fisher, *The Presidential Veto: Constitutional Developments, in* PORK BARRELS AND PRINCIPLES, at 17, 22.

164. Act of March 26, 1990, ch. 4, 1 Stat. 104–06; *see* Cooper, *The Line-Item Veto*, at 43–44.

165. Letter from George Washington to Edmund Pendleton (Sept. 23, 1793), 33 THE WRITINGS OF GEORGE WASHINGTON (John C. Fitzpatrick ed. 1940).

166. Sidak & Smith, *Four Faces of the Item Veto*, at 469–72; Douglas W. Kmiec, *OLC's Opinion Writing Function: The Legal Adhesive for a Unitary Executive*, 15 CARDOZO L. REV. 337, 353–59 (1993).

167. *See* Flaherty, *The Most Dangerous Branch*, at 1816–21; Greene, *Checks and Balances*, at 125–95.

168. *See* Easterbrook, *Presidential Review*, at 905–29; Paulsen, *The Most Dangerous Branch*, at 217–345.

169. Marbury v. Madison, 5 U.S. (1 Cranch) 137 (1803).

170. Easterbrook, *Presidential Review*, at 919–20.

171. Strauss, *Presidential Interpretation of the Constitution*, at 121–22.

172. Easterbrook, *Presidential Review*, at 921–22; *and see* Paulsen, *The Most Dangerous Branch*, at 234–35 & n.53 (quoting and citing same memorandum).

173. Paulsen, *The Most Dangerous Branch*, at 226–27.

174. *Id.* at 228–29.

175. *Id.* at 240.

176. *Id.* at 221–22.

177. *See id.* at 228–40.

178. *Id.* at 252–55, 270.

179. *Id.* at 269–70.

180. *Id.* at 288–92.

181. *Id.* at 288.

182. *Id.* at 221–22.

183. *Id.* at 290.

184. Easterbrook, *Presidential Review*, at 922.

185. New York Trust Co. v. Eisner, 256 U.S. 345, 349 (1921).

186. *See* GORDON WOOD, THE CREATION OF THE AMERICAN REPUBLIC, 1776–1787 453–63 (1969); SNOWISS, JUDICIAL REVIEW, at 13–44.

187. THE FEDERALIST No. 78, at 467 (Alexander Hamilton).

188. 5 U.S. (1 Cranch) 137, 180 (1803).

189. *See, e.g.*, ALEXANDER M. BICKEL, THE LEAST DANGEROUS BRANCH: THE SUPREME COURT AT THE BAR OF POLITICS 15–16 (1962). *See also* PAUL M. BATOR ET AL., HART AND WECHSLER'S THE FEDERAL COURTS AND THE FEDERAL SYSTEM 9 (2d ed. 1973); SNOWISS, JUDICIAL REVIEW, at 38–40.

190. 2 ELLIOT, DEBATES, at 445–46.

191. THE FEDERALIST No. 78, at 446 (Alexander Hamilton).

192. 3 ELLIOT, DEBATES, at 553–54.

193. 1 FARRAND, RECORDS OF THE FEDERAL CONVENTION, at 97.

194. 2 *id.* at 76.

195. 2 *id.* at 78.

196. *See Constitutionality of GAO's Bid Protest Function: Hearings Before a Subcomm. of the House Comm. on Gov't Operations*, 99th Cong., 1st Sess. 25 (1985) (statement of Mark Tushnet) [hereinafter *GAO Bid Protest Hearings*].

197. Letter from James Madison to James Monroe (Dec. 27, 1817), *in* 3 LETTERS AND OTHERS WRITINGS OF JAMES MADISON, at 56.

198. Others have reached this same conclusion sometimes by different reasoning; *see, e.g.*, CORWIN, THE PRESIDENT, at 68–72; 3 WILLOUGHBY, THE CONSTITUTIONAL LAW

OF THE UNITED STATES, at 1502–04; Eugene Gressman, *Take Care, Mr. President*, 64 N.C. L. REV. 381 (1986); Rex E. Lee, *The Provinces of Constitutional Interpretation*, 61 TUL. L. REV. 1009, 1012–15 (1987); Miller, *The President and Faithful Execution of the Laws*, at 396–98; Arthur S. Miller & Jefferey H. Bowman, *Presidential Attacks on the Constitutionality of Federal Statutes: A New Separation of Powers Problem*, 40 OHIO ST. L.J. 51, 72 (1979); Memorandum from Raymond J. Calada, Congressional Research Service, Library of Congress, to House Comm. on Gov't Operations (Feb. 6, 1985), *in GAO Bid Protest Hearings*, at 554–55 (1985).

199. JEFFERSON: WRITINGS. at 420–21 (emphasis added).

200. United States v. Smith, 27 F. Cas. 1192 (C.C.D. N.Y. 1806) (No. 16,342).

201. *See* MAX FARRAND, THE FRAMING OF THE CONSTITUTION OF THE UNITED STATES 18–19, 200 (1913); Reinstein, *An Early View of Executive Powers*, at 325–26 n. 70.

202. *See generally* Reinstein, *An Early View of Executive Powers*, at 309.

203. United States v. Smith, 27 F. Cas. at 1229–30.

204. *Id.* at 1229–30.

205. *Id.* at 1230.

206. Calabresi & Prakash, *The President's Power to Execute the Laws*, at 622 & n.352.

207. Marbury v. Madison, 5 U.S. (1 Cranch) 137, 180 (1803).

208. Message of Feb. 28, 1793, *in* 1 MESSAGES AND PAPERS, at 129.

209. *See* 1 CHARLES WARREN, THE SUPREME COURT IN UNITED STATES HISTORY 102–03 n.2 (rev. ed. 1937).

210. Letter from Thomas Jefferson to Abigail Adams (July 22, 1804), *in* 11 THE WRITINGS OF THOMAS JEFFERSON 43–44 (Andrew A. Lipscomb ed., 1905); SMITH, FREEDOM'S FETTERS, at 268–69 & n.67, 358 n.84.

211. Message of March 30, 1796, *in* 1 MESSAGES AND PAPERS, at 186–88.

212. Message of July 6, 1813, *in* 2 MESSAGES AND PAPERS, at 515–16.

213. *See* GEORGE C. EDWARDS III, PRESIDENTIAL INFLUENCE IN CONGRESS (1980); PIOUS, THE AMERICAN PRESIDENCY, at 176–202.

214. *See* EDWARD A. KOLODZIEJ, THE UNCOMMON DEFENSE AND CONGRESS, 1945–1963, 405–19 (1966); LOUIS FISHER, PRESIDENTIAL SPENDING POWER 163–65 (1975).

215. *See* Watson, *Origins and Early Development of the Veto Power*, at 408; CHESTER J. ANTIEAU, THE EXECUTIVE VETO 98 n.1 (1988).

216. Message of April 5, 1792, *in* 1 MESSAGES AND PAPERS, at 116.

217. Message of Feb. 21, 1811, *in* 2 MESSAGES AND PAPERS, at 474–75; message of Feb. 28, 1811, *in* 2 MESSAGES AND PAPERS, 2b 475.

218. Message of March 3, 1817, *in* 2 MESSAGES AND PAPERS, at 569–70.

219. Message of Aug. 17, 1916, *in* 38 PAPERS OF WOODROW WILSON 40–42 (Arthur S. Link ed., 1982); Statement of Aug. 29, 1916, *in* 38 PAPERS OF WOODROW WILSON, at 101–02.

220. *See* U.S. CONST. art. I, §7, cl. 2.

221. *See, e.g.*, Ulysses S. Grant, Message of Feb. 15, 1871, *in* 9 MESSAGES AND PAPERS, at 4076–77.

222. *See, e.g.*, Ulysses S. Grant, Message of Dec. 6, 1869, *in* 9 MESSAGES AND PAPERS, at 3992; Rutherford B. Hayes, Message of Dec. 6, 1880, *in* 10 MESSAGES AND PAPERS, at 4557; Grover Cleveland, Message of Mar. 1, 1886, *in* 11 MESSAGES AND PAPERS, at 4960–68; *and see* Act of March 3, 1887, ch. 353, 24 Stat. 500, *repealing* Tenure of Office Act, ch. 154, 14 Stat. 430 (1867).

223. *See* Harry S. Truman, Statement of May 12, 1949, *in* 1949 PUB. PAPERS 250 & n. (1964).

224. PUB. L. NO. 91–285, 84 Stat. 314 (1970); Statement of June 22, 1970, *in* 1970 PUB. PAPERS, at 512–13 (1971).

225. 123 CONG. REC. 2974 (1977) (remarks of Sen. Abourezk).

226. N.Y. TIMES, Oct. 20, 1970, at 25.

227. Oregon v. Mitchell, 400 U.S. 112 (1970).

228. *See* MILLER & BOWMAN, *Presidential Attacks on the Constitutionality of Federal Statutes* (documenting but objecting to practice); Michael T. Brady, Note, *Executive Discretion and the Congressional Defense of Statutes*, 92 YALE L.J. 970, 970–84 (1983) (documenting practice).

CHAPTER 3

1. McCulloch v. Maryland, 17 U.S. (4 Wheat.) 316, 415 (1819).

2. *See* ROBERT J. SPITZER, THE PRESIDENTIAL VETO: TOUCHSTONE OF THE AMERICAN PRESIDENCY 126–29 (1988); *Line-Item Veto: Hearing on S.J. Res. 26, S.J. Res. 178 and S. 1921 Before the Subcomm. on the Constitution of the Senate Comm. on the Judiciary*, 98th Cong., 2d Sess. (1984); S. Doc. No. 11, 87th Cong., 1st Sess. 236–44 (1961).

3. Line Item Veto Act, Pub. L. No. 104–130, 110 Stat. 1200 (1996) (codified at 2 U.S.C.A. §§ 691 et seq. (Supp. 1997)).

4. 37 U.S. (12 Pet.) 524 (1838).

5. *Id.* at 613.

6. *Id.* at 613.

7. 272 U.S. 52 (1926).

8. *See, e.g.*, Letter from Walter Dellinger, Office of Legal Counsel, to Abner J. Mikva, Counsel to the President (Nov. 2, 1994), *reprinted in* Note, *Recent Legal Opinions Concerning Presidential Powers*, 48 ARK. L. REV. 311, 313, 316–17, 329 (1995); Frank H. Easterbrook, *Presidential Review*, 40 CASE W. RES. L. REV. 905, 915 (1989–90); *The Attorney General's Duty to Defend and Enforce Constitutionally Objectionable Legislation*, 4A Op. O.L.C. 55, 59 (1980).

9. *Myers*, 272 U.S. at 179 (McReynolds, J., dissenting).

10. Pennhurst State School & Hosp. v. Halderman, 465 U.S. 89, 118–19 (1984); *see also* Hagans v. Lavine, 415 U.S. 528, 533 n.5 (1974).

11. *See* Arthur S. Miller, *Pretense and Our Two Constitutions*, 54 GEO. WASH. L. REV. 375, 379–82 (1986); Henry P. Monaghan, *The Protective Power of the Presidency*, 93 COLUM L. REV. 1, 1–2 (1993).

12. WALTER BAGEHOT, THE ENGLISH CONSTITUTION 1 (2d ed. London, Kegan, Paul, Trench, Trubner & Co., Ltd. 1872).

13. *See* WOODROW WILSON, CONGRESSIONAL GOVERNMENT: A STUDY IN AMERICAN POLITICS 30–31 (Meridian Books ed., 1956) (1885).

14. *Congress, the President, and the War Powers: Hearings Before the Subcomm. on National Security Policy and Scientific Developments of the House Comm. on Foreign Affairs*, 91st Cong., 2d Sess. 64 (1970).

15. *See* Immigration and Naturalization Service v. Chadha, 462 U.S. 919 (1983).

16. Louis Fisher, *The Legislative Veto: Invalidated, It Survives*, 56 LAW & CONTEMP. PROBS., Autumn 1993, at 273.

17. *See* S. Rep. No. 797, 90th Cong. 1st Sess. (1967); Allan Ides, *Congress, Constitutional Responsibility and the War Power*, 17 Loy. L.A. L. Rev. 599 (1984).

18. *See* Christopher N. May, In the Name of War: Judicial Review and the War Powers since 1918, at 260, 353–54 n.14 (1989).

19. *See* Miller, *Pretense and Our Two Constitutions*, at 382 & n.24; Monaghan, *Protective Power of the Presidency*, at 3–5; Henry P. Monaghan, *Stare Decisis and Constitutional Adjudication*, 88 Colum. L. Rev. 723, 727–39 (1988).

20. Bowsher v. Synar, 478 U.S. 714, 723–24 (1986) (quoting Marsh v. Chambers, 463 U.S. 783, 790 (1983)).

21. *See, e.g.*, Printz v. United States, 117 S.Ct. 2365, 2370 (1997); Harmelin v. Michigan, 501 U.S. 957, 980 (1991); Marsh v. Chambers, 463 U.S. 783, 788–90 (1983); Myers v. United States, 272 U.S. 52, 175 (1926).

22. Stuart v. Laird, 5 U.S. (1 Cranch) 299, 309 (1803); *see also* United States v. Midwest Oil Co., 236 U.S. 459, 472–74 (1915).

23. *See* Drew R. McCoy, The Last of the Fathers: James Madison and the Republican Legacy 79–82 (1989); Jefferson Powell, Languages of Power: A Sourcebook of Early American Constitutional History 11–13 (1991).

24. Letter from James Madison to Martin L. Hurlbert (May 30, 1830), *in* 9 The Writings of James Madison 370, 372 (Gaillard Hunt ed., 1906).

25. *Id.* at 372.

26. *See, e.g.*, Myers v. United States, 272 U.S. 52, 170–76 (1926) (congressional practice dating from 1789); United States v. Midwest Oil Co., 236 U.S. 459, 469 (1915) (executive practice dating from an "unknown" but early period of the government); Stuart v. Laird, 5 U.S. (1 Cranch) 299, 309 (1803) (judicial practice dating from 1789). *And see* Powell v. McCormack, 395 U.S. 486, 547 (1969).

27. *See* Bruce Ackerman, We the People: Foundations 47–50 (1991).

28. 453 U.S. 654, 675–83 (1981).

29. Touby v. United States, 500 U.S. 160, 163–65 (1991); *see* Forrest McDonald, The American Presidency: An Intellectual History 293–98 (1994); Monaghan, *The Protective Power of the Presidency*, 4–5, 38–61.

30. *See* Monaghan, *Stare Decisis and Constitutional Adjudication*, at 736–738.

31. *See* May, In the Name of War, at 260, 353–54 n.14.

32. *See, e.g.*, Schlesinger v. Reservists Committee to Stop the War, 418 U.S. 208 (1974) (plaintiffs lacked standing to enforce Art. I, § 6, cl. 2 ban against members of Congress holding other federal offices, as applied to members who were reserve officers in armed forces); United States v. Richardson, 418 U.S. 166 (1974) (plaintiffs lacked standing to enforce Art. I, § 9, cl. 7 command that government account for expenditures as applied to expenditures of Central Intelligence Agency).

33. U.S. Const. art. I, § 7, cl. 2.

34. For lists of all presidential vetoes, indicating which were overridden by Congress, and where the veto message may be found, see U.S. Congress, Senate Library, Presidential Vetoes, 1789–1976 (1978); U.S. Congress, Senate Library, Presidential Vetoes, 1977–1984, S. Pub. No. 5, 99th Cong., 1st Sess. (1985). Veto Messages are printed in the Congressional Record and in the two major series of Public Papers of the presidents: A Compilation of the Messages and Papers of the Presidents (James D. Richardson ed., 1897, 1917), and Public Papers of the Presidents of the United States (1958–1996).

35. *See* Spitzer, The Presidential Veto, at 115–19.

36. *See* Frank B. Cross, *The Constitutional Legitimacy and Significance of Presidential "Signing Statements,"* 40 ADMIN. L. REV. 209 (1988); Marc N. Garber & Kurt A. Wimmer, *Presidential Signing Statements as Interpretations of Legislative Intent: An Executive Aggrandizement of Power*, 24 HARV. J. ON LEGIS. 363 (1987); Brad Waites, Note, *Let Me Tell You What You Mean: An Analysis of Presidential Signing Statements*, 21 GA. L. REV. 755. (1987).

37. Act of July 12, 1943, ch. 218, 57 Stat. 431 (1943).

38. Statement of Sept. 14, 1943, *in* 12 PUBLIC PAPERS AND ADDRESSES OF FRANKLIN D. ROOSEVELT 385–86 (Samuel I. Rosenman ed., 1950). *See infra* chapter 6, "Obtaining Judicial Resolution."

39. A COMPILATION OF THE MESSAGES AND PAPERS OF THE PRESIDENTS (James D. Richardson ed., 1897, 1917, 1926).

40. PUBLIC PAPERS AND ADDRESSES OF FRANKLIN D. ROOSEVELT (Samuel I. Rosenman ed., 1950).

41. *See* 9 PUBLIC PAPERS AND ADDRESSES OF FRANKLIN D. ROOSEVELT, at 127.

42. Arthur S. Miller, *The President and Faithful Execution of the Laws*, 40 VAND. L. REV. 389, 398–99 (1987).

CHAPTER 4

1. *See* ROBERT J. SPITZER, THE PRESIDENTIAL VETO: TOUCHSTONE OF THE AMERICAN PRESIDENCY 71–75 (1988).

2. Vetoes are compiled in U.S. CONGRESS, SENATE LIBRARY, PRESIDENTIAL VETOES, 1789–1976 (1978) and in U.S. CONGRESS, SENATE LIBRARY, PRESIDENTIAL VETOES, 1977–84, S. PUB. NO. 5, 99th Cong., 1st Sess. (1985).

3. Act of July 8, 1856, ch. 54, 11 Stat. 24 (Miss. River at Southwest Pass and Pass à l'Outre); Act of July 8, 1856, ch. 55, 11 Stat. 25 (St. Mary's River, Mich.); Act of July 8, 1856, ch. 56, 11 Stat. 25 (St. Clair Flats, Mich.); Act of Aug. 16, 1856, ch. 121, 11 Stat. 44 (Patapsco River and Port of Baltimore); Act of Aug. 16, 1856, ch. 126, 11 Stat. 51 (Des Moines Rapids in Miss. River). Pierce's five vetoes appear in 7 A COMPILATION OF THE MESSAGES AND PAPERS OF THE PRESIDENTS 2919–21 (James D. Richardson ed., 1897, 1917) [hereinafter MESSAGES AND PAPERS].

4. U.S. CONST., art. I, § 8, cls. 1, 3; *see* EDWARD C. MASON, THE VETO POWER 94–106 (Boston, Ginn 1890) (re: nineteenth-century view on internal improvements); 7 MESSAGES AND PAPERS 2790–2804 (re: Pierce's view on internal improvements).

5. *See* S. EXEC. DOC. No. 5, 34th Cong., 3d Sess. 340. 345, 365, 367 (1857); S. EXEC. DOC. No. 11, 35th Cong., 1st Sess., vol. 2, at 219, 287–88, 290, 291, 305–06, 356–63, 393–95 (1858).

6. *See* SPITZER, THE PRESIDENTIAL VETO, at 74.

7. The 14 measures were (1) Act of April 9, 1866 (1866 Civil Rights Act), ch. 31, 14 Stat. 27; (2) Act of July 16, 1866 (Freedmen's Bureau Act), ch. 200, 14 Stat. 173; (3) Act of Jan. 8, 1867 (elective franchise in D.C.), ch. 6, 14 Stat. 375; (4) Act of Feb. 9, 1867 (admission of Nebraska), ch. 36, 14 Stat. 391; (5) Act of March 2, 1867 (First Reconstruction Act), ch. 153, 14 Stat. 428; (6) Act of March 2, 1867 (Tenure of Office Act), ch. 154, 14 Stat. 430 (17) Act of March 23, 1867 (Second Reconstruction Act), ch. 6, 15 Stat. 2; (8) Act of July 19, 1867 (Third Reconstruction Act) ch. 30,15 Stat. 14; (9) Act of July 19, 1867 (reconstruction), Res. No. 39, 15 Stat. 30; (10) Act of March 27, 1868 (judiciary act), ch. 34, 15 Stat. 44; (11) Act of June 22, 1868 (admit Arkansas

to Congress), ch. 69, 15 Stat. 72; (12) Act of June 25, 1868 (admit six states to Congress), ch. 70, 15 Stat. 73; (13) Act of July 25, 1868 (Freedmen's Bureau), ch. 245, 15 Stat. 193; (14) Act of July 20, 1868 (Electoral College), Res. No. 58, 15 Stat. 257. *See* 8–9 MESSAGES AND PAPERS 3603–3852.

8. *See generally* ERIC FONER, RECONSTRUCTION: AMERICA'S UNFINISHED REVOLUTION, 1863–1877 (1988); ERIC L. MCKITRICK, ANDREW JOHNSON AND RECONSTRUCTION (reprint ed. 1988) (1960); KENNETH M. STAMPP, THE ERA OF RECONSTRUCTION, 1865–1877 (paper ed. 1965).

9. *See, e.g.*, Message of July 16, 1866, *in* 8 MESSAGES AND PAPERS 3620–24; Message of March 2, 1867, *in* 8–9 MESSAGES AND PAPERS 3696–3709.

10. MCKITRICK, ANDREW JOHNSON, at 85–93, 108–09.

11. Message of July 16, 1866, *in* 8 MESSAGES AND PAPERS 3620, 3622.

12. Mississippi v. Johnson, 71 U.S. (4 Wall.) 475, 492 (1867).

13. Message of Dec. 3, 1867, *in* 9 MESSAGES AND PAPERS 3756, 3766–67.

14. 11 Op. Att'y Gen. 209, 213–15 (1865).

15. *See* Table 4.1.

16. Message of Dec. 3, 1867, *in* 9 MESSAGES AND PAPERS 3756, 3760–69.

17. MCKITRICK, ANDREW JOHNSON, at 493.

18. MICHAEL LES BENEDICT, THE IMPEACHMENT AND TRIAL OF ANDREW JOHNSON 49, 60 (1973).

19. MCKITRICK, ANDREW JOHNSON, at 491.

20. 9 MESSAGES AND PAPERS 3907–16.

21. Tenure of Office Act, ch. 154, § 1, 14 Stat. 430 (1867) (emphasis added).

22. 272 U.S. 52 (1926).

23. *See* DAVID M. DEWITT, THE IMPEACHMENT AND TRIAL OF ANDREW JOHNSON 232–87 (reprint ed. 1967) (1903); RAOUL BERGER, IMPEACHMENT: THE CONSTITUTIONAL PROBLEMS 259–60 (1973); BENEDICT, IMPEACHMENT OF JOHNSON, at 95–97; MCKITRICK, ANDREW JOHNSON, at 495, 497.

24. DEWITT, IMPEACHMENT OF JOHNSON, at 373.

25. 8 MESSAGES AND PAPERS 3907–16. *See* SAMUEL E. MORISON, THE OXFORD HISTORY OF THE AMERICAN PEOPLE 720–21 (1965); BERGER, IMPEACHMENT, at 271–72.

26. DEWITT, IMPEACHMENT OF JOHNSON, at 366–70.

27. *Id.* at 197–98.

28. Message of Feb. 22, 1868, *in* 9 MESSAGES AND PAPERS 3820, 3823.

29. *Id.* at 3822.

30. *Id.* at 3823.

31. MCKITRICK, ANDREW JOHNSON, at 497.

32. DEWITT, IMPEACHMENT OF JOHNSON, at 193–99, 577–78; MCKITRICK, ANDREW JOHNSON, at 495–97.

33. BENEDICT, IMPEACHMENT OF JOHNSON, at 151, 157–58.

34. *See* DEWITT, IMPEACHMENT OF JOHNSON, at 424–26; MCKITRICK, ANDREW JOHNSON, at 507; BERGER, IMPEACHMENT, at 274–80.

35. *See* DEWITT, IMPEACHMENT OF JOHNSON, at 411–12, 448–51; BERGER, IMPEACHMENT, at 278–80; *but see* BENEDICT, IMPEACHMENT OF JOHNSON, at 148–51 (concluding it was unclear whether Stanton was protected by the act).

36. *See* BENEDICT, IMPEACHMENT OF JOHNSON, at 105–06.

37. *See id.* at 153–56; DEWITT, IMPEACHMENT OF JOHNSON, at 427–32.

38. CONG. GLOBE, 40th Cong., 2d Sess. supp. at 301 (1868).

39. *Id.* at 373–74.

40. *Id.* at 302.

41. *Id.* at 314.

42. *Id.* at 314.

43. CONG. GLOBE, 40th Cong., 2d Sess. supp. at 126 (1868); *see* DEWITT, IMPEACHMENT OF JOHNSON, at 427–32.

44. CONG. GLOBE, 40th Cong., 2d Sess. supp. at 126–27 (1868).

45. JOHN N. POMEROY, AN INTRODUCTION TO THE CONSTITUTIONAL LAW OF THE UNITED STATES 444–45 (N.Y., Hurd & Houghton 1868).

46. *Id.* at 245.

47. *See* CONG. GLOBE, 40th Cong., 2d Sess. supp. at 332 (1868) (House Manager Thomas Williams agreeing it was necessary for Johnson to issue order removing Stanton); *and see* EDWARD S. CORWIN, THE PRESIDENT: OFFICE AND POWERS 1787–1957, at 70–72 (5th rev. ed. 1984).

48. CONG. GLOBE, 40th Cong., 2d Sess. supp. at 36 (1868).

49. *Id.* at 279.

50. *Id.* at 279.

51. *Id.* at 405.

52. *Id.* at 412, 414–15.

53. Letter from Salmon P. Chase to Gerrit Smith (April 19, 1868), *in* SALMON P. CHASE PAPERS, Library of Congress. *See also* ROBERT B. WARDEN, AN ACCOUNT OF THE PRIVATE LIFE AND PUBLIC SERVICES OF SALMON PORTLAND CHASE 684–85 (Cincinnati, Wilstach, Baldwin 1874) (reprinting letter in slightly different form); Jerome Mushkat ed., *The Impeachment of Andrew Johnson: A Contemporary View*, 48 N.Y. HISTORY 275, 280 (1967) (noting that Chase shared similar views with a congressman during the trial).

54. Letter from Salmon P. Chase to Gerrit Smith (April 19, 1868), *quoted in* CHARLES FAIRMAN, RECONSTRUCTION AND REUNION 1864–88, pt. 1, at 524 (1971).

55. *See* JAMES G. RANDALL & DAVID DONALD, THE CIVIL WAR AND RECONSTRUCTION 614–17 (2d rev. ed. 1969); BENEDICT, IMPEACHMENT OF JOHNSON, at 110, 126, 140; HANS L. TREFOUSSE, ANDREW JOHNSON: A BIOGRAPHY 328–31 (1989) [hereinafter TREFOUSSE, A BIOGRAPHY].

56. *See., e.g.*, CONG. GLOBE, 40th Cong., 2d Sess. supp. at 463–64, 473 (1868) (remarks of Charles Summer).

57. *See* HANS L. TREFOUSSE, IMPEACHMENT OF A PRESIDENT: ANDREW JOHNSON, THE BLACKS, AND RECONSTRUCTION 172–79 (1975); BENEDICT, IMPEACHMENT OF JOHNSON, at 126–43; JAMES E. SEFTON, ANDREW JOHNSON AND THE USES OF CONSTITUTIONAL POWER 182 (1980).

58. *See, e.g.*, CONG. GLOBE, 40th Cong., 2d Sess. supp. at 417–20 (1868) (opinion of Lyman Trumbull); *id.* at 452–57 (opinion of William P. Fessenden).

59. *See., e.g.*, CONG. GLOBE, 40th Cong., 2d Sess. supp. at 417–526 (1868). Senators Grimes, Johnson, Davis, Vickers, Buckalew, Doolittle, Henderson, and Frelinghuysen appear to have recognized a presidential right to violate a law in order to test its constitutionality, while Senators Edmunds, Sherman, Ferry, Williams, Wilson, Sumner, Morrill (Vt.), Yates, Tipton, Howard, Patterson (N. H.), and Cattell rejected such a right. *Id.*

60. BENEDICT, IMPEACHMENT OF JOHNSON, at 153–57.

61. CONG. GLOBE, 40th Cong., 2d Sess. supp. at 225–27 (1868).

62. *Id.* at 169–171, 200–01, 201–02.

63. *See id.* at 170, 200–02, 447, 471–72.

64. The thirteen senators who voted for at least one of the three motions to admit evidence concerning the test-case defense but then voted to find the president guilty were Republican Senators Anthony, Cole, Corbett, Frelinghuysen, Howe, Morgan, Morton, Sherman, Sprague, Sumner, Wiley, Morrill (Me.), and Patterson (N. H.). *See id.* at 169–71, 200–02, 411. Of this group, only Frelinghuysen, Howe, Sherman, Sumner, Morrill, and Patterson wrote opinions explaining their impeachment vote.

65. *See* BENEDICT, IMPEACHMENT OF JOHNSON, at 157–58.

66. CONG. GLOBE, 40th Cong., 2d Sess. supp. at 140 (1868) (testimony of Gen. Lorenzo Thomas); *id.* at 170, 173 (testimony of Gen. William T. Sherman); *id.* at 200 Testimony of Walter S. Cox).

67. *See* TREFOUSSE, A BIOGRAPHY, at 306–08; DEWITT, IMPEACHMENT OF JOHNSON, at 282–85, 322–38.

68. Message of Feb. 22, 1868, *in* 9 MESSAGES AND PAPERS 3820, 3823.

69. *See* CONG. GLOBE, 40th Cong., 2d Sess. supp. at 168–69 (1868). Section 5 of the Tenure of Office Act made it a crime, punishable by a fine of up to $10,000 and imprisonment for up to five years, to accept an appointment contrary to the terms of the act. Ch. 154, § 5, 14 Stat. 430, 431 (1867).

70. CONG. GLOBE, 40th Cong., 2d Sess. supp. at 200 (1868).

71. *Id.* at 201–04 (testimony of Walter S. Cox); *id.* at 204–06 (testimony of Richard T. Merrick); DEWITT, IMPEACHMENT OF JOHNSON, at 377.

72. *See* CONG. GLOBE, 40th Cong., 2d Sess. supp. at 198–200 (1868).

73. *Id.* at 203 (testimony of Walter S. Cox).

74. *Id.* at 203–04 (testimony of Walter S. Cox).

75. *See* BENEDICT, IMPEACHMENT OF JOHNSON, at 157–58.

76. CONG. GLOBE, 40th Cong., 2d Sess. supp. at 37 (1868) (opening argument of Rep. Benjamin Butler); *id.* at 271 (closing argument of Rep. George Boutwell); *id.* at 332–33 (closing argument of Thomas Williams).

77. *Id.* at 522 (Sen. Frelinghuysen); *id.* at 471, 473 (Sen. Sumner).

78. Act of Oct. 2, 1986, Pub. L. No. 99–440, 100 Stat. 1086; Message of Sept. 26, 1986, *in* 1986 PUBLIC PAPERS OF THE PRESIDENTS OF THE UNITED STATES 1278–80 (1989) [hereinafter PUB. PAPERS].

79. *See* LAWYERS COMM. FOR CIVIL RIGHTS UNDER LAW, IMPLEMENTATION OF THE COMPREHENSIVE ANTI-APARTHEID ACT OF 1986 (1988); 134 CONG. REC. H6917 (Aug. 11, 1988); WASH. POST, Aug. 20, 1989, at A12; 136 CONG. REC. E2150–01 (June 26, 1990).

80. Act of Aug. 2, 1882, ch. 375, 22 Stat. 191.

81. H.R. EXEC. DOC. No. 222, 47th Cong., 1st Sess. 1–2 (1882).

82. 2 GEORGE F. HOAR, AUTOBIOGRAPHY OF SEVENTY YEARS 118 (1903).

83. H.R. EXEC. DOC. No. 64, 48th Cong., 1st Sess. i (1884).

84. *Id.* at ii, iii.

85. 22 Stat. at 199.

86. H.R. EXEC. DOC. No. 64, 48th Cong., 1st Sess. 37, 41–42 (1884).

87. *Id.* at 4–5.

88. Act of June 3, 1896, ch. 314, 29 Stat. 202; H.R. DOC. No. 2, 54th Cong., 2d Sess., vol. II, at 21–22 (1896).

89. Message of May 29, 1896, *in* 14 MESSAGES AND PAPERS 6109, 6110.

90. *Id.* at 6111.

91. HORACE S. MERRILL, BOURBON LEADER: GROVER CLEVELAND AND THE DEM-

OCRATIC PARTY 137 (1957); *see also* REXFORD G. TUGWELL, GROVER CLEVELAND 126 (1968).

92. *See* H.R. DOC. No. 2, 54th Cong., 2d Sess., vol. I, at 40–41 (1896); *id.*, vol. II, at 21 et seq. (1896); H.R. DOC. No. 2, 55th Cong., 2d Sess., vol I., at 37–39 (1897).

93. *See, eg.*, 21 Op. Att'y Gen. 391 (1896); 21 Op. Att'y Gen. 414 (1896); 21 Op. Att'y Gen. 471 (1897).

94. 21 Op. Att'y Gen. 420, 421 (1896).

95. *Id.* at 421–22.

96. Act of March 1, 1913, ch. 90, 37 Stat. 699.

97. 49 CONG. REC. 4291 (1913). The Court upheld the Webb-Kenyon Act in Clark Distilling Co. v. Western Maryland Ry., 242 U.S. 311 (1917).

98. *See* CHRISTOPHER N. MAY, IN THE NAME OF WAR: JUDICIAL REVIEW AND THE WAR POWERS SINCE 1918, at 60–73 (1989).

99. National Prohibition Act (Act of Oct. 28, 1919), ch. 85, title I, 41 Stat. 305; MAY, IN THE NAME OF WAR, at 86–91.

100. Message of Oct. 27, 1919, *in* 63 PAPERS OF WOODROW WILSON 601 (Arthur S. Link ed., 1990).

101. *Id.* at 601.

102. MAY, IN THE NAME OF WAR, at 91–93.

103. N.Y. TIMES, Oct. 29, 1919, at 1, col. 1; *id.*, Nov. 21, 1919, at 10, col. 8.

104. Ruppert v. Caffey, 251 U.S. 264 (1920); *see* MAY, IN THE NAME OF WAR, at 191, 203–06.

105. Act of Sept. 23, 1950, ch. 1024, 64 Stat. 987.

106. 96 CONG. REC. 15631 (1950).

107. *Id.* at 15630 (1950).

108. N.Y. TIMES, Sept. 24, 1950, at 1, col. 1.

109. *Id.*, Sept. 25, 1950, at 1, col. 4.

110. THOMAS I. EMERSON, ET AL., POLITICAL AND CIVIL RIGHTS IN THE UNITED STATES 160 (student ed. 1967).

111. 1951 *Att'y Gen. Ann. Rep.* 6; 1952 *Att'y Gen. Ann. Rep.* 11–12; EMERSON, POLITICAL AND CIVIL RIGHTS, at 160–61.

112. EMERSON, POLITICAL AND CIVIL RIGHTS, at 186.

113. Act of June 27, 1952, ch. 477, 66 Stat. 163.

114. 98 CONG. REC. 8084 (1952).

115. § 401(f), 66 Stat. at 274; 98 CONG. REC. 8084 (1952).

116. *See* 98 CONG. REC. 8621, 9750 (1952); 99 CONG. REC. 574, 824 (1953).

117. § 407, 66 Stat. at 281.

118. *See* N.Y. TIMES, Nov. 12, 1952, at 12, col. 5; *id.*, Dec. 17, 1952, at 6, col. 5; *id.*, Dec. 21, 1952, at 1, col. 6; 1953 *Att'y Gen. Ann. Rep.* 46.

119. 17 Fed. Reg. 11469–11564 (1952).

120. Message of Jan. 9, 1953, *in* 1952–53 PUB. PAPERS 1128, 1163 (1966).

121. N.Y. TIMES, June 26, 1952, at 1, col. 8; *id.*, Sept. 5, 1952, at 9, col. 1; *id.*, Oct. 12, 1952, at 77, col. 4, and at 79, col. 3; *id.*, Dec. 24, 1952, at 7, col. 4.

122. War Powers Resolution, Pub. L. No. 93–148, 87 Stat. 555 (1973) (codified as amended at 50 U.S.C. §§ 1541 to 1548 (1994)).

123. Message of Oct. 24, 1973, *in* 1973 PUB. PAPERS 893, 893–95 (1975).

124. *Id.* at 893.

125. WASH. STAR, Nov. 9, 1973, at C-back page, *quoted in* JOHN H. SULLIVAN, STAFF

OF HOUSE COMM. ON FOREIGN AFFAIRS, REPORT ON THE WAR POWERS RESOLUTION, 97th Cong., 2d Sess. 169 (Comm. Print 1982). [hereinafter SULLIVAN REPORT].

126. *See* John H. Ely, *The American War in Indochina, Part I: The (Troubled) Constitutionality of the War They Told Us About*, 42 STAN. L. REV. 877, 908, 910 (1990).

127. SULLIVAN REPORT, at 173–76.

128. Clement J. Zablocki, *War Powers Resolution: Its Past Record and Future Promise*, 17 LOY. L. A. L. REV. 579, 580–83 (1984); SULLIVAN REPORT, at 179–220.

129. Act of Nov. 21, 1974, Pub. L. No. 93–502, 88 Stat. 1561, 1562 (codified as 5 U.S.C. § 552(a) (4) (B) (1988)).

130. Message of Oct. 17, 1974, *in* 1974 PUB. PAPERS 374, 375 (1975).

131. Act of Nov. 21, 1974, Pub. L. No. 93–502, 88 Stat. 1561.

132. JUSTIN D. FRANKLIN & ROBERT F. BOUCHARD, GUIDEBOOK TO THE FREEDOM OF INFORMATION AND PRIVACY ACTS, § 1.04, at p. 1–36 (2d ed. 1992).

133. *See, e.g.*, Clark Distilling Co. v. Western Maryland Ry. Co., 242 U.S. 311 (1917) (upholding Webb-Kenyon Act vetoed by President Taft); Ruppert v. Caffey, 251 U.S. 264 (1920) (sustaining the National Prohibition Act, title I, vetoed by President Wilson).

CHAPTER 5

1. Charles J. Zinn, *The Veto Power of the President*, 12 F.R.D. 207, 238–40 (1952).

2. ROBERT J. SPITZER, THE PRESIDENTIAL VETO: TOUCHSTONE OF THE AMERICAN PRESIDENCY 126–29 (1988); *Line-Item Veto: Hearing on S.J. Res. 26, S.J. Res. 178 and S. 1921 Before the Subcomm. on the Constitution of the Senate Comm. on the Judiciary*, 98th Cong., 2d Sess. (1984); S. Doc. No. 11, 87th Cong., 1st Sess. 236–44 (1961).

3. Line Item Veto Act, Pub. L. No. 104–130, 110 Stat. 1200 (1996) (to be codified as 2 U.S.C. §§ 691 to 692).

4. 2 U.S.C. § 691 (e) (7)–(9).

5. 2 U.S.C. § 691 (d).

6. Line Item Veto Act, § 5, 110 Stat. at 1212.

7. *See* Byrd v. Raines, 956 F. Supp. 25 (D.D.C. 1997) (declaring Line Item Veto Act unconstitutional), *rev'd on other grounds*, 117 S.Ct. 2312 (1997) (Members of Congress lack standing to challenge Line Item Veto Act); City of New York v. Clinton, No. Civ. 97–2393 TFH, 1998 WL 63070 (D.D.C. Feb. 12, 1998) (declaring Line Item Veto Act unconstitutional), *prob. juris. noted*, 118 S.Ct. 1123 (1998).

8. 25–28 WEEKLY COMP. PRES. DOC. (1989–92).

9. *See* Table 5.1.

10. *See* Message of Dec. 17, 1819, *in* 2 A COMPILATION OF THE MESSAGES AND PAPERS OF THE PRESIDENTS 632 (James D. Richardson ed., 1897, 1917) [hereinafter MESSAGES AND PAPERS]; Message of April 13, 1822, *in* 2 *id.*, at 698; neither statement objected to the validity of the law.

11. Message of May 29, 1830, *in* 3 MESSAGES AND PAPERS 1045; Message of May 30, 1830, *in* 3 *id.*, at 1046; only the second statement raised a constitutional objection.

12. H.R. REP. No. 909, 27th Cong., 2d Sess. 2, 12 (1842).

13. Message of Aug. 14, 1848, *in* 6 MESSAGES AND PAPERS 2456; the message did not question the validity of the law.

14. Message of July 22, 1854, *in* 7 MESSAGES AND PAPERS 2776; the message did not question the validity of the law.

15. Message of Jan. 14, 1875, *in* 10 MESSAGES AND PAPERS 4268.

16. *See* 1–15 MESSAGES AND PAPERS.

17. Message of March 7, 1906, *in* 17 MESSAGES AND PAPERS 7667.

18. *See* 17–18 MESSAGES AND PAPERS.

19. *See* Table 5.1.

20. *See* 1945–1953 PUBLIC PAPERS OF THE PRESIDENTS OF THE UNITED STATES (1961–66) [hereinafter PUB. PAPERS].

21. *See* 1974—1980–1981 PUB. PAPERS (1975–82).

22. *See* 1980–1981 PUB. PAPERS (1982).

23. 1992 U.S. CODE CONG. & ADMIN. NEWS, Table 4A.

24. *See* 29–32 WEEKLY COMP. PRES. DOC. (1993–97).

25. These figures were calculated by dividing the number of signing statements shown in Table 7.1 by the number of public laws enacted during the president's term, as shown in the *Statutes at Large* volumes for the years in question.

26. *See, e.g.*, Harry S. Truman, Statement of May 22, 1947, *in* 1947 PUB. PAPERS 254–55 (1963).

27. *See* Table 5.1; 8 WEEKLY COMP. PRES. DOC. (1972); 12 WEEKLY COMP. PRES. DOC. (1976); 16 WEEKLY COMP. PRES. DOC. (1980–81); 1984 PUB. PAPERS (1986–87); 1992 U.S. CODE CONG. & ADMIN. NEWS, Table 4A; 1996 U.S. CODE CONG. & ADMIN. NEWS, Table 4A.

28. *See, e.g.*, Ronald W. Reagan, Statement of Oct. 24, 1984, *in* 1984 PUB. PAPERS 1643 (1987).

29. *See, e.g.*, Harry S. Truman, Statement of July 3, 1946, *in* 1946 PUB. PAPERS 336–37 (1962) (interpreting Hobbs Bill as not infringing rights of organized labor).

30. Fred Strasser, *Executive Intent*, NAT'L L.J., Mar. 10, 1986, at 2.

31. *Compare* Douglas W. Kmiec, *Judges Should Pay Attention to Statements by President*, NAT'L L.J., Nov. 10, 1986, at 13; Frank B. Cross, *The Constitutional Legitimacy and Significance of Presidential 'Signing Statements'*, 40 ADMIN. L. REV. 209 (1988); *and* Kathyryn M. Dessayer, Note, *The First Word: The President's Place in 'Legislative History'*, 89 MICH. L. REV. 399 (1990) (defending the practice), *with* Marc N. Garber & Kurt A. Wimmer, *Presidential Signing Statements as Interpretations of Legislative Intent: An Executive Aggrandizement of Power*, 24 HARV. J. ON LEGIS. 363 (1987); Brad Waites, Note, *Let Me Tell You What You Mean: An Analysis of Presidential Signing Statements*, 21 GA. L. REV. 755 (1987); *and* William D. Popkin, *Judicial Use of Presidential Legislative History: A Critique*, 66 IND. L.J. 699 (1991) (criticizing the practice).

32. *See, e.g.*, Lyndon B. Johnson, Statement of July 17, 1964, *in* 1963–64 PUB. PAPERS 861–62 (1965) (praising the Water Resources Research Act and the senator who guided it through Congress but requesting deletion of a provision that violated the spirit of the Constitution).

33. The fifteen statements were issued by Presidents Jackson, Tyler, Buchanan, Lincoln, Johnson (2), Grant, Arthur, Cleveland, Taft, Wilson (2), Hoover, and Franklin Roosevelt (2).

34. During this twenty-nine-year period, thirty-two constitutionally based signing statements were issued as follows: Truman (4), Eisenhower (9), Kennedy (1), Lyndon Johnson (9), and Nixon (9).

35. *See* 1980–1988 PUB. PAPERS (1982–1990).

36. The 102d Congress, which met during 1991 and 1992, approved 590 public laws;

Bush issued constitutionally based signing statements objecting to 59 of them. *See* 1992 U.S. CODE CONG. & ADMIN. NEWS, Table 1; 1991—1992–93 PUB. PAPERS (1992–93).

37. For a list of constitutionally based signing statements issued from 1972 to 1988, without indication of the president's response to the law, *see* Popkin, *Presidential Legislative History*, at 718–22.

CHAPTER 6

1. Message of June 25, 1842, *in* 5 A COMPILATION OF THE MESSAGES AND PAPERS OF THE PRESIDENTS 2012–13 (James D. Richardson ed., 1897, 1917) [hereinafter MESSAGES AND PAPERS]; Act of June 25, 1842, ch. 47, 5 Stat. 491.

2. Act of July 24, 1866, Res. No. 73, 14 Stat. 364.

3. Message of July 24, 1866, *in* 8 MESSAGES AND PAPERS 3593–95.

4. Message of March 2, 1867, *in* 8 MESSAGES AND PAPERS 3670; Act of March 2, 1867, ch. 170, § 6, 14 Stat. 485, 486–87.

5. Act of March 23, 1932, ch. 90, 47 Stat. 70.

6. Statement of March 23, 1932, *in* 1932 PUBLIC PAPERS OF THE PRESIDENTS OF THE UNITED STATES 112–13 (1977) [hereinafter PUB. PAPERS].

7. Statement of Dec. 17, 1973, *in* 1973 PUB. PAPERS 1015–16 (1975); Act of Dec. 18, 1973, Pub. L. No. 93–190, 87 Stat. 736–37.

8. Act of July 14, 1960, Pub. L. No. 86–648, 74 Stat. 504.

9. Statement of July 14, 1960, *in* 1960–61 PUB. PAPERS 579 (1961).

10. Statement of Aug. 5, 1974, *in* 1974 PUB. PAPERS 620 (1975); Act of Aug. 5, 1974, Pub. L. No. 93–365, 88 Stat. 399, 408.

11. Act of Oct. 15, 1976, Pub. L. No. 94–502, 90 Stat. 2383, 2397–98.

12. Statement of Oct. 15, 1976, *in* 1976–77 PUB. PAPERS 2538–39 (1979).

13. Statement of Dec. 12, 1980, *in* 1980–81 PUB. PAPERS 2804–06 (1982); Act of Dec. 12, 1980, Pub. L. No. 96–516, 94 Stat. 3007.

14. Statement of Jan. 2, 1981, *in* 1980–81 PUB. PAPERS 2856 (1982); Act of Dec. 24, 1980, Pub. L. No. 96–593, 94 Stat. 3452.

15. The statutes were: (1) Act of Dec. 12, 1980, Pub. L. No. 96–515, 94 Stat. 2987, 3004; Statement of Dec. 12, 1980, *in* 1980–81 PUB. PAPERS 2802–03 (1982); (2) Act of Dec. 16, 1980, Pub. L. No. 96–533, 94 Stat. 3131, 3136, 3142; Statement of Dec. 16, 1980, *in* 1980–81 PUB. PAPERS 2813–14 (1982); (3) Act of Dec. 17, 1980, Pub. L. No. 96–539, 94 Stat. 3194, 3195; Statement of Dec. 17, 1980, *in* 1980–81 PUB. PAPERS 2814–15 (1982); (4) Act of Dec. 24, 1980, Pub. L. No. 96–592, 94 Stat. 3437, 3449–50; Statement of Dec. 24, 1980, *in* 1980–81 PUB. PAPERS 2837 (1982).

16. Immigration and Naturalization Service v. Chadha, 462 U.S. 919 (1983).

17. *See, e.g.*, Harry Truman, Statement of July 5, 1949, *in* 1949 PUB. PAPERS 346–47 (1964); Dwight Eisenhower, Message of July 13, 1955, *in* 1955 PUB. PAPERS 688–90 (1959).

18. The statutes to which Ford objected were: (1) Act of Aug. 21, 1974, Pub. L. No. 93–380, 88 Stat. 484, 545; Statement of Aug. 21, 1974, *in* 1974 PUB. PAPERS 35–37 (1975); *see* Harold H. Bruff & Ernest Gellhorn, *Congressional Control of Administrative Regulation: A Study of Legislative Vetoes*, 90 HARV. L. REV. 1369, 1382–90 (1977) (noting absence of legislative of vetoes under act); (2) Act of Aug. 9, 1975, Pub. L. No. 94–88, 89 Stat. 433, 436–37; Statement of Aug. 11, 1975, *in* 1975 PUB. PAPERS 1148–

49 (1977); *see* 43 Fed. Reg. 2170 (1978) (final regulations subject to legislative veto provision not issued until 1978 after Ford left office); (3) Act of June 30, 1976, Pub. L. No. 94–329, 90 Stat. 729, 743; Statement of July 1, 1976, *in* 1976–77 PUB. PAPERS 1936–38 (1979); (4) Act of Sept. 14, 1976, Pub. L. No. 94–412, 90 Stat. 1255; Statement of Sept. 14, 1976, *in* 1976–77 PUB. PAPERS 2249–50 (1979).

19. The statutes to which Carter objected were: (1) Act of July 27, 1977, Pub. L. No. 95–75, 91 Stat. 308; Statement of July 28, 1977, *in* 1977 PUB. PAPERS 1374–75 (1978); (2) Act of Aug. 4, 1977, Pub. L. No. 95–92, 91 Stat. 614, 622–23; Statement of Aug. 5, 1977, *in* 1977 PUB. PAPERS 1431–32 (1978); (3) Act of Dec. 28, 1977, Pub. L. No. 95–223, 91 Stat. 1625, 1628; Statement of Dec. 28, 1977, *in* 1977 PUB. PAPERS 2186–87 (1978); (4) Act of Mar. 10, 1978, Pub. L. No. 95–242, 92 Stat. 120, 123; Statement of Mar. 10, 1978, *in* 1978 PUB. PAPERS 500–02 (1979); (5) Act of Sept. 18, 1978, Pub. L. No. 95–372, 92 Stat. 629, 641, 668; Statement of Sept. 18, 1978, *in* 1978 PUB. PAPERS 1530–31 (1979); (6) Act of Sept. 30, 1978, Pub. L. No. 95–405, 92 Stat. 865, 877; Statement of Oct. 2, 1978, *in* 1978 PUB. PAPERS 1696–97 (1979); (7) Act of Oct. 5, 1978, Pub. L. No. 95–421, 92 Stat. 923, 925–26; Statement of Oct. 5, 1978, *in* 1978 PUB. PAPERS 1718 (1979); (8) Act of Oct. 6, 1978, Pub. L. No. 95–424, 92 Stat. 937, 956; Statement of Oct. 6, 1978, *in* 1978 PUB. PAPERS 1721 (1979); (9) Act of Aug. 15, 1979, Pub. L. No. 96–60, § 408, 93 Stat. 395, 405–06, Statement of Aug. 15, 1979, *in* 1979 PUB. PAPERS 1434–35 (1980); (10) Act of Mar. 5, 1980, Pub. L. No. 96–199, 94 Stat. 67, 73; Statement of Mar. 5, 1980, *in* 1980–81 PUB. PAPERS 432–33 (1981); (11) Act of May 23, 1980, Pub. L. No. 96–247, 94 Stat. 349, 352–53; Statement of May 23, 1980, *in* 1980–81 PUB. PAPERS 965–66 (1981); (12) Act of May 28, 1980, Pub. L. No. 96–252, 94 Stat. 374, 393–96; Statement of May 28, 1980, *in* 1980–81 PUB. PAPERS 982–83 (1982); (13) Act of Aug. 29, 1980, Pub. L. No. 96–332, 94 Stat. 1057; Statement of Aug. 29, 1980, *in* 1980–81 PUB. PAPERS 1592 (1982); (14) Act of Oct. 17, 1980, Pub. L. No. 96–464, 94 Stat. 2060, 2067; Statement of Oct. 18, 1980, *in* 1980–81 PUB. PAPERS 2335–36 (1982).

20. Message of June 21, 1978, *in* 1978 PUB. PAPERS 1146–49 (1979).

21. Act of May 31, 1830, ch. 232, 4 Stat. 427; Message of May 30, 1830, *in* 3 MESSAGES AND PAPERS 1046.

22. Message of May 27, 1830, *in* 3 MESSAGES AND PAPERS 1046–56.

23. *See* 1830 SECRETARY OF WAR ANN. REPORT 97, 102–03; 1831 SECRETARY OF WAR ANN. REPORT 84, 104–05; 1832 SECRETARY OF WAR ANN. REPORT 99–103; *but see* H.R. REP. No. 909, 27th Cong., 2d Sess. 5–6 (1842) (charging Jackson with "arresting the road at the limits of the Territory instead of extending it to Chicago").

24. Act of June 17, 1944, ch. 262, 58 Stat. 280; Statement of June 17, 1944, N.Y. TIMES, June 18, 1944, at 30, col. 1, *reprinted in* 90 CONG. REC. 6154 (1944).

25. Act of June 17, 1944, ch. 263, 58 Stat. 283.

26. Act of Nov. 16, 1973, Pub. L. No. 93–153, § 404, 87 Stat. 576, 590.

27. Statement of Nov. 16, 1973, *in* 1973 PUB. PAPERS 945–46 (1975).

28. Exec. Order No. 11,748, 38 Fed. Reg. 33,575 (1973); Exec. Order No. 11,775, 39 Fed. Reg. 11,415 (1974); N.Y. TIMES, Dec. 4, 1973, at 1, col. 5; *id.*, Dec. 5, 1973, at 1, col. 6.

29. Act of Jan. 8, 1980, Pub. L. No. 96–187, 93 Stat. 1339, 1367 (amending 18 U.S.C. § 603).

30. Statement of Jan. 8, 1980, *in* 1980–81 PUB. PAPERS 37–38 (1981).

31. Act of Dec. 12, 1980, Pub. L. No. 96–515, 94 Stat. 2987, 2999; Statement of Dec. 12, 1980, *in* 1980–81 PUB. PAPERS 2802–03 (1982).

32. *See* 1981 ANN. REPORT OF ADV. COUNCIL ON HISTORIC PRESERVATION 56, 72.

33. Act of July 17, 1862, ch. 195, 12 Stat. 589; Act of July 17, 1862, Res. No. 63, 12 Stat. 627; Message of July 17, 1862, *in* 8 MESSAGES AND PAPERS 3286–88.

34. Act of Aug. 6, 1959, Pub. L. No. 86–137, 73 Stat. 280, 282; Statement of Aug. 6, 1959, *in* 1959 PUB. PAPERS 566 (1960).

35. Act of Aug. 14, 1959, Pub. L. No. 86–157, 73 Stat. 338.

36. Act of July 24, 1959, Pub. L. No. 86–108, 73 Stat. 246, 253–54.

37. Statement of July 24, 1959, *in* 1959 PUB. PAPERS 549 (1960).

38. Act of Sept. 28, 1959, Pub. L. No. 86–383, § 111(d), 73 Stat. 717, 720; Act of Sept. 2, 1960, Pub. L. No. 86–704, § 101(d), 74 Stat. 776, 778.

39. Letter of Nov. 12, 1959, *in* 1959 PUB. PAPERS 776–77 (1960); Letter of Dec. 22, 1959, *in* 1959 *id.* at 874–75; Certification of Dec. 2, 1960, *in* 1960–61 *id.* at 881–83 (1961).

40. *See* 41 Op. Att'y Gen. 507, 511–12 (1960); Bowsher v. Synar, 478 U.S. 714, 727–32 (1986) (finding comptroller general to be an agent of Congress).

41. 41 Op. Att'y Gen. 507 (1960).

42. *See* CHARLES J. ZINN, EXTENT OF THE CONTROL OF THE EXECUTIVE BY THE CONGRESS OF THE UNITED STATES, 87th Cong., 2d Sess. 18 n.5 (Comm. Print 1962); CLARK R. MOLLENHOFF, WASHINGTON COVER-UP 169–76 (1962) (but also claiming that Eisenhower failed to comply with the law).

43. Act of May 27, 1972, Pub. L. No. 92–306, 86 Stat. 163, 175; Statement of May 28, 1972, *in* 1972 PUB. PAPERS 627–28 (1974).

44. Act of July 13, 1972, Pub. L. No. 92–351, 86 Stat. 481.

45. Act of Sept. 8, 1980, Pub. L. No. 96–342, 94 Stat. 1082–83.

46. Statement of Sept. 8, 1980, *in* 1980–81 PUB. PAPERS 1667–68 (1982).

47. Act of Dec. 23, 1980, Pub. L. No. 96–579, 94 Stat. 3359, 3368; S. REP. No. 96–1051, 96th Cong., 2d Sess. 8 (1980).

48. Act of June 23, 1913, ch. 3, 38 Stat. 4, 53.

49. Statement of June 23, 1913, *in* 27 PAPERS OF WOODROW WILSON 558 (Arthur S. Link ed., 1978).

50. *See* 1914 ATT'Y GEN. ANN. REPORT 11–22, 174.

51. Act of Dec. 20, 1975, Pub. L. No. 94–158, 89 Stat. 844.

52. Statement of Dec. 20, 1975, *in* 1975 PUB. PAPERS 1990–91 (1977) (noting constitutional objections and invoking authority under Act of Sept. 29, 1965, Pub. L. No. 89–209, § 9(b), 79 Stat. 851, to order that when council performs executive functions, the members in question not serve as members of the council).

53. Act of Aug. 6, 1956, ch. 972, 70 Stat. 1044, 1045.

54. Statement of Aug. 6, 1956, *in* 1956 PUB. PAPERS 648–50 (1958).

55. Act of June 5, 1957, Pub. L. No. 85–47, 71 Stat. 48.

56. Act of Aug. 26, 1957, Pub. L. No. 85–167, 71 Stat. 419–20; *see* Act of Sept. 2, 1958, Pub. L. No. 85–863, 72 Stat. 1576.

57. Act of July 17, 1964, Pub. L. No. 88–379, § 200, 78 Stat. 329, 331.

58. Statement of July 17, 1964, *in* 1963–64 PUB. PAPERS 861–62 (1965).

59. *See* RICHARD M. PIOUS, THE AMERICAN PRESIDENCY 258, 276–77 (1979); ALAN SCHICK, CONGRESS AND MONEY: BUDGETING, SPENDING AND TAXING 169–77 (1980).

60. Act of April 19, 1966, Pub. L. No. 89–404, 80 Stat. 129; *Water Resources Re-*

search: Hearings on H.R. 3606 and S. 22 Before the Subcomm. on Irrigation and Reclamation of the House Comm. on Interior and Insular Affairs, 89th Cong., 2d Sess. 6, 8, 15, 32 (1966); OFFICE OF WATER RESOURCES RESEARCH, U.S. DEP'T OF THE INTERIOR, 1965 ANN. REPORT xv–xvi, 27–28 (1965); OFFICE OF WATER RESOURCES RESEARCH, U.S. DEP'T OF THE INTERIOR, 1966 ANN. REPORT 3, 132, 135 (1966).

61. Act of Oct. 27, 1965, Pub. L. No. 89–298, 79 Stat. 1073.

62. Statement of Oct. 26, 1965, *in* 1965 PUB. PAPERS 1082–84 (1966). *See Separation of Powers: Hearings Before the Subcomm. on Separation of Powers of the Senate Judiciary Comm.*, pt. I, 90th Cong., 1st Sess. 148, 153 (1967).

63. S. REP. No. 549, 91st Cong., 1st Sess. 14–15 (1969).

64. Act of Oct. 27, 1965, Pub. L. No. 89–298, 79 Stat. 1073.

65. *But see* LOUIS FISHER, PRESIDENTIAL SPENDING POWER 166, 308 n.52 (1975) (stating that Johnson impounded funds under this act when it was in fact the 1954 Watershed Protection and Flood Control Act).

66. Act of July 12, 1943, ch. 218, 57 Stat. 431, 450.

67. Statement of Sept. 14, 1943, *in* PUBLIC PAPERS AND ADDRESSES OF FRANKLIN D. ROOSEVELT 1943, at 385–86 (Samuel I. Rosenman ed., 1950), and *in* 89 CONG. REC. 7521 (1943).

68. *See* John H. Ely, United States v. Lovett: *Litigating the Separation of Powers*, 10 HARV. C. R.-C. L. L. REV. 1, 4–6 n.20 (1975).

69. Lovett v. United States, 66 F. Supp. 142 (Ct. Cl. 1945).

70. United States v. Lovett, 328 U.S. 303 (1946).

71. Act of June 22, 1970, Pub. L. No. 91–285, 84 Stat. 314, 318.

72. Statement of June 22, 1970, *in* 1970 PUB. PAPERS 512–13 (1971).

73. N.Y. TIMES, July 15, 1970, at 16, col. 5; *id.*, July 18, 1970, at 11, col. 4; *id.*, Aug. 11, 1970, at 24, col. 1; *id.*, Aug. 18, 1970, at 25, col. 3; *id.*, Aug. 20, 1970, at 27, col. 5.

74. *See* Oregon v. Mitchell, 400 U.S. 112, 117 n.1 (1970); Oregon v. Mitchell, 400 U.S. 802 (1970).

75. 123 CONG. REC. 2974 (1977) (remarks of Sen. James Abourezk).

76. N.Y. TIMES, Aug. 18, 1970, at 25, col. 3; *id.*, Oct. 20, 1970, at 25, cols. 1–3; 123 CONG. REC. 2974 (1977).

77. Oregon v. Mitchell, 400 U.S. 112 (1970).

78. Act of Oct. 15, 1974, Pub. L. No. 93–443, 88 Stat. 1263–64.

79. Statement of Oct. 15, 1974, *in* 1974 PUB. PAPERS 303–04 (1975).

80. *See* Buckley v. Valeo, 519 F.2d 821 (D.C. Cir. 1975); Buckley v. Valeo, 424 U.S. 1 (1976).

81. Buckley v. Valeo, 424 U.S. 1 (1976).

82. Act of Oct. 15, 1974, Pub. L. No. 93–443, § 209, 88 Stat. 1263, 1287–88.

83. *See* FEDERAL ELECTION COMM'N, 1976 ANN. REPORT iii, 45 (1977); FEDERAL ELECTION COMM'N, 1977 ANN. REPORT 6 n.*, 7 (1978); 121 CONG. REC. 32321 (1975); S. REP. No. 94–409, 94th Cong. 1st Sess. (1975); 121 CONG. REC. 33664, 33674 (1975); H.R. REP. No. 94–552, 94th Cong., 1st Sess. (1975).

84. Act of May 11, 1976, Pub. L. No. 94–283, 90 Stat. 475, 477.

85. Statement of May 11, 1976, *in* 1976–77 PUB. PAPERS 1529–31 (1979).

86. N.Y. TIMES, July 2, 1976, at A9, col. 5; *id.*, Aug. 7, 1976, at 7, col. 4; Clark v. Valeo, 559 F.2d 642, 644 (D.C. Cir. 1977) (en banc).

87. *Clark*, 559 F.2d at 647, *aff'd sub nom.* Clark v. Kimmitt, 431 U.S. 950 (1977).

88. Act of Dec. 9, 1977, Pub. L. No. 95–205, 91 Stat. 1460–61.

89. Statement of Dec. 9, 1977, *in* 1977 PUB. PAPERS 2087–88 (1978).

90. *See* Brown v. Califano, 627 F.2d 1221, 1229 n.42, 1237–38 (D.C. Cir. 1980).

91. Brown v. Califano, 455 F. Supp. 837 (D.D.C. 1978), *aff'd*, 627 F.2d 1221 (D.C. Cir. 1980).

92. Act of Mar. 2, 1867, ch. 170, § 2, 14 Stat. 485, 486–87.

93. Message of Mar. 2, 1867, *in* 8 MESSAGES AND PAPERS 3670.

94. Message of Dec. 9, 1868, *in* 9 MESSAGES AND PAPERS 3870, 3871–72.

95. Article IX, *in* 9 MESSAGES AND PAPERS 3911; CONG. GLOBE, 40th Cong., 2d Sess. supp. at 15–16 (1868) (Johnson's denial that he ever gave orders violating command of army provision).

96. Act of Aug. 2, 1886, ch. 840, 24 Stat. 209; Message of Aug. 2, 1886, *in* 11 MESSAGES AND PAPERS 4992–94.

97. *See* N.Y. TIMES, Dec. 6, 1886, at 4, col. 7; *id.*, Dec. 15, 1886, at 1, col. 6, and at 2, col. 2; *id.*, Dec. 20, 1886, at 5, col. 3. A later version of this tax was upheld in McCray v. United States, 195 U.S. 27 (1904).

98. Act of June 29, 1948, ch. 754, 62 Stat. 1112, 1126, and Act of May 12, 1949, ch. 101, 63 Stat. 67 (both barring payment of salary to certain Bureau of Reclamation employees unless they met certain educational and training requirements).

99. Statement of June 30, 1948, *in* 1948 PUB. PAPERS 390–91 (1964); Statement of May 12, 1949, *in* 1949 PUB. PAPERS 250 (1964); N.Y. TIMES, July 1, 1948, at 1, col. 6; *id.*, May 13, 1949, at 17, col. 1.

100. Act of Oct. 12, 1949, ch. 680, 63 Stat. 765; Act of Oct. 28, 1949, ch. 783, 63 Stat. 973, 980; N.Y. TIMES, Oct. 20, 1949, at 36, col. 2.

101. Act of July 5, 1949, ch. 296, 63 Stat. 405, 406.

102. Statement of July 5, 1949, *in* 1949 PUB. PAPERS 346–47 (1964).

103. *See* 44 U.S.C. §§ 501, 504 (1994).

104. Act of Oct. 8, 1964, Pub. L. No. 88–638, § 1(10), 78 Stat. 1035, 1036.

105. Statement of Oct. 8, 1964, *in* 1963–64 PUB. PAPERS 1249–51 (1965).

106. Act of Nov. 11, 1966, Pub. L. No. 89–808, 80 Stat. 1526, 1530–31; H.R. REP. No. 1558, 89th Cong., 2d Sess. 5–6 (1966).

107. *See World War on Hunger: Hearings on H.R. 12152, H.R. 12784, and H.R. 12785 Before the House Comm. on Agriculture*, 89th Cong., 2d Sess. 251–56 (1966); 112 Cong. Rec. 21111 (remarks of Sen. Ellender).

108. Act of Aug. 15, 1970, Pub. L. No. 91–379, 84 Stat. 796–98.

109. Statement of Aug. 17, 1970, *in* 1970 PUB. PAPERS 674–76 (1971).

110. *See Defense Production Act Amendments—1972: Hearings on S. 669 and S. 1901 Before the Subcomm. on Production and Stabilization of the Senate Comm. on Banking, Housing and Urban Affairs*, 92d Cong., 2d Sess. 1–2, 8–9, 25–29, 105–07 (1972).

111. Act of June 16, 1972, Pub. L. No. 92–313, 86 Stat. 216, 217, 220.

112. Statement of June 17, 1972, *in* 1972 PUB. PAPERS 686–88 (1974).

113. *See* H.R. REP. No. 1624, 92d Cong., 2d Sess. 17–18 (1972); STAFF OF SENATE COMM. ON PUBLIC WORKS, 92D CONG., 2D SESS., SUMMARY OF LEGISLATIVE ACTIVITIES AND ACCOMPLISHMENTS 77–83 (Comm. Print 1972); STAFF OF HOUSE COMM. ON PUBLIC WORKS, LEGISLATIVE HISTORY NINETY-THIRD CONGRESS, 92D CONG., 2D SESS. 15–16 (Comm. Print 1975); STAFF OF SENATE COMM. ON PUBLIC WORKS, 94TH CONG., 1ST SESS., SUMMARY OF LEGISLATIVE ACTIVITIES AND ACCOMPLISHMENTS 29–32 (Comm. Print 1975).

114. Act of Aug. 15, 1876, ch. 288, 19 Stat. 170, 175; Message of Aug. 14, 1876, *in* 10 MESSAGES AND PAPERS 4331–32.

115. Message of Dec. 5, 1876, *in* 10 MESSAGES AND PAPERS 4353, 4356.

116. Act of Sept. 6, 1950, ch. 896, 64 Stat. 595, 758.

117. Statement of Sept. 6, 1950, *in* 1950 PUB. PAPERS 616 (1965).

118. N.Y. TIMES, Aug. 29, 1950, at 1, col. 3; *id.*, Sept. 7, 1950, at 1, col. 6; *id.*, Sept. 10, 1950, at 24, col. 4.

119. N.Y. TIMES, Nov. 16, 1950, at 1, col. 5; *id.*, Nov. 17, 1950, at 10, col. 5; *id.*, Nov. 19, 1950, pt. IV, at 2, col. 7.

120. Act of Aug. 2, 1955, ch. 491, 69 Stat. 435.

121. Statement of Aug. 2, 1955, *in* 1955 PUB. PAPERS 753–54 (1959).

122. *See* H.R. DOC. No. 369, 84th Cong., 2d Sess. 35 (1955); H.R. DOC. No. 481, 84th Cong., 2d Sess. 18, 28–29 (1956).

123. Act of July 31, 1956, ch. 803, 70 Stat. 733–34.

124. Statement of July 31, 1956, *in* 1956 PUB. PAPERS 619 (1958).

125. *See* SENATE SPECIAL COMM. TO STUDY THE FOREIGN AID PROGRAM, REPORT ON UNITED STATES FOREIGN ASSISTANCE PROGRAMS: WESTERN EUROPE II, 85TH CONG., 1ST SESS. 66–67 (Comm. Print. 1957); SENATE SPECIAL COMM. TO STUDY THE FOREIGN AID PROGRAM, REPORT ON UNITED STATES FOREIGN ASSISTANCE PROGRAMS: CENTRAL AMERICA AND THE CARIBBEAN AREA, 85TH CONG., 1ST SESS. 15 (Comm. Print. 1957).

126. Act of Aug. 8, 1956, ch. 1036, 70 Stat. 1119, 1123.

127. Statement of Aug. 8, 1956, *in* 1956 PUB. PAPERS 672–73 (1958).

128. Act of Apr. 13, 1976, Pub. L. No. 94–265, 90 Stat. 331, 339–40.

129. Statement of Apr. 13, 1976, *in* 1976 PUB. PAPERS 1116–18 (1979).

130. *See Implementation of the Fishery Conservation and Management Act: Hearings Before the Senate Comm. on Commerce*, 95th Cong., 1st Sess. 1–13 (1977).

131. Act of Aug. 17, 1977, Pub. L. No. 95–108, 91 Stat. 871–72; Statement of Aug. 18, 1977, *in* 1977 PUB. PAPERS 1480 (1978).

132. Act of Sept. 12, 1966, Pub. L. No. 89–568, 80 Stat. 739, 757.

133. Statement of Sept. 12, 1966, *in* 1966 PUB. PAPERS 1008–09 (1967).

134. Act of Apr. 4, 1967, Pub. L. No. 90–8, 81 Stat. 8, 9.

135. Statement of Apr. 4, 1967, *in* 1967 PUB. PAPERS 421 (1968); N.Y. TIMES, Apr. 5, 1967, at 3, col. 2.

136. S. REP. No. 494, 90th Cong., 1st Sess. 5, 18, 20 (1967).

137. Act of Oct. 21, 1967, Pub. L. No. 90–110, §§ 809, 810, 1001, 81 Stat. 279, 309–10; Statement of Oct. 21, 1967, *in* 1967 PUB. PAPERS 935–36 (1968).

138. Pub. L. No. 90–110, § 809, 81 Stat. 279, 309.

139. *Joint Hearings of the Investigations, Readiness, and Military Installations and Facilities Subcomms. of the House Comm. on Armed Services*, 99th Cong., 2d Sess. 371–72 (1986); SUBCOMMS. ON INVESTIGATIONS, READINESS, AND MILITARY INSTALLATIONS AND FACILITIES OF THE HOUSE COMM. ON ARMED SERVICES, PRESENT USE, REQUIREMENTS, AND FUTURE UTILIZATION OF FORT DERUSSY, HAWAII, 99TH CONG., 2D SESS. 1–7 (Comm. Print 1987).

140. Pub. L. No. 90–110, § 810, 81 Stat. 279, 309.

141. L.A. TIMES, Apr. 16, 1989, at 19, col. 1.

142. Statement of Oct. 21, 1967, *in* 1967 PUB. PAPERS 935 (1968).

143. *See* L.A. TIMES, Apr. 16, 1989, at 19, col. 1.

144. Pub. L. No. 90–110, § 1001, 81 Stat. 279, 310.

145. N.Y. TIMES, Jan. 19, 1967, at 5, col. 3; *id.*, Jan. 20, 1967, at 13, col. 6; *id.*, Aug. 13, 1967, at 58, col. 1; S. REP. No. 570, 90th Cong., 1st Sess. 15–16 (1967).

146. Act of July 13, 1955, ch. 358, 69 Stat. 301, 321.

147. Statement of July 13, 1955, *in* 1955 PUB. PAPERS 688–90 (1959).

148. *See Section 638, Dep't of Defense Appropriations Act, 1956: Hearings Before the Subcomm. on Defense Appropriations of the House Comm. on Appropriations*, 84th Cong., 2d Sess. 6, 39–49, 88, 109, 124 (1956); SUBCOMM. ON DEP'T OF DEFENSE, HOUSE COMM. ON APPROPRIATIONS, 84TH CONG., 2D SESS., REPORT ON SECTION 638, DEP'T OF DEFENSE APPROPRIATIONS ACT, 1956, at 1 (Comm. Print 1956); SUBCOMM. ON DEP'T OF DEFENSE, HOUSE COMM. ON APPROPRIATIONS, 84TH CONG., 2D SESS., REPORT ON SECTION 638, DEP'T OF DEFENSE APPROPRIATIONS ACT, 1956, at 1 (Comm. Print 1956); N.Y. TIMES, Jan. 13, 1956, at 13, col. 2; *id.*, Jan. 18, 1956, at 15, col. 4; FISHER, PRESIDENTIAL SPENDING POWER, at 74.

149. Act of Dec. 31, 1963, Pub. L. No. 88–257, 77 Stat. 844, 847; Statement of Dec. 31, 1963, *in* 1963–64 PUB. PAPERS 104 (1965).

150. *See Panama Canal Problems: Hearings on H.R. 3999 Before the Subcomm. on Panama Canal of the House Comm. on Merchant Marine and Fisheries*, 88th Cong., 1st Sess. (1963); 109 CONG. REC. 18172–76 (1963).

151. Act of Oct. 13, 1964, Pub. L. No. 88–643, 78 Stat. 1043.

152. Statement of Oct. 14, 1964, *in* 1963–64 PUB. PAPERS 1336 (1965).

153. *Hearings on H.R. 16306 Before Subcomm. No. 1 of the House Comm. on Armed Services*, 89th Cong., 2d Sess. 10321 (1966).

154. Act of July 9, 1973, Pub. L. No. 93–66, 87 Stat. 152, 158–59.

155. Statement of July 11, 1973, *in* 1973 PUB. PAPERS 642–43 (1975).

156. *See* 38 Fed. Reg. 19911 (1973); *id.*, 24872 (1973); *id.*, 30072 (1973); 39 Fed. Reg. 1443 (1974).

157. Act of May 26, 1975, Pub. L. No. 94–25, 89 Stat. 90, 91.

158. Statement of May 26, 1975, *in* 1975 PUB. PAPERS 724–25 (1977).

159. *Hearings on Criteria and Procedures for Making Route and Service Decisions by Amtrak Before the Surface Transportation Subcomm. of the Senate Comm. on Commerce*, 94th Cong., 2d Sess. 19–20, 39, 46, 113 (1976); *Hearings on Amtrak Discontinuance Criteria Before the Subcomm. on Transportation and Commerce of the House Comm. on Interstate and Foreign Commerce*, 94th Cong., 2d Sess. 13–16 (1976).

160. Act of Feb. 9, 1976, Pub. L. No. 94–212, 90 Stat. 153, 161–62.

161. *See* H.R. REP. No. 94–517, 94th Cong., 1st Sess. 206–12 (1975); S. REP. No. 94–446, 94th Cong., 1st Sess. 185–87 (1975); H.R. REP. No. 94–710, 94th Cong., 1st Sess. 46–47 (1975).

162. Statement of Feb. 10, 1976, *in* 1976 PUB. PAPERS 241–42 (1979).

163. *See Dep't of Defense Appropriations for Fiscal Year 1977: Hearings on H.R. 14262 Before a Subcomm. of the Senate Comm. on Appropriations*, 94th Cong., 2d Sess, pt. 4, at 182–90 (1976); *Dep't of Defense Appropriations for Fiscal Year 1978: Hearings on H.R. 7933 Before a Subcomm. of the Senate Comm. on Appropriations*, 95th Cong., 1st Sess., 1st Sess., pt. 4, at 275–76, 293 (1976).

164. Act of June 30, 1976, Pub. L. No. 94–330, 90 Stat. 771, 773–74.

165. Statement of July 1, 1976, *in* 1976–77 PUB. PAPERS 1935–36 (1979).

166. Act of June 17, 1944, ch. 262, 58 Stat. 280, 281–82.

167. Statement of June 17, 1944, *reprinted in* 90 CONG. REC. 6154 (1944).

168. *See* Act of Apr. 4, 1944, ch. 165, 58 Stat. 189, 190; 97 CONG. REC. 5435–37; Robert W. Ginnane, *The Control of Federal Administration by Congressional Resolutions and Committees*, 66 HARV. L. REV. 569, 602–03 (1953) (but confusing the Elk Hills Act with the earlier statute dealing with real property).

169. Act of Sept. 7, 1966, Pub. L. No. 89–556, 80 Stat. 689, 690.

170. Statement of Sept. 8, 1966, *in* 1966 PUB. PAPERS 980–81 (1967).

171. THE BUDGET OF THE UNITED STATES GOVERNMENT, FOR THE FISCAL YEAR ENDING JUNE 30, 1968, app. at 101–02 (1967).

172. Act of Nov. 18, 1969, Pub. L. No. 91–120, 83 Stat. 203; Statement of Nov. 19, 1969, *in* 1969 PUB. PAPERS 948 (1971).

173. S. REP. No. 91–285, 91st Cong., 1st Sess. 28–29 (1969).

174. *See* S. REP. No. 983, 91st Cong., 2d Sess. (1970); H.R. REP. No. 991, 91st Cong., 2d Sess. (1970).

175. *See* Act of July 24, 1970, Pub. L. No. 91–356, 84 Stat. 471–72.

176. Act of Nov. 16, 1973, Pub. L. No. 93–153, § 405, 87 Stat. 576, 590.

177. Statement of Nov. 16, 1973, *in* 1973 PUB. PAPERS 945–46 (1975).

178. *See* N.Y. TIMES, Aug. 21, 1974, at 55, col. 7; 120 CONG. REC. 1186 (1974).

179. *See* N.Y. TIMES, Nov. 21, 1974, at 15, col. 1; 120 CONG. REC. 36226 (1974).

180. Act of Jan. 2, 1976, Pub. L. No. 94–201, 89 Stat. 1129, 1130.

181. Statement of Jan. 3, 1976, *in* 1976–77 PUB. PAPERS 6–7 (1979).

182. Act of Oct. 1, 1980, Pub. L. No. 96–369, 94 Stat. 1351, 1356.

183. Statement of Oct. 2, 1980, *in* 1980–81 PUB. PAPERS 2015–16 (1982).

184. 45 Fed. Reg. 52052–76 (1980); *id.*, 58145–46 (1980).

185. 46 Fed. Reg. 10516 (1981).

186. Act of Oct. 8, 1977, Pub. L. No. 95–126, 91 Stat. 1106.

187. Statement of Oct. 8, 1977, *in* 1977, *in* 1977 PUB. PAPERS 1757–58 (1978); N.Y. TIMES, Oct. 9, 1977, at 1, col. 6.

188. 43 Fed. Reg. 15152–54 (1978) (to be codified at 38 C.F.R. § 3.12(c) (6)); *and see* Op. Veterans Admin. Gen. Counsel 30–79 (Aug. 11, 1978).

189. Neal Devins, *Congressional-Executive Information Access Disputes: A Modest Proposal—Do Nothing*, 48 ADMIN. L. REV. 109, 120–21, 134–35 (1996); *see also* LOUIS FISHER, THE POLITICS OF SHARED POWER: CONGRESS AND THE EXECUTIVE 89–92 (2d ed. 1987); DANIEL P. FRANKLIN, EXTRAORDINARY MEASURES: THE EXERCISE OF PREROGATIVE POWER IN THE UNITED STATES 63–64 (1991); Steven G. Calabresi, *Some Normative Arguments for the Unitary Executive*, 48 ARK. L. REV. 23, 50–55 (1995).

190. Louis Fisher, *The Legislative Veto: Invalidated, It Survives*, 56 LAW & CONTEMP. PROBS., Autumn 1993, at 273, 288.

191. Act of Oct. 23, 1962, Pub. L. No. 87–872, 76 Stat. 1163, 1164.

192. Memorandum of Jan. 8, 1963, *in* 1963 PUB. PAPERS 6 (1964).

193. *Foreign Assistance and Related Agencies Appropriations for 1964: Hearings on H.R. 9499 Before the Senate Comm. on Appropriations*, 88th Cong., 1st Sess. 312–13 (1963).

194. Act of Nov. 10, 1978, Pub. L. No. 95–625, 92 Stat. 3467, 3549; *Additions to the National Wilderness Preservation System: Hearings Before the Subcomm. on Public Lands of the House Comm. on Interior and Insular Affairs*, 96th Cong., 1st Sess. 24–26 (1979) [hereinafter *Wilderness Hearings*].

195. Statement of Nov. 10, 1978, *in* 1978 PUB. PAPERS 1999–2000 (1979).

196. *Wilderness Hearings* at 244–45.

197. *Id.*

198. *Id.* at 35, 42–47.

CHAPTER 7

1. *See* Cass R. Sunstein, *What's Standing After Lujan? Of Citizen Suits, 'Injuries,' and Article III*, 91 MICH. L. REV. 163, 168–97 (1992).

2. *See* Warth v. Seldin, 422 U.S. 490, 498–500 (1975); Lujan v. Defenders of Wildlife, 504 U.S. 555, 560–61 (1992).

3. Act of June 25, 1860, ch. 211, 12 Stat. 104, 106. *See* S. MISC. DOC. No. 83, 38th Cong., 1st Sess. 1–4 (1864).

4. Statement of June 25, 1860, *in* 7 A COMPILATION OF THE MESSAGES AND PAPERS OF THE PRESIDENTS 3128, 3129 (James D. Richardson ed., 1897, 1917) [hereinafter MESSAGES AND PAPERS].

5. RUSSELL F. WEIGLEY, QUARTERMASTER GENERAL OF THE UNION ARMY: A BIOGRAPHY OF M. C. MEIGS 78–112 (1959); S. EXEC. DOC. No. 1, 37th Cong., 2d Sess. 84 (1861).

6. WEIGLEY, QUARTERMASTER GENERAL, at 126–30; S. EX. DOC. No. 1, 37th Cong., 2d Sess. 84–85, 89–91 (1861).

7. 9 Op. Att'y Gen. 463, 468–69 (1860).

8. *Id.* at 469–70.

9. CONG. GLOBE, 36th Cong., 1st Sess. 3209–13 (1860).

10. WEIGLEY, QUARTERMASTER GENERAL, at 101–04; 9 Op. Att'y Gen. at 467–68; CONG. GLOBE, 36th Cong., 1st Sess. 3210 (1860).

11. *See* LAURENCE H. TRIBE, AMERICAN CONSTITUTIONAL LAW 259 n. 13 (2d ed. 1988).

12. S. EXEC. DOC. No. 1, 37th Cong., 2d Sess. at 92–93.

13. Act of June 14, 1862, Res. 34, 12 Stat. 619; CONG. GLOBE, 37th Cong., 2d Sess. 1723, 2061 (1862); H.R. EXEC. DOC. No. 1, 37th Cong., 3d Sess. 615 (1862).

14. Act of Jan. 16, 1883, ch. 27, 22 Stat. 403, 404.

15. Message of March 1, 1883, *in* 11 MESSAGES AND PAPERS 4745.

16. 17 Op. Att'y Gen. 504 (Jan. 22, 1883).

17. *Id.* at 508–09.

18. 11 MESSAGES AND PAPERS 4745.

19. 23 J. OF EXEC. PROC. OF U.S. SENATE 712 (1901); N.Y. TIMES, March 3, 1883, at 1, col. 2.

20. 23 J. OF EXEC. PROC. OF U.S. SENATE 723 (1901).

21. H.R. DOC. No. 854, 62d Cong., 2d Sess. (1912); *see* Frederick A. Cleveland, *The Federal Budget: What the President Is Trying to Do by Way of Budget Making for the National Government*, 3 PROC. ACAD. POL. SCI. 165, 165–66 (1912–13).

22. *See* LOUIS FISHER, CONSTITUTIONAL CONFLICTS BETWEEN CONGRESS AND THE PRESIDENT 189–90 (3d ed. rev. 1991).

23. 48 CONG. REC. 8500–01 (June 27, 1912).

24. Cleveland, *The Federal Budget*, at 166–68.

25. Act of Aug. 23, 1912, ch. 350, 37 Stat. 360, 415.

26. Message of Feb. 26, 1913, S. DOC. No. 1113, 62d Cong., 3d Sess. 5 (1913) (quoting U.S. CONST. art. I, § 9 & art. II, § 3); *see* FISHER, CONSTITUTIONAL CONFLICTS, at 189.

27. Act of Aug. 23, 1912, ch. 350, § 9, 37 Stat. at 415.

28. Fisher, Presidential Spending Power 30 (1975).

29. Fisher, Constitutional Conflicts, at 189; Fisher, Presidential Spending, at 31.

30. *See* Message of Feb. 26, 1913, H.R. Doc. No. 1113, 62d Cong., 3d Sess. 9 (1913).

31. Act of June 5, 1920, ch. 250, § 28, 41 Stat. 988, 999–1000; *see* Jeffrey J. Safford, Wilsonian Maritime Diplomacy 1913–1921, at 221–32 (1978).

32. Act of June 5, 1920, ch. 250, § 34, 41 Stat. 988, 1007.

33. Letter from Woodrow Wilson to Bainbridge Colby (Sept. 2, 1920), *in* 66 Papers of Woodrow Wilson 89 (Arthur S. Link ed. 1992).

34. Letter and Enclosure from Bainbridge Colby to Woodrow Wilson (Sept. 23, 1920), *in* 66 *id.* at 136.

35. Safford, Wilsonian Maritime Diplomacy, at 237.

36. *Id.* at 229.

37. Act of March 4, 1915, ch. 153, 38 Stat. 1164, 1184; *see* Jesse S. Reeves, *The Jones Act and the Denunciation of Treaties*, 15 Am. J. Int'l Law 33, 37 (1921); Edward S. Corwin, The President: Office and Powers, 1787–1984, at 220–21 (5th rev. ed. 1984).

38. Letter from Woodrow Wilson to Sen. Albert Fall (Dec. 8, 1920), *in* 64 Papers of Woodrow Wilson, at 152 (Arthur S. Link ed., 1991).

39. *See* Donald G. Morgan, Congress and the Constitution: A Study of Responsibility 150 (1966).

40. Letter and Enclosure from Bainbridge Colby to Woodrow Wilson (Sept. 23, 1920), *in* 66 Papers of Woodrow Wilson, at 136–37; *see* Safford, Wilsonian Maritime Diplomacy, at 232–39.

41. Reeves, *The Jones Act*, at 37–38.

42. H.R. Doc. No. 227, 67th Cong., 2d Sess. 27–28 (1921); H.R. Doc. No. 407, 67th Cong., 3d Sess. 13 (1921); Safford, Wilsonian Maritime Diplomacy, at 233, 244.

43. Safford, Wilsonian Maritime Diplomacy, at 233.

44. *See* N.Y. Times, May 20, 1921, at 12, col. 7; *id.*, Oct. 8, 1921, at 4, col. 1; *id.*, Nov. 26, 1921, at 10, col. 3; *id.*, Dec. 2, 1921, at 5, col. 2.

45. *See* Duane Tananbaum, The Bricker Amendment Controversy: A Test of Eisenhower's Political Leadership (1988).

46. Act of July 29, 1958, Pub. L. No. 85–568, 72 Stat. 426, 432.

47. Statement of July 29, 1958, *in* 1958 Public Papers of the Presidents of the United States 573 (1959) [hereinafter Pub. Papers].

48. Agreement on Tracking Stations, Feb. 19, 1959, U.S.-Chile, 10 U.S.T. 783–86.

49. Act of Oct. 23, 1974, Pub. L. No. 93–463, 88 Stat. 1389, 1390.

50. Statement of Oct. 24, 1974, *in* 1974 Pub. Papers 461–62 (1975).

51. *See* Buckley v. Valeo, 424 U.S. 1, 126 n.162 (1976) (noting that Art. II, § 2 is inapplicable to mere ''employees'' or ''lesser functionaries'').

52. Staff of the House Comm. on Appropriations, 95th Cong., 2d Sess., Investigative Study on the Commodity Futures Trading Commission 30–31 (Comm. Print 1978) [hereinafter CFTC Study].

53. Act of Sept. 30, 1978, Pub. L. No. 95–405, § 2, 92 Stat. 865.

54. H.R. Rep. No. 1181, 95th Cong., 2d Sess. 22 (1978); *Reauthorization of the*

Commodity Futures Trading Commission: Hearing Before the Subcomm. on Agricultural Research and General Legislation of the Senate Comm. on Agriculture, Nutrition, and Forestry, 95th Cong., 2d Sess. 17, 22, 29–30 (1978); CFTC STUDY, at 30.

55. CFTC STUDY, at 30.

56. Act of Oct. 20, 1975, Pub. L. No. 94–118, 89 Stat. 603, 604.

57. Statement of Oct. 21, 1975, *in* 1975 PUB. PAPERS 1718–19 (1977).

58. Regulations of the Japan-United States Friendship Commission (adopted Oct. 5, 1976); telephone interview with Eric J. Gangloff, Exec. Dir., Japan-U.S. Friendship Comm'n (April 15, 1993).

59. *See* Hutchinson v. Proxmire, 443 U.S. 111 (1979); United States v. Brewster, 408 U.S. 501 (1972).

60. Proclamation No. 4483, 91 Stat. 1719 (1977). *See* 123 CONG. REC. 20835 (June 24, 1977) (remarks of Sen. Dole).

61. Act of Aug. 2, 1977, Pub. L. No. 95–86, 91 Stat. 419, 444.

62. Letter from Robert J. Lipshutz, Counsel to the President, to Sen. Mark Hatfield (June 23, 1977), *in* 123 CONG. REC. 20834–35 (1977).

63. Statement of Aug. 3, 1977, *in* 1977 PUB. PAPERS 1409–10 (1978).

64. Exec. Order No. 11,967, 50 U.S.C. app. § 462 (1988).

65. N.Y. TIMES, June 25, 1977, at 1, col. 5; 123 CONG. REC. 20834 (1977).

66. 123 CONG. REC. 20834 (1977).

67. N.Y. TIMES, Mar. 17, 1977, at 15, col. 1; *id.*, June 25, 1977, at 1, col. 5, and 7 col. 3.

68. 54 INTERPRETER RELEASES 369 (Maurice A. Roberts ed., Oct. 19, 1977).

69. 42 Fed. Reg. 59562–63 (1977).

70. *See* Daughtrey v. Carter, 584 F.2d 1050, 1054–55 (D.C. Cir. 1978).

71. Daughtrey v. Carter, 584 F.2d at 1053, 1058.

72. *See* LOUIS HENKIN, FOREIGN AFFAIRS AND THE CONSTITUTION 416 (1972); United States v. Klein, 80 U.S. (13 Wall.) 128 (1872).

73. Act of Nov. 2, 1978, Pub. L. No. 95–567, 92 Stat. 2405, amending Act of Nov. 7, 1967, Pub. L. No. 90–129, 81 Stat. 365.

74. Pub. L. No. 90–129, § 201(8), 81 Stat. at 368; 47 U.S.C. § 399(a) (amended 1981).

75. Statement of Nov. 2, 1978, *in* 1978 PUB. PAPERS 1927–28 (1979).

76. 125 CONG. REC. 35416 (1979); *Department of Justice Authorization and Oversight, 1981: Hearings Before the Senate Judiciary Comm.*, 96th Cong., 2d Sess. 853–54 (1980); FCC v. League of Women Voters, 468 U.S. 364, 370–71 & n.8 (1984).

77. FCC v. League of Women Voters, 468 U.S. at 370–71 & n.8.

78. League of Women Voters v. FCC, 489 F.Supp. 517, 519–20 (C.D. Calif. 1980).

79. 489 F.Supp. at 520.

80. League of Women Voters v. FCC, 547 F.Supp. 379, 382 (C.D. Calif. 1982); *see* Michael T. Brady, Note, *Executive Discretion and the Congressional Defense of Statutes*, 92 YALE L.J. 970, 976 n.21 (1983).

81. FCC v. League of Women Voters, 468 U.S. 364 (1984).

82. Act of Nov. 10, 1978, Pub. L. No. 95–629, 92 Stat. 3635, 3636–39.

83. Statement of Nov. 10, 1978, *in* 1978 PUB. PAPERS 2001 (1979).

84. *Department of the Interior and Related Agencies Appropriations for 1980: Hearings Before a Subcomm. of the House Appropriations Comm.*, 96th Cong., 1st Sess. 50 (1979).

85. *See* 45 Fed. Reg. 49689 (1980); *id.* at 84159 (1980).

86. Cooperative Agreement, Feb. 20, 1983, Clerk's Office, Bexar County, Texas, file no. 627684, vol. 3901, at 562–69.

87. *See* Flast v. Cohen, 392 U.S. 83 (1968); Valley Forge Christian College v. Americans United for Separation of Church and State, Inc., 454 U.S. 464 (1982).

88. Act of Aug. 15, 1979, Pub. L. No. 96–60, 93 Stat. 395, 397.

89. Statement of Aug. 15, 1979, *in* 1979 PUB. PAPERS 1434–35 (1980).

90. 126 CONG. REC. 21515–16, 28513 (1980) (noting closure of consulates in Salzburg, Bremen, Nice, Turin, Goteborg, Mandalay, and Brisbane).

91. *See supra* chapter 6, "President's Conduct of Foreign Affairs."

92. *See* 126 CONG. REC. 28513 (1980).

93. Statement of Dec. 12, 1980, *in* 1980–81 PUB. PAPERS 2802–03 (1982).

94. Act of Dec. 12, 1980, Pub. L. No. 96–515, § 301, 94 Stat. 2987, 2998.

95. ADVISORY COUNCIL ON HISTORIC PRESERVATION, 1981 ANN. REPORT 20, 54.

96. ROBERT J. SPITZER, THE PRESIDENTIAL VETO: TOUCHSTONE OF THE AMERICAN PRESIDENCY 126, 158 nn. 6, 8 (1988); GA. CONST. art. III, § V.

97. *See* NORMAN J. ORNSTEIN ET AL., VITAL STATISTICS OF CONGRESS, 1991–1992, at 40–42 (1992).

98. Act of March 2, 1821, ch. 13, 3 Stat. 615.

99. Message of April 13, 1822, *in* 2 MESSAGES AND PAPERS 698.

100. *Id.* at 702; (emphasis added).

101. *Id.* at 702; Letter from J. C. Calhoun, Secretary of War, to Rep. William Eustis (Jan. 29, 1822), *reprinted in* 22 *Niles Weekly Register* 413–14 (1822).

102. *See* 22 *Niles' Weekly Register* 415–21 (1822).

103. *See, e.g.*, Michael S. Paulsen, *The Most Dangerous Branch: Executive Power to Say What the Law Is*, 83 GEO. L.J. 217, 327 (1994); *but cf.* William M. Meigs, *The Independence of the Departments of Government*, 23 AM. L. REV. 594, 600–01 (1889).

104. HENKIN, FOREIGN AFFAIRS, at 418–19 n.136.

105. Act of Feb. 9, 1865, Res. No. 13, 13 Stat. 568.

106. *See* Reeves, *The Jones Act*, at 35–36.

107. Act of Aug. 14, 1876, ch. 267, 19 Stat. 132; Message of Aug. 14, 1876, *in* 10 MESSAGES AND PAPERS 4331.

108. *See* 1876 ANN. REPORT OF THE SECRETARY OF WAR, H.R. EXEC. DOC. NO. 1, 44th Cong., 2d Sess., pt. 2, at 12, 35–37 (1876); 1877 ANN. REPORT OF THE SECRETARY OF WAR, H.R. EXEC. DOC. No. 1, 45th Cong., 2d Sess., vol. 2, at 31 (1877).

109. *See* Act of June 10, 1872, ch. 416, 17 Stat. 370; Act of March 3, 1873, ch. 233, 17 Stat. 560.

110. Message of Aug. 14, 1876, *in* 10 MESSAGES AND PAPERS 4331.

111. Act of October 29, 1949, ch. 787, 63 Stat. 987.

112. FISHER, PRESIDENTIAL SPENDING, at 162–63.

113. Statement of Oct. 29, 1949, *in* 1949 PUB. PAPERS 538–39 (1964).

114. Letter from Harry S. Truman to Louis A. Johnson, Secretary of War (Nov. 8, 1949), *reprinted in Executive Impoundment of Appropriated Funds: Hearings Before the Subcomm. on Separation of Powers of the Senate Comm. on the Judiciary*, 92d Cong., 1st Sess. 524–25 (1971) [hereinafter *Impoundment* Hearings].

115. Letter from John F. Kennedy to Rep. Carl Vinson (March 20, 1962), *reprinted in Impoundment Hearings*, at 526.

116. Act of April 26, 1962, Pub. L. No. 87–436, 76 Stat. 55; Gerald W. Davis,

Congressional Power of Require Defense Expenditures, 33 FORDHAM L. REV. 39, 40–44 (1964).

117. *See* EDWARD A. KOLODZIEJ, THE UNCOMMON DEFENSE AND CONGRESS, 1945–1963, at 408–19 (1966).

CHAPTER 8

1. *See* 9 A COMPILATION OF THE MESSAGES AND PAPERS OF THE PRESIDENTS 3992 (James D. Richardson ed., 1897, 1917) (President Grant) [hereinafter MESSAGES AND PAPERS]; 10 *id.* at 4557 (President Hayes); 11 *id.* at 4960 (President Cleveland); LOUIS FISHER, CONSTITUTIONAL CONFLICTS BETWEEN CONGRESS AND THE PRESIDENT 60–61 (3d ed. rev. 1991).

2. *See Separation of Powers: Hearings Before the Subcomm. on Separation of Powers of the Senate Judiciary Comm.*, pt. I, 90th Cong., 1st Sess. 222 (1967) [hereinafter SEPARATION OF POWER HEARINGS].

3. *See* Michael T. Brady, Note, *Executive Discretion and the Congressional Defense of Statutes*, 92 YALE L.J. 970 (1983); Arthur S. Miller & Jefferey H. Bowman, *Presidential Attacks on the Constitutionality of Federal Statutes: A New Separation of Powers Problem*, 40 OHIO ST. L.J. 51 (1979).

4. Simkins v. Moses H. Cone Memorial Hosp., 323 F.2d 959, 962 (4th Cir. 1963) (en banc), *cert. denied*, 376 U.S. 1938 (1964).

5. Gavett v. Alexander, 477 F. Supp. 1035, 1039, 1043–44 & n.19 (D.D.C. 1979).

6. *See* Statement of Dec. 31, 1963, *in* 1963–64 PUBLIC PAPERS OF THE PRESIDENTS OF THE UNITED STATES 104 (1965) [hereinafter PUB. PAPERS].

7. *See* Message of June 7, 1965, 111 CONG. REC. 12669–70 (1965), S. DOC. NO. 34, 89th Cong., 1st Sess. 1–2 (1965).

8. *See* Statement of July 17, 1964, *in* 1963–64 PUB. PAPERS 861–62 (1965); Statement of Oct. 8, 1964, *in id.* at 1249–51; Statement of Oct. 14, 1964, *in id.* at 1336; Statement of Oct. 26, 1965, *in* 1965 PUB. PAPERS 1082–84 (1966).

9. *See* Statement of Nov. 8, 1966, *in* 1966 PUB. PAPERS 1354 (1967); *Separation of Powers Hearings*, at 38, 108–09, 153–55, 214–15.

10. *See Separation of Powers Hearings*, at 106–07; Statement of Nov. 8, 1966, *in* 1966 PUB. PAPERS 1354 (1967); S. REP. NO. 549, 91st Cong., 1st Sess. 14–15 (1969).

11. Bankhead-Jones Farm Tenant Act of 1937, ch. 517, 50 Stat. 522 (codified as amended at 7 U.S.C. § 1011 (1980)); Watershed Protection and Flood Prevention Act of 1954, Pub. L. No. 83–566, ch. 656, 68 Stat. 666 (codified as amended at 16 U.S.C. § 1002 (1985); Small Reclamation Projects Act of 1956, ch. 972, 70 Stat. 1044, 1045 (codified as amended at 43 U.S.C. § 422a (1988)); Public Buildings Act of 1959, Pub. L. No. 86–249, § 7(a), 73 Stat. 479 (codified as amended at 40 U.S.C. § 605 (1988)). *See Separation of Powers Hearings*, at 81–138, 150–55, 214–15.

12. 18 Op. Att'y Gen. 409 (1886).

13. Act of Jan. 16, 1883, ch. 27, § 3, 22 Stat. 403, 404.

14. 25 J. OF EXEC. PROC. OF U.S. SENATE 601, 683 (1901).

15. Myers v. United States, 58 Ct. Cl. 199, 199–200 (1923).

16. Act of July 12, 1876, ch. 179, § 6, 19 Stat. 78, 80–81.

17. *Myers*, 58 Ct. Cl. at 201–02.

18. WOODROW WILSON, CONGRESSIONAL GOVERNMENT: A STUDY IN AMERICAN POLITICS 180 (Meridian Books ed., 1956) (1885).

19. *See* Myers v. United States, 272 U.S. 52, 168–69 (1926).

20. Message of June 4, 1920, *in* 65 PAPERS OF WOODROW WILSON 362–63 (Arthur S. Link ed., 1991); Myers v. United States, 272 U.S. 52, 169 (1926).

21. *Myers*, 58 Ct. Cl. at 206.

22. *Myers*, 272 U.S. at 176. Justices McReynolds, Brandeis and Holmes dissented.

23. Federal Trade Commission Act, ch. 311, § 1, 38 Stat. 717, 717–18 (1914).

24. Humphrey's Executor v. United States, 295 U.S. 602, 618–19, 626 (1935).

25. *Id.* at 627–32.

26. *See Separation of Powers Hearings*, at 106–07.

27. Watershed Protection and Flood Prevention Act of 1954, ch. 566, § 2, 68 Stat. 666 (codified as amended at 16 U.S.C. § 1001 (1985)); *Separation of Powers Hearings*, at 82–83, 108–110.

28. 115 CONG. REC. 5923–24 (1969); *Separation of Powers Hearings*, at 92, 138.

29. *See Separation of Powers Hearings*, at 115.

30. *See* 28 U.S.C. § 2201 (1988).

31. *See Separation of Powers Hearings*, at 92, 99.

32. LOUIS FISHER, PRESIDENTIAL SPENDING POWER 166 (1975).

33. War Powers Resolution, Pub. L. No. 93–148, 87 Stat. 555 (codified as amended at 50 U.S.C. §§ 1541 to 1548 (1994); Message of Oct. 24, 1973, *in* 1973 PUB. PAPERS 893–95 (1975).

34. 50 U.S.C. § 1542 (1994); *see* John H. Ely, *Suppose Congress Wanted a War Powers Act That Worked*, 88 COLUM. L. REV. 1379, 1400 & n.63 (1988).

35. 50 U.S.C. §§ 1543 to 1544 (1994).

36. JOHN H. SULLIVAN, STAFF OF HOUSE COMM. ON FOREIGN AFFAIRS, REPORT ON THE WAR POWERS RESOLUTION, 97th Cong., 2d Sess. 179–246 (Comm. Print 1982) [hereinafter SULLIVAN REPORT]; LOUIS FISHER, PRESIDENTIAL WAR POWER 134–40 (1995); Ely, *War Powers Act*, at 1381 & n.8; Michael Ratner & David Cole, *The Force of Law: Judicial Enforcement of the War Powers Resolution*, 17 LOY. L.A. L. REV. 715, 742–44 (1984); Clement J. Zablocki, *War Powers Resolution: Its Past Record and Future Promise*, 17 LOY. L.A. L. REV. 579, 579–87 (1984).

37. SULLIVAN REPORT, at 247–54; FISHER, PRESIDENTIAL WAR POWER, at 140–45; Allan Ides, *Congress, Constitutional Responsibility and the War Power*, 17 LOY. L.A. L. REV. 599, 631–52 (1984); Zablocki, *War Powers Resolution*, at 587–97; Ratner & Cole, *Force of Law*, at 744–50; *see also* David L. Hall, THE REAGAN WARS: A CONSTITUTIONAL PERSPECTIVE ON WAR POWERS AND THE PRESIDENCY 156–59, 197–99, 225–27, 255–62 (1991) (but arguing that in some instances Reagan was not required to give notice under §4 (a) (1)).

38. *See* FISHER, PRESIDENTIAL WAR POWER, at 145–61.

39. Ely, *War Powers Act*, at 1406–17; Ratner & Cole, *Force of Law*, at 717; *but see* Raines v. Byrd, 117 S.Ct. 2312 (1997) (Members of Congress lack standing to challenge validity of actions taken by president).

40. *See* Zablocki, *War Powers Resolution*, at 580–86.

41. *See, e.g.*, Ange v. Bush, 752 F. Supp. 509 (D.D.C. 1990) (Operation Desert Shield); Dellums v. Bush, 752 F. Supp. 1141 (D.D.C. 1990) (Operation Desert Shield); Lowry v. Reagan, 676 F. Supp. 333 (D.D.C. 1987) (Persian Gulf War); Sanchez-Espinoza v. Reagan, 568 F. Supp. 596 (D.D.C. 1983), *aff'd*, 770 F.2d 202 (D.C. Cir. 1985) (Nicaragua); Conyers v. Reagan, 578 F. Supp. 324 (D.D.C. 1984), *dismissed as moot*, 765 F.2d 1124 (D.C. Cir. 1985) (Grenada); Crockett v. Reagan, 558 F. Supp. 893 (D.D.C.

1982), *aff'd*, 720 F.2d 1355 (D.C. Cir. 1983), *cert. denied*, 467 U.S. 1251 (1984) (El Salvador).

42. Statement of Aug. 21, 1974, *in* 1974 PUB. PAPERS 35–37 (1975).

43. Act of Aug. 21, 1974, Pub. L. No. 93-380, § 509, 88 Stat. 484, 566–68 (amending § 431 of the General Education Provisions Act, 20 U.S.C. § 1232 (d) (1988)).

44. H.R. CON. RES. 318, 96th Cong., 2d Sess., 94 Stat. 3651 (1980) (disapproving 45 Fed. Reg. 22634 (1980)); H.R. CON. RES. 319, 96th Cong., 2d Sess., 94 Stat. 3651 (disapproving 45 Fed. Reg. 22742 (1980)); H.R. CON. RES. 332, 96th Cong., 2d Sess., 94 Stat. 3652 (disapproving 45 Fed. Reg. 27880)); S. CON. RES. 91, 96th Cong., 2d Sess., 94 Stat. 3653 (disapproving 45 Fed. Reg. 23602 (1980)).

45. 43 Op. Att'y Gen. 231, 232 (1980).

46. *See* 45 C.F.R. § 100d (Education Appeals Bd.), § 134 (Grants for Educational Improvement, Resources, and Support), § 161c (Arts Education Program), § 161g (Law Related Education Program) (1980).

47. 43 Op. Att'y Gen. 231, 241 (1980).

CHAPTER 9

1. Frank H. Easterbrook, *Presidential Review*, 40 CASE W. RES. L. REV. 905, 923 (1989–90).

2. *See, e.g.*, Stuart v. Laird, 5 U.S. (1 Cranch) 299, 309 (1803); United States v. Midwest Oil Co., 236 U.S. 459, 472–73 (1915); Myers v. United States, 272 U.S. 52, 170–76 (1926).

3. Powell v. McCormack, 395 U.S. 486, 547 (1969).

4. Youngstown Sheet & Tube Co. v. Sawyer, 343 U.S. 579, 610–11 (1952) (Frankfurter, J., concurring); *and see* The Laura, 114 U.S. 411, 414 (1885) (as a result of longstanding usage, the president's power to remit fines under the pardoning power may be delegated by Congress to subordinates in the executive branch).

5. *See* Immigration and Naturalization Service v. Chadha, 462 U.S. 919, 942 n.13, 944–45 (1983).

6. New York v. United States, 505 U.S. 144, 182 (1992); *see also* Buckley v. Valeo, 424 U.S. 1, 118–37 (1976); Powell v. McCormack, 395 U.S. 486, 547 (1969).

7. *See* Henry P. Monaghan, *The Protective Power of the Presidency*, 93 COLUM. L. REV. 1, 46–47 n.222 (1992).

8. JEFFREY J. SAFFORD, WILSONIAN MARITIME DIPLOMACY, 1913–1921, at 237 (1978).

9. *See Separation of Powers: Hearings Before the Subcomm. on Separation of Powers of the Senate Judiciary Comm.*, 90th Cong, 1st Sess. (1967).

10. *See War Powers: A Test of Compliance Relative to the Danang Sealift, the Evacuation of Phnom Penh, the Evacuation of Saigon, and the Mayaguez Incident: Hearings Before the Subcomm. on Int'l Security & Scientific Affairs of the House Comm. on Int'l Relations*, 94th Cong., 1st Sess. (1975); *War Powers Resolution: Hearings on the Operation and Effectiveness of the War Powers Resolution Before the Senate Comm. on Foreign Relations*, 95th Cong., 1st Sess. (1977).

11. *See* Letter from Benjamin R. Civiletti to Senator Max Baucus (July 30, 1980), *reprinted in Constitutionality of GAO's Bid Protest Function: Hearings Before a Subcomm. of the House Comm. on Gov't Operations*, 99th Cong., 1st Sess. 745 (1985) [hereinafter *GAO Bid Protest Hearings*].

12. *See, e.g.*, Michael S. Paulsen, *The Most Dangerous Branch: Executive Power to Say What the Law Is*, 83 GEO. L.J. 217, 267–68 (1994); Michael B. Rappaport, *The President's Veto and the Constitution*, 87 NW. U.L. REV. 735, 767 & n.125 (1993); Easterbrook, *Presidential Review*, at 923.

13. Letter from Walter Dellinger, Office of Legal Counsel, to Abner J. Mikva, Counsel to the President (Nov. 2, 1994), *reprinted in* Note, *Recent Legal Opinions Concerning Presidential Powers*, 48 ARK. L. REV. 311, 313 (1995).

14. *Id.* at 323–27.

15. Douglas W. Kmiec, *Judges Should Pay Attention to Statements by President*, NAT'L L.J., Nov. 10, 1986, at 13.

16. Pub. L. No. 98–369, Title VII, 98 Stat. 494, 1199, 31 U.S.C. §§ 3551 to 3556 (1988).

17. Statement of July 18, 1984, *in* 1984 PUBLIC PAPERS OF THE PRESIDENTS OF THE UNITED STATES 1053 (1987) [hereinafter PUB. PAPERS].

18. *See* H.R. REP. NO. 99–138, 99th Cong., 1st Sess. 3–8 (1985); Lear Siegler, Inc. v. Lehman, 842 F.2d 1102, 1104–06 (9th Cir. 1988).

19. Ameron, Inc. v. United States Army Corps of Engineers, 809 F.2d 979 (3d Cir. 1986), *cert. dismissed*, 488 U.S. 918 (1988); Lear Siegler, Inc. v. Lehman, 842 F.2d 1102 (9th Cir. 1988); Parola v. City of Monterey, 848 F.2d 956 (9th Cir. 1988).

20. 31 U.S.C. § 3554 (c) (1988); *see* United States v. Instruments, S.A., Inc., 807 F. Supp. 811 (D.D.C. 1992).

21. Act of Oct. 2, 1986, Pub. L. No. 99–440, 100 Stat. 1086; Message of Sept. 26, 1986, *in* 1986 PUB. PAPERS 1278–80 (1989).

22. LAWYERS COMMITTEE FOR CIVIL RIGHTS UNDER LAW, IMPLEMENTATION OF THE COMPREHENSIVE ANTI-APARTHEID ACT OF 1986 (1988); PHILA. INQUIRER, May 13, 1990, *reprinted in* 136 CONG. REC. E2150 01 (June 26, 1990); 134 CONG. REC. H6917 (Aug. 11, 1988); WASH. POST, Aug. 20, 1989, at A12.

23. Act of Dec. 22, 1987, Pub. L. No. 100–202, § 630, 101 Stat. 1329, 1329–1432; Act of Sept. 22, 1988, Pub. L. No. 100–440, § 619, 102 Stat. 1721, 1756; Act of Nov. 3, 1989, Pub. L. No. 101–136, § 618, 103 Stat. 783, 820.

24. Statement of Sept. 22, 1988, *in* 1988–89 PUB. PAPERS 1204–05 (1991); Statement of Nov. 3, 1989, *in* 1989 PUB. PAPERS 1448–49 (1990); L.A. TIMES, Sept. 24, 1988, at 2, col. 4; *id.*, Nov. 4, 1989, at A18, col. 2; National Fed'n of Fed. Employees v. United States, 688 F. Supp. 671 (D.D.C. 1988), *vacated sub nom.* American Foreign Service Ass'n v. Garfinkel, 490 U.S. 153 (1989) (per curiam); American Foreign Service Ass'n v. Garfinkel, 732 F. Supp. 13 (D.D.C. 1990).

25. Foreign Relations Authorization Act, Fiscal Years 1990 & 1991, Pub. L. No. 101–246, § 102, 104 Stat. 15, 19 (1990).

26. Statement of Feb. 16, 1990, *in* 1990 PUB. PAPERS 239, 240 (1991); William P. Barr, *Attorney General's Remarks, Benjamin N. Cardozo School of Law, November 15, 1992*, 15 CARDOZO L. REV. 31, 39 (1993).

27. *See* chapter 8, "Gerald Ford and Jimmy Carter: The War Powers Resolution." For other laws that President Reagan refused to comply with because of their alleged unconstitutionality, see Christine E. Burgess, Note, *When May a President Refuse to Enforce the Law?* 72 TEX. L. REV. 631, 642 n.64 (1994).

28. Act of July 22, 1994, Pub. L. No. 103–283, 108 Stat. 1423, 1440.

29. Statement of July 22, 1994, *in* 1994 PUB. PAPERS 1301 (1995).

30. Letter from Comptroller General to Sen. Wendell H. Ford, Chairman of the Joint Comm. on Printing, B-251481.4 (Sept. 30, 1994).

31. Memorandum from Walter Dellinger, Asst. Atty Gen., Office of Legal Counsel, to Emily C. Hewitt, General Counsel, General Services Administration (May 31, 1996), at 1.

32. *Id.* at 18.

33. *See* Testimony of Wayne P. Kelly, Superintendent of Documents, before Sen. Comm. on Rules and Admin., June 18, 1996; Testimony of Michael F. DiMario, Public Printer, before Sen. Comm. on Rules and Admin., July 24, 1996.

34. Telecommunications Act of 1996, Pub. L. No. 104–104, 110 Stat. 56 (1996).

35. Statement of Feb. 12, 1996, *in* 1996 U.S. CODE CONG. & ADMIN. NEWS 228–1, 228–3.

36. 4A Op. Off. Legal Counsel 55, 56 (1980).

37. *Id.* at 55, 58.

38. *GAO Bid Protest Hearings*, at 434 (statement of William French Smith, Att'y Gen.).

39. *Id.* at 318 (statement of D. Lowell Jensen, Acting Deputy Att'y Gen.); *see also id.* at 299–300, 329.

40. *GAO Bid Protest Hearings*, at 300–01, 322, 434–35, 438.

41. N.Y. TIMES, Nov. 13, 1985, at A24, col. 3.

42. Barr, *Attorney General's Remarks*, at 39.

43. Letter from Walter Dellinger, Office of Legal Counsel, to Abner J. Mikva, Counsel to the President (Nov. 2, 1994), *reprinted in* Note, *Recent Legal Opinions*, at 313.

44. *Id.* at 318.

45. *Id.* at 315.

46. *Id.* at 315.

47. *Id.* at 315.

48. *See Line-Item Veto: Hearing on S.J. Res. 26, S.J. Res. 178 and S. 1921 Before the Subcomm. on the Constitution of the Senate Comm. on the Judiciary*, 98th Cong., 2d Sess. 1–3 (1984) [hereinafter *Line-Item Veto Hearing*]; ROBERT J. SPITZER, THE PRESIDENTIAL VETO: TOUCHSTONE OF THE AMERICAN PRESIDENCY 121, 158, n.8 (1988); LOUIS FISHER, CONSTITUTIONAL CONFLICTS BETWEEN CONGRESS AND THE PRESIDENT 131 (3d ed. rev. 1991); 1984 Republican Party Platform, *in* 1984 CONG. Q. ALMANAC 43-B (1985); 1988 Republican Party Platform, *in* 1988 CONG. Q. ALMANAC 50-A (1989); George Bush, 1989 PUB. PAPERS 1053–54, 1055 (1990); George Bush, 1990 PUB. PAPERS 1014, 1035, 1526, 1533, 1548 (1991).

49. Nelson Lund, *Rational Choice at the Office of Legal Counsel*, 15 CARDOZO L. REV. 437, 455–58 & nn.46–47 (1993); Douglas W. Kmiec, *OLC's Opinion Writing Function: The Legal Adhesive for a Unitary Executive*, 15 CARDOZO L. REV. 337, 353–59 (1993); Barr, *Attorney General's Remarks*, at 35.

50. *See* Rappaport, *The President's Veto*, at 740 n.12.

51. Andrew Taylor, *Congress Hands President a Budgetary Scalpel*, 54 CONG. Q. 864–67 (1996).

52. H.R. REP. NO. 99–138, 99th Cong., 1st Sess. 16 (1985).

53. *Line-Item Veto Hearing*, at 1.

54. *See* 1981–1988–89 PUB. PAPERS (1982–91).

55. DANIEL P. FRANKLIN, EXTRAORDINARY MEASURES: THE EXERCISE OF PREROGATIVE POWERS IN THE UNITED STATES 66–67 (1991).

56. Statement of Sept. 26, 1986, *in* 1986 PUB. PAPERS 1278–80 (1989).

57. *GAO Bid Protest Hearings*, at 434.

58. *Id.* at 334.

59. *Id.* at 254.

60. The twenty incidents are listed in Table 9.1. Those that involved omnibus bills were Buchanan; Carter (pardon); Carter (San Antonio Missions); Carter (Department of Education regulations). Those that involved riders were Taft; Wilson; Carter (consulates).

61. Barr, *Attorney General's Remarks*, at 38.

62. Kmiec, *OLC's Opinion Writing Function*, at 355.

63. Line Item Veto Act, Pub. L. No. 104–130, 110 Stat. 1200 (1996) (codified at 2 U.S.C.A. §§ 691 et seq. (Supp. 1997)). *See Line-Item Veto Provisions*, 1996 CONG. Q. ALMANAC 2-30–2-31.

64. *See* American Enterprise Institute for Public Policy, Proposals for Line-Item Veto Authority (1984), *reprinted in Line-Item Veto Hearing*, at 102–36. *See also* Rappaport, *The President's Veto*, at 770–71.

65. Three incidents concerned spending items: Buchanan's use of the Washington Aqueduct funds; Lyndon Johnson's refusal to undertake watershed projects; and Carter's refusal to restore the San Antonio Missions. In addition, Taft's failure to follow the budget format prescribed by Congress involved a fiscal matter. *See* Table 9.1.

66. J. Gregory Sidak & Thomas A. Smith, *Four Faces of the Item Veto: A Reply to Tribe and Kurland*, 84 NW. U.L. REV. 437, 460–61 (1990).

67. *See* DOUGLAS W. KMIEC, THE ATTORNEY GENERAL'S LAWYER: INSIDE THE MEESE JUSTICE DEPARTMENT 54 (1992); *GAO Bid Protest Hearings*, at 326–27.

68. Statement of Oct. 21, 1967, *in* 1967 PUB. PAPERS 935 (1968).

69. NANCY V. BAKER, CONFLICTING LOYALTIES: LAW AND POLITICS IN THE ATTORNEY GENERAL'S OFFICE, 1789–1990, at 6–7, 11–15 (1992).

70. Robert B. Shanks, *Office of Legal Counsel—The President's "Outside" Law Firm," in* 2 DEP'T OF JUSTICE MANUAL, 1–36, 1–43 (1990–1 Supp. 1991); BAKER, CONFLICTING LOYALTIES, at 10–11.

71. *See* BAKER, CONFLICTING LOYALTIES, at 67–125; DANIEL J. MEADOR, THE PRESIDENT, THE ATTORNEY GENERAL, AND THE DEPARTMENT OF JUSTICE 25–43 (1980); Michel Rosenfeld, *Executive Autonomy, Judicial Authority and the Rule of Law: Reflections on Constitutional Interpretation and the Separation of Powers*, 15 CARDOZO L. REV. 137, 150–51 (1993); Harold H. Koh, *Protecting the Office of Legal Counsel from Itself*, 15 CARDOZO L. REV. 513, 514, 523 (1993); *GAO Bid Protest Hearings*, at 42 (statement of Sanford Levinson); *id.* at 52 (statement of Mark Tushnet); *id.* at 276 (statement of Steven R. Ross & Charles Tiefer); *contra*, Barr, *Attorney General's Remarks*, at 34–37 (denying that OLC tempers its legal advice based on political considerations).

72. KMIEC, THE ATTORNEY GENERAL'S LAWYER, at 52.

73. Shanks, *Office of Legal Counsel*, at 1-41–1-42. *Accord*, Lund, *Rational Choice*, at 486–505; John O. McGinnis, *Models of the Opinion Function of the Attorney General: A Normative, Descriptive, and Historical Prolegomenon*, 15 CARDOZO L. REV. 375, 420–35 (1993).

74. *See, e.g.*, Ronald Reagan, Statement of Oct. 27, 1986, *in* 1986 PUB. PAPERS 1450–51 (1989) (4 provisions); Ronald Reagan, Statement of Nov. 14, 1986, *in* 1986 PUB. PAPERS 1557–58 (1989) (6 provisions); Ronald Reagan, Statement of Sept. 29, 1987, *in* 1987 PUB. PAPERS 1096–97 (1989) (4 provisions); George Bush, Statement of Nov. 30, 1989, *in* 1989 PUB. PAPERS 1609–11 (1990) (4 provisions).

75. Statement of Nov. 29, 1989, *in* 1989 PUB. PAPERS 1599–1600 (1990).

76. *See* Carolyn A. Edie, *Tactics and Strategies: Parliament's Attack Upon the Royal Dispensing Power 1597–1689*, 29 AM. J. LEGAL HIST. 197, 222–24 (1985).

CHAPTER 10

1. 37 U.S. (12 Pet.) 524, 613 (1838).

2. 27 F. Cas. 1192 (C.C.D. N.Y. 1806) (No. 16,342).

3. Myers v. United States, 272 U.S. 52 (1926) (invalidating act, defied by Woodrow Wilson, barring removal of postmasters without the Senate's consent); Humphrey's Executor v. United States, 295 U.S. 602 (1935) (upholding law, defied by Franklin Roosevelt, allowing removal of FTC commissioners only for cause).

4. *See* Wayte v. United States, 470 U.S. 598, 607 (1985); Nader v. Saxbe, 497 F.2d 676, 679–80 & n.19 (D.C. Cir. 1974).

5. *See, e.g.*, Thunder Basin Coal Co. v. Reich, 510 U.S. 200, 215 (1994); Johnson v. Robison, 415 U.S. 361, 368 (1974); Oestereich v. Selective Service Bd., 393 U.S. 233, 242 (1968) (Harlan, J., concurring); *see also* Riggin v. Office of Senate Fair Employment Practices, 61 F.3d 1563, 1569–70 (Fed. Cir. 1995), *cert. denied*, 116 S.Ct. 773 (1996); Continental Airlines v. Department of Transp., 843 F.2d 1444, 1456 (D.C. Cir. 1988); Meredith Corp. v. FCC, 809 F.2d 863, 872 (D.C. Cir. 1987); *but see* Marozsan v. United States, 852 F.2d 1469, 1492 n.4 (7th Cir. 1988) (Easterbrook, Coffey & Manion, JJ., dissenting) (voicing "doubt" that executive agencies "lacked the authority to disregard statues on constitutional grounds").

6. 422 U.S. 749 (1975).

7. *Id.* at 767.

8. *See Hearings on the Executive Impoundment of Appropriated Funds Before the Subcomm. on Separation of Powers of the Senate Comm. on the Judiciary*, 92d Cong., 1st Sess. 279, 283 (1971).

9. Thunder Basin Coal Co. v. Reich, 510 U.S. at 215; Riggin v. Office of Senate Fair Employment Practices, 61 F.3d at 1569.

10. 1 William and Mary sess. 2 ch. 2 § i 1.

11. Riggin v. Office of Senate Fair Employment Practices, 61 F.3d at 1569.

12. Morrison v. Olson, 487 U.S. 654, 711 (1988) (Scalia, J., dissenting).

13. 328 U.S. 303 (1946).

14. *See supra* chapter 6, "Obtaining Judicial Resolution."

15. 501 U.S. 868, 906 (1991) (Scalia, J., concurring in part and concurring in the judgment).

16. Frank H. Easterbrook, *Presidential Review*, 40 CASE W. RES. L. REV. 905 (1989–90); *see supra* chapter 2, "Logical Arguments for Executive Review."

17. *See* Antonin Scalia, *Originalism: The Lesser Evil*, 57 U. CIN. L. REV. 849 (1989).

18. Lear Siegler, Inc. v. Lehman, 842 F.2d 1102, 1121 (9th Cir. 1988), *withdrawn in part*, 893 F.2d 205 (9th Cir. 1989) (en banc) (emphasis in original).

19. Ameron, Inc. v. U.S. Army Corps of Eng'rs, 787 F.2d 875, 889 & n.11 (3d Cir. 1986) (dictum); *see also* Haring v. Blumenthal, 471 F. Supp. 1172, 1178–79 (D.D.C. 1979) (holding that each executive branch employee is, like the president, required to enforce measures even if they are thought to be unconstitutional, and cannot "take it upon himself to decide which particular laws, regulations, and policies are legal or illegal,

and to base his official actions upon that private determination''). *But see* United States v. Instruments, S.A., Inc., Civ.A. No. 91-1574-LFO, 1993 WL 198842 (D.D.C. May 26, 1993) (mem. and order) (stating that the Justice Department's decision to file declaratory judgment action challenging validity of fee-recovery provision of the Competition in Contracting Act, rather than complying with act by paying defendants their fees and costs, was ''nothing more than the department's good faith attempt to do its job in subtle and difficult areas of law.'' (*id.* at *4); while the court thus implied that a president might ignore an allegedly unconstitutional law, it noted that there may not have been a failure to honor the law because defendants had not pursued available remedies for securing payment under the act and because the executive's conduct may have reflected a valid reading of the act). *Id.* at *3.

20. *See, e.g.*, EDWARD S. CORWIN, THE PRESIDENT: OFFICE AND POWERS 1787–1957, at 71–72 (Randall W. Bland et al. eds., 5th rev. ed. 1984); 3 WESTEL W. WILLOUGHBY, THE CONSTITUTIONAL LAW OF THE UNITED STATES 1502–04 (2d ed. 1929); Eugene Gressman, *Take Care, Mr. President*, 64 N.C. L. REV. 381 (1986); Letter from Arthur S. Miller to Rep. Jack Brooks (Feb. 27, 1985), *reprinted in Constitutionality of GAO's Bid Protest Functions: Hearings Before a Subcomm. of the House Comm. on Gov't Operations*, 99th Cong., 1st Sess. 497–98 (1985) [hereinafter *GAO Bid Protest Hearings*].

21. For similar conclusions, *see* JOHN N. POMEROY, AN INTRODUCTION TO THE CONSTITUTIONAL LAW OF THE UNITED STATES 244–45, 444–45 (N.Y., Hurd & Houghton 1868); Letter from Salmon P. Chase to Gerrit Smith (April 19, 1868), *in* ROBERT B. WARDEN, AN ACCOUNT OF THE PRIVATE LIFE AND PUBLIC SERVICES OF SALMON PORTLAND CHASE 684–85 (Cincinnati, Wilstach, Baldwin 1874).

22. *See* THE FEDERALIST NO. 48 (James Madison); *id.* Nos. 71, 73 & 78 (Alexander Hamilton); GORDON WOOD, THE CREATION OF THE AMERICAN REPUBLIC, 1776–1787, at 403–13, 474, 507 (1969).

23. *See* RAOUL BERGER, EXECUTIVE PRIVILEGE: A CONSTITUTIONAL MYTH 307–09 (1974); *U.S. Government Information Policies and Practices, The Pentagon Papers: Hearings Before the Subcomm. on Foreign Operations and Gov't Information of the House Comm. on Gov't Operations*, 92d Cong., 1st Sess., pt. 2, at 381 (1971) (statement of William H. Rehnquist) [hereinafter *Pentagon Papers Hearings*].

24. *See* Thomas W. Merrill, *Judicial Opinions as Binding Law and as Explanations for Judgments*, 15 CARDOZO L. REV. 43, 46–47 (1993); David A. Strauss, *Presidential Interpretation of the Constitution*, 15 CARDOZO L. REV. 113, 123–24 (1993); *but see* Gary Lawson & Christopher D. Moore, *The Executive Power of Constitutional Interpretation*, 81 IOWA L. REV. 1267, 1313–29 (1996); Michael S. Paulsen, *The Most Dangerous Branch: Executive Power to Say What the Law Is*, 93 GEO L.J. 217, 276–88 (1994); Michael S. Paulsen, *The Merryman Power and the Dilemma of Autonomous Executive Branch Interpretation*, 15 CARDOZO L. REV. 81 (1993).

25. Letter from Ass't Att'y Gen. Walter Dellinger to Abner J. Mikva, Counsel to the President (Nov. 2, 1994), *reprinted in* Note, *Recent Legal Opinions Concerning Presidential Powers*, 48 ARK. L. REV. 311, 313 (1995).

26. See Michael T. Brady, Note, *Executive Discretion and the Congressional Defense of Statutes*, 92 YALE L.J. 970 (1983); Arthur S. Miller & Jefferey H. Bowman, *Presidential Attacks on the Constitutionality of Federal Statutes: A New Separation of Powers Problem*, 40 OHIO ST. L.J. 51 (1979); *and see supra* 6, ''Obtaining Judicial Resolution''; chapter 7, ''The Ban on Editorializing by Public Broadcasters.''

27. *See supra* chapter 7, ''Chester A. Arthur: Appointing the Chief Examiner,'' ''The

Commodity Futures Commission,'' ''The Japan-United States Friendship Commission''; chapter 8, ''Grover Cleveland: The Civil Service Chief Examiner.''

28. *See GAO Bid Protest Hearings*, at 273 (statement of Steven R. Ross & Charles Tiefer).

29. 43 Op. Att'y Gen. No. 25, at 11 (1980); 4A Op. Office Legal Counsel 21, 29 (1980). *See supra* chapter 8, ''Jimmy Carter: Issuing Vetoed Regulations.''

30. Edwin Meese, *On Separation of Powers: President's Right to Challenge a Law*, N.Y. TIMES, May 21, 1985, at A26 (letter to editor); *GAO Bid Protest Hearings*, at 300–01, 322–23 (statement of D. Lowell Jensen, Deputy Att'y Gen.); *id.* at 438 (statement of Att'y Gen. William French).

31. H.R. REP. NO. 99–138, 99th Cong., 1st Sess. 17 (1985); *GAO Bid Protest Hearings*, at 52, 81–82 (statement of Eugene Gressman); *id.* at 56 (statement of Mark Tushnet); *id.* at 274–75 (statement of Steven R. Ross & Charles Tiefer); Letter from Peter W. Rodino to William French Smith (Jan. 31, 1985), *reprinted in id.* at 431.

32. Letter from Ass't Att'y Gen. Walter Dellinger to Abner J. Mikva, Counsel to the President (Nov. 2, 1994), *reprinted in* Note, *Recent Legal Opinions*, at 315.

33. *See* Letter from Salmon P. Chase to Gerrit Smith (April 19, 1868), *in* WARDEN, AN ACCOUNT OF THE PRIVATE LIFE AND PUBLIC SERVICES OF SALMON PORTLAND CHASE, at 684–85; *Pentagon Papers Hearings*, at 381 (statement of William H. Rehnquist); BERGER, EXECUTIVE PRIVILEGE, at 309; *GAO Bid Protest Hearings*, at 272–74 (statement of Steven R. Ross & Charles Tiefer).

34. H.R. REP. NO. 99–138, 99th Cong., 1st Sess. 21 (1985); *GAO Bid Protest Hearings*, at 273–74 (statement of Steven R. Ross & Charles Tiefer).

35. 31 U.S.C. § 3554(c) (1988).

36. *See* United States v. Instruments, S.A., Inc., 807 F. Supp. 811, 816 (D.D.C. 1992).

37. Charles J. Zinn, *The Veto Power of the President*, 12 F.R.D. 207, 214–15 (1952); ROBERT J. SPITZER, THE PRESIDENTIAL VETO: TOUCHSTONE OF THE AMERICAN PRESIDENCY 18 (1988).

38. *See* 49 CONG. REC. 4291–92 (1913) (President Taft's message vetoing Webb-Kenyon Act); WILLIAM H. TAFT, OUR CHIEF MAGISTRATE AND HIS POWERS 19–23 (1916); SPITZER, THE PRESIDENTIAL VETO, at 25–70; EDWARD C. MASON, THE VETO POWER 129–31 (Boston, Ginn 1890).

39. Katzenbach v. Morgan, 384 U.S. 641, 670 (1966) (Harlan, J., dissenting); *and see* United States v. Carolene Products Co., 304 U.S. 144, 152–53 & n.4 (1938); INS v. Chadha, 462 U.S. 919, 944 (1983).

40. *See* Paulsen, *The Most Dangerous Branch*, at 332–34.

41. *See* Strauss, *Presidential Interpretation of the Constitution*, at 127–35 (rejecting complete executive autonomy and arguing that president should act as though he were a Supreme Court justice especially when, as here, there is a constitutional disagreement between Congress and the executive branch); *but see* Lawson & Moore, *The Executive Power of Constitutional Interpretation*, at 1303–13 (generally endorsing ''independent presidential review'' of federal laws).

42. *See, e.g.*, 31 OP. ATT'Y GEN. 475, 489 (1919); Letter from Att'y Gen. Benjamin R. Civiletti to Sen. Max Baucus (July 30, 1980), *reprinted in GAO Bid Protest Hearings*, at 745, 746 n.*, 749; Letter from Att'y Gen. William French Smith to Rep. Peter W. Rodino, Jr. (Feb. 22, 1985), *reprinted in GAO Bid Protest Hearings*, at 432 434–35 (endorsing position taken by Andrew Johnson's defense counsel); Letter from Ass't Att'y Gen. Walter Dellinger to Abner J. Mikva, Counsel to the President (Nov. 2, 1994), *reprinted in* Note, *Recent Legal Opinions*, at 313–15.

43. *See, e.g., GAO Bid Protest Hearings*, at 50 (statement of Sanford Levinson); *id.* at 50, 55 (statement of Mark Tushnet); Douglas W. Kmiec, *OLC's Opinion Writing Function: The Legal Adhesive for a Unitary Executive*, 15 CARDOZO L. REV. 337, 347 n.37 (1993); John O. McGinnis, *Models of the Opinion Function of the Attorney General: A Normative, Descriptive, and Historical Prolegomenon*, 15 CARDOZO L. REV. 375, 387–89 (1993); Michael B. Rappaport, *The President's Veto and the Constitution*, 87 NW. U.L. REV. 735, 769–70 (1993).

44. Letter from Ass't Att'y Gen. Walter Dellinger to Abner J. Mikva, Counsel to the President (Nov. 2, 1994), *reprinted in* Note, *Recent Legal Opinions*, at 315.

45. Arthur S. Miller, *The President and Faithful Execution of the Laws*, 40 VAND. L. REV. 389, 405 (1987).

46. *GAO Bid Protest Hearings*, at 334–35.

47. Parola v. City of Monterey, 848 F.2d 956 (9th Cir. 1988); Lear Siegler, Inc. v. Lehman, 842 F.2d 1102 (9th Cir. 1988); Ameron, Inc. v. U.S. Army Corps of Eng'rs, 809 F.2d 979 (3d Cir. 1986), *cert. dismissed*, 488 U.S. 918 (1988); Universal Shipping Co. v. United States, 652 F. Supp. 668 (D.D.C. 1987).

48. *See GAO Bid Protest Hearings*, at 42–43 (statement of Sanford Levinson); *but see* LINCOLN CAPLAN, THE TENTH JUSTICE: THE SOLICITOR GENERAL AND THE RULE OF LAW 113–14, 255–67 (1987); Richard G. Wilkins, *An Officer and an Advocate: The Role of the Solicitor General*, 21 LOY. L.A. L. REV. 1167 (1988).

49. 462 U.S. 919 (1983) (one-house legislative veto provision violates bicameralism and presentment requirements of Art. I, § 7).

50. *But see* John H. Ely, *Suppose Congress Wanted a War Powers Act That Worked*, 88 COLUM. L. REV. 1379, 1395–97 (1988); LOUIS FISHER, PRESIDENTIAL WAR POWER 194–97 (1995).

51. Statement of Oct. 21, 1967, *in* 1967 PUBLIC PAPERS OF THE PRESIDENTS OF THE UNITED STATES 935 (1968).

52. *See, e.g., GAO Bid Protest Hearings*, at 50 (statements of Mark Tushnet & Sanford Levinson); *and see* Ameron, Inc. v. U.S. Army Corps Eng'rs, 787 F.2d 875, 889 n.11 (3d Cir. 1986).

53. *See, e.g.*, Regional Rail Reorganization Act Cases, 419 U.S. 102, 138 (1974); Railroad Comm'n of Texas v. Pullman Co., 312 U.S. 496, 500 (1941); Ashwander v. TVA, 297 U.S. 288, 346–48 (1936) (Brandeis, J., concurring); Siler v. Louisville & Nashville R.R., 213 U.S. 175 (1909).

54. Letter from Ass't Att'y Gen. Walter Dellinger to Abner J. Mikva, Counsel to the President (Nov. 2, 1994), *reprinted in* Note, *Recent Legal Opinions*, at 314.

55. *See supra* chapter 2, "The Translationist Argument for Executive Review."

56. *See* Rappaport, *The President's Veto and the Constitution*, at 771–76 (arguing that a president who is prepared to ignore an allegedly unconstitutional law must, if he has the opportunity, veto the measure); *but see* Memorandum from Walter Dellinger to Bernard N. Nussbaum (Nov. 3, 1993), *in* Note, *Recent Legal Opinions*, at 338 (denying that "the President is under any duty to veto legislation containing a constitutionally infirm provision").

57. *See supra* chapter 2, "Presidential Invocation of the Constitution."

58. *Id.*

59. *See supra* chapter 8, "Lyndon Johnson: Impounding Watershed Funds."

60. *See supra* chapter 4, "The Debatable Case of the Tenure of Office Act."

61. *Id.*

62. *Id.*

63. *See* Papasan v. Allain, 478 U.S. 265, 300 (1986) (Powell, Burger & Rehnquist, JJ., concurring and dissenting) (arguing that Equal Protection Clause is not concerned with de minimis variations in treatment); Mississippi Univ. for Women v. Hogan, 458 U.S. 718, 736 (1982) (Powell & Rehnquist, JJ., dissenting) (arguing that claimed disparate treatment was too inconsequential to trigger Equal Protection Clause).

64. *See supra* chapter 7, "Woodrow Wilson: The Termination of Treaties."

65. *See supra* chapter 7, "Closing American Consulates Abroad."

66. *See* Goldwater v. Carter, 444 U.S. 996 (1979).

67. *See supra* chapter 6, "Simple Compliance."

68. *See supra* chapter 7, "Chester A. Arthur: Appointing the Chief Examiner."

69. *See* Myers v. United States, 272 U.S. 52 (1926); Humphrey's Executor v. United States, 295 U.S. 602 (1935).

70. *See supra* chapter 4, "The Debatable Case of the Tenure of Office Act."

71. *See supra* chapter 7, "William Howard Taft: The Presidential Budget."

72. *See supra* chapter 8, "Woodrow Wilson: Removing a Postmaster"; Myers v. United States, 272 U.S. 52, 178, 240, 295 (1926); Letter from Ass't Att'y Gen. Walter Dellinger to Abner J. Mikva, Counsel to the President (Nov. 2, 1994), *reprinted in* Note, *Recent Legal Opinions*, at 316 (noting that law invalidated in *Myers* "was not manifestly unconstitutional").

73. *See supra* chapter 8, "Franklin Roosevelt: Removing a Trade Commissioner"; Humphrey's Executor v. United States, 295 U.S. 602 (1935).

74. *See supra* chapter 8, "Gerald Ford and Jimmy Carter: The War Powers Resolution."

75. *See, e.g.*, POMEROY, AN INTRODUCTION TO THE CONSTITUTIONAL LAW OF THE UNITED STATES, at 444–45; Christine E. Burgess, *When May a President Refuse to Enforce the Law?* Note, 72 TEX. L. REV. 631, 645–46 & n.86, 657–65 (1994); Rappaport, *The President's Veto and the Constitution*, at 769–70.

76. *GAO Bid Protest Hearings*, at 434–35 (statement of Att'y Gen. William French Smith); *see also id.* at 299–300, 322 (statement of Deputy Att'y Gen. D. Lowell Jensen).

77. *See* William P. Barr, *Attorney General's Remarks, Benjamin N. Cardozo School of Law, November 15, 1992*, 15 CARDOZO L. REV. 31, 39 (1993); Letter from Ass't Att'y Gen. Walter Dellinger to Abner J. Mikva, Counsel to the President (Nov. 2, 1994), *reprinted in* Note, *Recent Legal Opinions*, at 315–16.

78. *See supra* chapter 2, "The Rejection of an Absolute Veto."

79. *See supra* Table 5.2 and chapter 5, "The Constitutional Grounds for Objection."

80. *GAO Bid Protest Hearings*, at 44.

81. *See, e.g.*, *GAO Bid Protest Hearings*, at 44, 50 (statement of Sanford Levinson); *id.* at 55 (statement of Mark Tushnet); Ameron, Inc. v. U.S. Army Corps. of Eng'rs, 787 F.2d 875, 889 n.11 (3d Cir. 1986) (dictum); Geoffrey P. Miller, *The President's Power of Interpretation: Implications of a Unified Theory of Constitutional Law*, LAW & CONTEMP. PROBS., Autumn 1993, at 35, 59.

82. *See* Easterbrook, *Presidential Review*, at 922.

83. *See* LAURENCE. H. TRIBE, AMERICAN CONSTITUTIONAL LAW 44–50 (2d ed. 1988).

84. *See supra* chapter 7, "The Ban on Editorializing by Public Broadcasters."

85. *See supra* chapter 7, "Restoration of the San Antonio Missions."

86. *See supra* chapter 7, "The Presidential Pardon for Draft Resisters."

87. *See supra* chapter 6, "Obtaining Judicial Resolution."

Selected Bibliography

Adams, George B. *Constitutional History of England.* Revised by Robert L. Schuyler. New York: Henry Holt & Co., 1934.

Anson, William R. *The Law and Custom of the Constitution.* Oxford: Clarendon Press, 1886. Reprint, New York: Johnson Reprint Corp., 1970.

Baker, Nancy V. *Conflicting Loyalties: Law and Politics in the Attorney General's Office, 1789–1990.* Lawrence: University Press of Kansas, 1992.

Barr, William P. "Attorney General's Remarks, Benjamin N. Cardozo School of Law, November 15, 1992." 15 *Cardozo Law Review* 31 (1993).

Benedict, Michael Les. *The Impeachment and Trial of Andrew Johnson.* New York: W. W. Norton & Co., 1973.

Brady, Michael T. "Executive Discretion and the Congressional Defense of Statutes." 92 *Yale Law Journal* 970 (1983).

Brest, Paul. "The Misconceived Quest for the Original Understanding." 60 *Boston University Law Review* 204 (1980).

Burgess, Christine E. "When May a President Refuse to Enforce the Law?" 72 *Texas Law Review* 631 (1994).

Calabresi, Steven G. "The Vesting Clauses as Power Grants." 88 *Northwestern University Law Review* 1377 (1994).

Calabresi, Steven G., and Saikrishna B. Prakash. "The President's Power to Execute the Laws." 104 *Yale Law Journal* 541 (1994).

Conley, Patrick T., and John P. Kaminski, eds. *The Bill of Rights and the States: Colonial and Revolutionary Origins of American Liberties.* Madison: Madison House, 1992.

Cooper, Charles J. "The Line-Item Veto: The Framers' Intentions." In *Pork Barrels and Principles: The Politics of the Presidential Veto*, 29–46. Washington, D.C.: National Legal Center for the Public Interest, 1988.

Corwin, Edward S. *The President: Office and Powers 1787–1957*. 5th rev. ed. New York: New York University Press, 1984.

Cronin, Thomas E. "The President's Executive Power." In *Inventing the American Presidency*, edited by Thomas E. Cronin, 180–208. Lawrence: University Press of Kansas, 1989.

Cross, Frank B. "The Constitutional Legitimacy and Significance of Presidential 'Signing Statements.' " 40 *Administrative Law Review* 209 (1988).

Dessayer, Kathyryn M. "The First Word: The President's Place in 'Legislative History.' " 89 *Michigan Law Review* 399 (1990).

DeWitt, David M. *The Impeachment and Trial of Andrew Johnson*. 1903. Reprint, Madison: State Historical Society of Wisconsin, 1967.

Duker, William F. "The President's Power to Pardon: A Constitutional History." 18 *William and Mary Law Review* 475 (1977).

Dumbauld, Edward. *The Bill of Rights and What It Means Today*. Norman: University of Oklahoma Press, 1957.

Easterbrook, Frank H. "Presidential Review." 40 *Case Western Reserve Law Review* 905 (1989–90).

Edie, Carolyn A. "Tactics and Strategies: Parliament's Attack upon the Royal Dispensing Power 1597–1689." 29 *American Journal of Legal History* 197 (1985).

Edwards, George C., III. *Presidential Influence in Congress*. San Francisco: W. H. Freeman, 1980.

Elliot, Jonathan. *Debates in the Several State Conventions on the Adoption of the Federal Constitution*. 2d ed. 5 vols. Philadelphia: J. B. Lippincott & Co., 1881. Reprint, Charlottesville: The Michie Company, 1937.

Ely, John H. "Suppose Congress Wanted a War Powers Act That Worked." 88 *Columbia Law Review* 1379 (1988).

Farber, Daniel A. "The Originalism Debate: A Guide for the Perplexed." 49 *Ohio State Law Journal* 1085 (1989).

Farrand, Max. *The Records of the Federal Convention of 1787*. 4 vols. New Haven: Yale University Press, 1966.

Fisher, Louis. *Constitutional Conflicts Between Congress and the President*. 3d ed. rev. Princeton: Princeton University Press, 1985.

———. *The Politics of Shared Power: Congress and the Executive*. 2d ed. Washington, D.C.: Congressional Quarterly Press, 1987.

———. *President and Congress: Power and Policy*. New York: Free Press, 1972.

———. *Presidential Spending Power*. Princeton: Princeton University Press, 1975.

———. "The Presidential Veto: Constitutional Developments." In *Pork Barrels and Principles: The Politics of the Presidential Veto*, 17–28. Washington, D.C.: National Legal Center for the Public Interest, 1988.

———. *Presidential War Power*. Lawrence: University Press of Kansas, 1995.

Flaherty, Martin S. "The Most Dangerous Branch." 105 *Yale Law Journal* 1725 (1996).

Foner, Eric. *Reconstruction: America's Unfinished Revolution, 1863–1877*. New York: Harper & Row, 1988.

Franklin, Daniel P. *Extraordinary Measures: The Exercise of Prerogative Powers in the United States*. Pittsburgh: University of Pittsburgh Press, 1991.

Garber, Marc N., and Kurt A. Wimmer. "Presidential Signing Statements as Interpretations of Legislative Intent: An Executive Aggrandizement of Power." 24 *Harvard Journal on Legislation* 363 (1987).

Gerhardt, Michael J., and Thomas D. Rowe, Jr., *Constitutional Theory: Arguments and Perspectives*. Charlottesville: The Michie Co., 1993.

Greene, Abner S. "Checks and Balances in an Era of Presidential Lawmaking." 61 *University of Chicago Law Review* 123 (1994).

Gressman, Eugene. "Take Care, Mr. President." 64 *North Carolina Law Review* 381 (1986).

Hall, David L. *The Reagan Wars: A Constitutional Perspective on War Powers and the Presidency*. Boulder: Westview Press, 1991.

Henkin, Louis. *Foreign Affairs and the Constitution*. Mineola, N.Y.: Foundation Press, 1972.

Holdsworth, William S. *A History of English Law*. 4th ed. Vol. 2. Boston: Little, Brown & Co., 1936.

———. *A History of English Law*. 2d ed. Vol. 6. Boston: Little, Brown & Co., 1937.

Humbert, W. H. *The Pardoning Power of the President*. Washington, D.C.: American Council on Public Affairs, 1941.

Ides, Allan. "Congress, Constitutional Responsibility and the War Power." 17 *Loyola of Los Angeles Law Review* 599 (1984).

Kmiec, Douglas W. *The Attorney General's Lawyer: Inside the Meese Justice Department*. New York: Praeger, 1992.

———. "OLC's Opinion Writing Function: The Legal Adhesive for a Unitary Executive." 15 *Cardozo Law Review* 337 (1993).

Kobil, Daniel T. "The Quality of Mercy Strained: Wresting the Pardoning Power from the King." 69 *Texas Law Review* 569 (1991).

Koh, Harold H. "Protecting the Office of Legal Counsel from Itself." 15 *Cardozo Law Review* 513 (1993).

Kurland, Philip B., and Ralph Lerner, eds. *The Founders' Constitution*. 5 vols. Chicago: University of Chicago Press, 1987.

Lawson, Gary, and Christopher D. Moore. "The Executive Power of Constitutional Interpretation." 81 *Iowa Law Review* 1267 (1996).

Lee, Rex E. "*The Provinces of Constitutional Interpretation*." 61 *Tulane Law Review* 1009 (1987)

Lessig, Lawrence. "Fidelity and Constraint." 65 *Fordham Law Review* 1365 (1997).

———. "Fidelity in Translation." 71 *Texas Law Review* 1165 (1993).

Lessig, Lawrence, and Cass R. Sunstein. "The President and the Administration." 94 *Columbia Law Review* 1 (1994).

Lovell, Colin R. *English Constitutional and Legal History: A Survey*. New York: Oxford University Press, 1962.

McDonald, Forrest. *The American Presidency: An Intellectual History*. Lawrence: University Press of Kansas, 1994.

McGinnis, John O. "Models of the Opinion Function of the Attorney General: A Normative, Descriptive, and Historical Prolegomenon." 15 *Cardozo Law Review* 375 (1993).

McKittrick, Eric L. *Andrew Johnson and Reconstruction*. New York: Oxford University Press, 1960.

Maitland, Frederic W. *The Constitutional History of England: A Course of Lectures Delivered*. 1908. Reprint, Cambridge: Cambridge University Press, 1926.

Mason, Edward C. *The Veto Power*. Boston: Ginn & Co., 1890.

May, Christopher N. *In the Name of War: Judicial Review and the War Powers since 1918*. Cambridge: Harvard University Press, 1989.

Meador, Daniel J. *The President, The Attorney General, and the Department of Justice*. Charlottesville: White Burkett Miller Center of Public Affairs, 1980.

Miller, Arthur S. "The President and Faithful Execution of the Laws." 40 *Vanderbilt Law Review* 389 (1987).

———. "Pretense and Our Two Constitutions." 54 *George Washington Law Review* 375 (1986).

Miller, Arthur S., and Jefferey H. Bowman. "Presidential Attacks on the Constitutionality of Federal Statutes: A New Separation of Powers Problem." 40 *Ohio State Law Journal* 51 (1979).

Miller, Geoffrey P. "The President's Power of Interpretation: Implications of a Unified Theory of Constitutional Law." *Law and Contemporary Problems*, Autumn 1993, at 35.

Monaghan, Henry P. "The Protective Power of the Presidency." 93 *Columbia Law Review* 1 (1993).

———. "Stare Decisis and Constitutional Adjudication." 88 *Columbia Law Review* 723 (1988).

Paulsen, Michael S. "The Most Dangerous Branch: Executive Power to Say What the Law Is." 83 *Georgetown Law Journal* 217 (1994).

Perry, Michael. "The Legitimacy of Particular Conceptions of Constitutional Interpretation." 77 *Virginia Law Review* 669 (1991).

Pious, Richard M. *The American Presidency*. New York: Basic Books, 1979.

Plucknett, Theodore F. T. *Taswell-Langmead's English Constitutional History*. 11th ed. London: Sweet & Maxwell Ltd., 1960.

Pomeroy, John Norton. *An Introduction to the Constitutional Law of the United States*. New York: Hurd & Houghton, 1868.

Popkin, William D. "Judicial Use of Presidential Legislative History: A Critique." 66 *Indiana Law Journal* 699 (1991).

Public Papers of the Presidents of the United States: Herbert Hoover, 1929–33. 4 vols. Washington, D.C.: GPO, 1974–77.

Public Papers of the Presidents of the United States: Harry Truman, 1945–53. 8 vols. Washington, D.C.: GPO, 1961–66.

Public Papers of the Presidents of the United States: Dwight D. Eisenhower, 1953–61. 8 vols. Washington, D.C.: GPO, 1958–61.

Public Papers of the Presidents of the United States: John F. Kennedy, 1961–63. 3 vols. Washington, D.C.: GPO, 1962–64.

Public Papers of the Presidents of the United States: Lyndon B. Johnson, 1963–69. 10 vols. Washington, D.C.: GPO, 1965–70.

Public Papers of the Presidents of the United States: Richard Nixon, 1969–74. 6 vols. Washington, D.C.: GPO, 1971–75.

Public Papers of the Presidents of the United States: Gerald R. Ford, 1974–77. 6 vols. Washington, D.C.: GPO, 1975–79.

Public Papers of the Presidents of the United States: Jimmy Carter, 1977–81. 9 vols. Washington, D.C.: GPO, 1977–82.

Public Papers of the Presidents of the United States: Ronald Reagan, 1981–89. 15 vols. Washington, D.C.: GPO, 1982–91.

Public Papers of the Presidents of the United States: George Bush, 1989–93. 8 vols. Washington, D.C.: GPO, 1990–93.

Public Papers of the Presidents of the United States: William J. Clinton, 1993–95. 6 vols. Washington, D.C.: GPO, 1994–96.

Rappaport, Michael B. "The President's Veto and the Constitution." 87 *Northwestern University Law Review* 735 (1993).

Ratner, Michael, and David Cole. "The Force of Law: Judicial Enforcement of the War Powers Resolution." 17 *Loyola of Los Angeles Law Review* 715 (1984).

"Recent Legal Opinions Concerning Presidential Powers." 48 *Arkansas Law Review* 311 (1995).

Reinstein, Robert J. "An Early View of Executive Powers and Privilege: The Trial of Smith and Ogden." 2 *Hastings Constitutional Law Quarterly* 309 (1975).

Richardson, James D., ed. *A Compilation of the Messages and Papers of the Presidents.* 20 vols. New York: Bureau of National Literature, 1897, 1917, 1927.

Roosevelt, Franklin D. *Public Papers and Addresses of Franklin D. Roosevelt.* Edited by Samuel I. Rosenman. 13 vols. New York: Russell & Russell, 1938–50.

Rosenfeld, Michel. "Executive Autonomy, Judicial Authority and the Rule of Law: Reflections on Constitutional Interpretation and the Separation of Powers." 15 *Cardozo Law Review* 137 (1993).

Rossiter, Clinton, ed. *The Federalist Papers.* New York: New American Library, 1961.

Scalia, Antonin. "Originalism: The Lesser Evil." 57 *University of Cincinnati Law Review* 849 (1989).

Schlesinger, Arthur M., Jr. *The Imperial Presidency.* Boston: Houghton Mifflin Co., 1973.

Scigliano, Robert. "The President's 'Prerogative Power'." In *Inventing the American Presidency*, edited by Thomas E. Cronin, 236–56. Lawrence: University Press of Kansas, 1989.

Sidak, J. Gregory, and Thomas A. Smith, "Four Faces of the Item Veto: A Reply to Tribe and Kurland." 84 *Northwestern University Law Review* 437 (1990).

Solum, Lawrence. "Originalism as Transformative Politics." 63 *Tulane Law Review* 1599 (1986).

Spitzer, Robert J. *The Presidential Veto: Touchstone of the American Presidency.* Albany: State University of New York Press, 1988.

———. "The President's Veto Power." In *Inventing the American Presidency*, edited by Thomas E. Cronin, 154–79. Lawrence: University Press of Kansas, 1989.

Stephen, Henry J. *Commentaries on the Laws of England.* Edited by L. Crispin Warmington. 21st ed. 4 vols. London: Butterworth & Co., 1950.

Storing, Herbert J., ed. *The Complete Anti-Federalist.* 7 vols. Chicago: University of Chicago Press, 1981.

Strauss, David A. "Presidential Interpretation of the Constitution." 15 *Cardozo Law Review* 113 (1993).

Stubbs, William A. *The Constitutional History of England, In Its Origin and Development.* 2d ed. 3 vols. Oxford: Clarendon Press, 1877.

Sullivan, John H. *Report on the War Powers Resolution.* Staff of the House Committee on Foreign Affairs, 97th Cong., 2d Sess. Washington, D.C.: GPO, 1982.

Swindler, William F., ed. *Sources and Documents of the United States Constitution.* 10 vols. Dobbs Ferry: Oceana Publications, 1973–79.

Taft, William H. *Our Chief Magistrate and His Powers*. New York: Columbia University Press, 1916.

Tanner, Joseph R. *English Constitutional Conflicts of the Seventeenth Century, 1603–1689*. Cambridge: Cambridge University Press, 1966.

Trefousse, Hans L. *Impeachment of a President: Andrew Johnson, the Blacks, and Reconstruction*. Knoxville: University of Tennessee Press, 1975.

Tucker, St. George. *Blackstone's Commentaries*. 5 vols. Philadelphia: William Young Birch & Abraham Small, 1803. Reprint, Buffalo: Dennis & Co., 1965.

U.S. Congress. Senate Library. *Presidential Vetoes, 1789–1976*. Washington, D.C.: GPO, 1978.

———. *Presidential Vetoes, 1977–1984*. Senate Publication No. 99–5. Washington, D.C.: GPO, 1985.

Veit, Helen E., Kenneth R. Bowling, and Charles B. Bickford, eds. *Creating the Bill of Rights: The Documentary Record from the First Federal Congress*. Baltimore: Johns Hopkins University Press, 1991.

Waites, Brad. "Let Me Tell You What You Mean: An Analysis of Presidential Signing Statements." 21 *Georgia Law Review* 755 (1987).

Watson, Richard A. "Origins and Early Development of the Veto Power." 17 *Presidential Studies Quarterly* 401 (1987).

Weekly Compilation of Presidential Documents. Washington, D.C.: GPO, 1965–1998.

Willoughby, Westel W. *The Constitutional Law of the United States*. 2d ed. 3 vols. New York: Baker, Voorhis & Co., 1929.

Wilson, Woodrow. *The Papers of Woodrow Wilson*. Edited by Arthur S. Link. 69 vols. Princeton: Princeton University Press, 1966–94.

Wood, Gordon. *The Creation of the American Republic, 1776–1787*. New York: W. W. Norton: 1969.

Zablocki, Clement J. "War Powers Resolution: Its Past Record and Future Promise." 17 *Loyola of Los Angeles Law Review* 579 (1984).

Zinn, Charles J. *The Veto Power of the President*. U.S. Congress, House Committee on the Judiciary, 82d Cong., 1st Sess. Washington, D.C.: GPO, 1951. Reprinted in 12 *Federal Rules Decisions* 207 (1952).

Index

Advisory Council on Historic Preservation, 85, 115
Alien and Sedition Acts (1798), 22, 39
American Folklife Center, 97–98
Amtrak (National Railroad Passenger Corp.), 96
Anthony, Henry B., 172 n.64
Anti-Federalists, 13, 23, 26–29, 35, 37
Anti-Saloon League, 66
Army Corps of Engineers, 103–4
Arthur, Chester A., 116
  signing statements, generally, 175 n.33
    Civil Service Commission, 104–6, 121–22, 130, 149
  veto of river and harbor bill, 64–65, 69
Attorney general
  See Justice Department; Office of Legal Counsel; Solicitor general

B-70 bomber, 39–40
Bell, David E., 99
Benedict, Michael Les, 62
Bickel, Alexander M., 47
Bill of Rights, English (1689), 3, 5, 8, 11, 15, 16, 18, 19, 23–24, 34, 37, 139, 142, 153
Bill of Rights, U.S. (1791)
  and signing statements, 76, 83, 85, 90, 113–14, 133, 152–53
  and suspending power, 23–26
  and vetoes, 53, 67
  See also Individual rights
Bills of attainder, 89–90, 91, 153
Bingham, John A., 61
Black, Jeremiah S., 103
Blackstone, Sir William, 11, 22
Boutwell, George S., 60
Brandeis, Louis D., 151
Bricker, John, 109
Buchanan, James
  signing statement re Washington Aqueduct, 103–4, 115, 127, 130, 150, 175 n.33, 193 nn.60, 65
Buckalew, Charles R., 171 n.59
''Bundling'' of bills, 29–33, 136
Bureau of the Census, 133
Bureau of Reclamation, 91–92, 180 n.98
Burt, Silas W., 105
Bush, George, xiv, 153
  and Competition in Contracting Act, 146

constitutionally based vetoes, 72
and item veto, 135
and justification for noncompliance with laws, 134, 152
signing statements, generally, xiii, 30, 31, 72–76, 132, 135, 138, 175–76 n.36
Foreign Relations Authorization Act, 133
federal employee nondisclosure agreements, 133
and War Powers Resolution, 133
Butler, Benjamin F., 60, 172 n.76

Carter, Jimmy, xiv, 51, 86, 115, 116, 130, 149, 153
and item veto, 135
and justification for noncompliance with laws, 133, 146
and legislative veto of Department of Education regulations, 124–25, 131, 133, 145, 193 n.60
refusal to defend validity of law in court, 119, 121
signing statements, generally, xiii, 73, 74, 75
Advisory Council on Historic Preservation, 85, 115
arms control negotiations, 94
enforcement of 1964 Civil Rights Act, 91, 98
Federal Election Campaign Act, 85
legislative veto or approval provisions, 83, 84, 87
National Labor Relations Act, 83
National Parks and Recreation Act, 99–100
National Science Foundation, 83
pardon of Vietnam War draft resisters, 111–12, 153, 193 n.60
Public Telecommunications Act, 113, 121, 153
San Antonio Missions, 113–14, 153, 193 nn.60, 65
U.S. consulates, 114–15, 149, 150, 193 n.60
veterans benefits, 98
and War Powers Resolution, 124, 131, 150, 151
Cattell, Alexander G., 171 n.59
Central America, 124
Central Intelligence Agency (CIA), 95–96
Charles II (King of England), 5, 6–7, 8
Chase, Salmon P., 61
Chicago Road, 84–85
Chile, 109–10
Civil Rights Act of 1964, 91, 98
Civil Service Commission, 104–6, 121–22, 130
Clark, Ramsey, 90
Clark Distilling Co. v. Western Maryland Ry. (1917), 173 n.97, 174 n.133
Cleveland, Grover, 119, 149
and Civil Service Commission, 121–22, 125
signing statements
regulating oleomargarine, 91, 175 n.33
veto of river and harbor bill, 65–66, 69
Clinton, William J., xiv, 153
and item veto, 30, 135
and justification for noncompliance with laws, 134–35, 144, 145, 146, 152
signing statements, generally, xiii, 30–31, 73, 74–75, 76
Government Printing Office, 133
Telecommunications Act, 133
Coke, Sir Edward, 5, 6
Cole, Cornelius, 172 n.64
Colonial assemblies, 31
"Coming into agreement" provisions
See Legislative veto or approval provisions
Commodity Futures Trading Commission (CFTC), 110–11
Competition in Contracting Act, xiii, 132, 134, 136, 143, 145–46, 147, 148, 152, 194–95 n.19
A Compilation of the Messages and Papers of the Presidents, 50
Comprehensive Anti-Apartheid Act, 64, 132
Comptroller general, 87, 99, 132, 133
Congress
amendment or repeal of contested leg-

islation, 40–41, 86–87, 91–92, 100, 110, 119, 147–48
and "bundling" or use of omnibus bills, 29–33, 136, 148, 152, 193 n.60
and congressional districts, 40, 82
control over executive agencies, 98–100
denunciation of early signing statements, 73
opposition to executive noncompliance with the law, 131, 133, 134
and president's veto power, 29–33
representation of Southern states in, 56, 57
resolutions of, 39
and "tacking" or use of riders, 29–33, 136, 148, 152, 193 n.60
See also Legislative veto or approval provisions; *and names of specific legislation*
Constitutional Convention
See Original understanding
Constitutional interpretation
by courts, 35–37, 38
and governmental practice, 45–49, 130
and prescriptive process, 130–31
by president, 33–37, 38–41, 137–38, 146–47, 196 n.41
theories of, 9–10, 29, 141
Consulates, U.S., 93, 114–15, 149, 150, 187 n.90, 193 n.60
Coolidge, Calvin, 50, 130
Corbett, Henry W., 172 n.64
Corwin, Edward S., 18, 21
Cost Accounting Standards Board, 92
Council of Revision, 35–36
Cox, Walter S., 63–64
Curtis, Benjamin R., 59–60

Dames & Moore v. Regan (1981), 48
Davis, Garrett, 171 n.59
Day, James M., 97
Declarations of Indulgence, 7, 8
Dispensing power
royal, 4–8, 11
presidential, 11, 37–38, 46, 141
District of Columbia, 57
Doolittle, James R., 171 n.59

Easterbrook, Frank H., xiv, 33–34, 143
Edmunds, George F., 171 n.59
Edward III (King of England), 4
Eisenhower, Dwight D., 116, 119, 149
signing statements, generally, 175 n.34
agreement with Chile 109–10
commercial military operations, 95
executive privilege, 86–87
international fish and wildlife conferences, 93–94
legislative veto or approval provisions, 83, 86, 88
loans to Greece and Spain, 93
Elizabeth I (Queen of England), 5
Elk Hills Oil Bill, 85, 96–97
Emergency Detention Act (1950), 67
English Bill of Rights
See Bill of Rights, English (1689)
English crown
and American presidency, 19–21, 28–29, 37
powers of, 3–8
Executive power, 18–21
Executive privilege, 39, 68, 69, 86–87, 97
Executive review, 33–38, 142–44
Ex parte Bollman (1807), 16

Farrand, Max, 14
Federal Communications Commission (FCC), 113
Federal Council on the Arts and Humanities, 88
Federal Election Campaign Act, 85, 90–91
Federal Election Commission, 90
Federal Energy Office, 85
Federalism
as basis for signing statements, 76, 77
as basis for vetoes, 53
Federalist Papers, 13–14, 20, 26, 28, 34, 35
Federal Trade Commission (FTC), 122–23, 150, 151, 194 n.3

Ferry, Orris S., 171 n.59
Fielding, Fred, 134
Fisher, Louis, 99, 179 n.65
Flood Control Act (1965), 88–89
Floyd, John B., 103
Food For Peace Program, 92
Ford, Gerald R., 116, 149, 153
  signing statements, generally, xiii, 73, 74, 75
    American Folklife Center, 97–98
    Amtrak, 96
    Army ammunition plant, 96
    Commodity Futures Trading Commission, 110–11
    Federal Council on the Arts and Humanities, 88
    Federal Election Campaign Act, 90
    fishery conservation zone, 94
    Freedom of Information Act, 69
    Japan-United States Friendship Commission, 111
    legislative veto or approval provisions, 83, 84, 96, 125
  and War Powers Resolution, 124, 131, 150, 151
Forest Service, 90–100
Fort DeRussy (Hawaii), 94
"Four principles" limiting presidential defiance, 144–53
Frankfurter, Felix, 130–31
Franklin, Daniel P., 136
Freedmen's Bureau, 57
Freedom of Information Act, 69
Frelinghuysen, Frederick T., 171 n.59, 172 nn.64, 77
Freytag v. Commissioner (1991), 143

Gallatin-Beaverhead National Forest (Montana), 99–100
General Accounting Office, 86
General Services Administration (GSA), 92
George III (King of England), 20
Gerry, Elbridge, 13, 36
Godden v. Hales (1686), 7
Government Printing Office (GPO), 92, 133
Grant, Ulysses S., 119
  as interim secretary of war, 58, 62–63
  signing statements, generally, 73
    river and harbor bill, 117
    U.S. consulates, 93, 114, 150, 175 n.33
Graves, Edward O., 105
Grayson, William, 25
Greece, 93
Grenada, 124
Grimes, John W., 171 n.59
Griswold, Erwin, 90
Groesbeck, William S., 59
Guatemala, 93

Habeas corpus, 15–16, 24, 34, 67
Hales, Sir Edward, 7
Hamilton, Alexander, 13–14, 17, 20, 35, 38
Harding, Warren G., 130
Hayes, Rutherford B., 119
Henderson, John B., 171 n.59
Henry VII (King of England), 5
Hill-Burton Act, 119
Hoar, George F., 64
Holmes, Oliver W., Jr., 35, 151
Holmes, Sherlock, 26
Hoover, Herbert, 50, 82, 130, 175 n.33
Howard, Jacob M., 171 n.59
Howe, Timothy O., 172 n.64
Humphrey's Executor v. United States (1935), 122–23, 151, 194 n.3

Immigration and Nationality Act (1952), 67–68
Immigration and Naturalization Service (INS), 112
Immigration and Naturalization Service v. Chadha (1983), 84, 131, 147
Impoundment of funds, 88–89, 103–4, 117, 123–24
Independent Gazetteer (Philadelphia), 28–29
Individual rights, 53, 76, 80, 98, 133, 152–53
  See also Bill of Rights
Internal improvements, 40, 55, 64–66, 69, 84
Internal Security Act (1950), 67
International Cooperation Administration, 86

Interstate Commerce Commission (ICC), 108
Item veto, xiii–xiv, 30, 45, 71–72, 115, 132, 135–39
See also Line Item Veto Act of 1996

Jackson, Andrew
signing statements, generally, 73, 175 n.33
Chicago Road, 84–85, 130
James II (King of England), 7–8, 21, 61
Japan-United States Friendship Commission, 111
Jay's Treaty, 39
Jefferson, Thomas, 14, 37
and executive powers, 19
and Sedition Act, 22, 39
and veto power, 13, 37, 38
and Virginia's proposed constitutional amendments, 23
Johnson, Andrew
constitutionally based vetoes, 56–64
and duty to execute the laws, 56–57, 59–60
impeachment of, 57, 59–64, 91, 131
and justification for noncompliance with laws, 146
and Reconstruction, 56–57, 82
signing statements, generally, 73, 175 n.33
command of the army, 91, 180 n.95
disbanding state militias, 82
restoring Tennessee to the Union, 82
and Tenure of Office Act, 41, 53, 57–59, 119, 122, 130, 131, 148, 150, 151
and "test-case defense," 59–64, 148–49
vetoes overridden, 56–57
Johnson, Lyndon B., 131
bypassing legislative veto provisions, 121
impoundment of Watershed Protection and Flood Prevention Act funds, 123–24, 131, 193 n.65
and repeal of legislative veto provisions, 148
signing statements, generally, 175 n.34
agriculture budget, 97
Air National Guard and Air Force Reserve, 94
Central Intelligence Agency, 95–96
Flood Control Act, 88–89
Food for Peace Program, 92
Fort DeRussy, 94
military base closures, 94
Naval Academy dairy farm, 95, 137–38, 147
naval districts, 95
Panama Canal Company, 95
Water Resources Research Act, 88
Johnson, Reverdy, 171 n.59
Jones Act, 107–9
Judicial review
availability of and signing statements, 115–16
as factor in decision not to comply with law, 135, 144–49
Founders' view of, 24–25, 35–37, 38
influence of government practices on, 48–49
of laws enacted over a veto, 69
presidents' efforts to secure, 41, 89–91, 148–52
of refusals to comply with the laws, 141–42
and War Powers Resolution, 124
See also Standing to see; "Test-case defense"; *and discussion of specific laws to whose validity presidents objected*
Justice Department, 146
and Arthur administration, 105
and Buchanan administration, 103
and Bush administration, 30, 134, 138, 146
and Carter administration, 85, 91, 99, 111–12, 113, 119–20, 125, 131, 133
and Cleveland administration, 65–66, 121
and Clinton administration, xiii, 131, 133, 134–35, 144, 145, 146, 147–48
and Eisenhower administration, 87
and Hoover administration, 82
and A. Johnson administration, 56–57, 59, 63, 148
and Kennedy administration, 99, 119
and Nixon administration, 90

and Reagan administration, xiii, 30, 132, 134, 136, 138, 147, 148
and F. Roosevelt administration, 89–90, 123
and Truman administration, 67, 68
and Wilson administration, 87–88, 122
See also Office of Legal Counsel; Solicitor general

Kendall v. United States ex rel Stokes (1838), 46, 141
Kennedy, Anthony M., 143
Kennedy, John F., 95, 130
and B-70 bomber, 39–40
and Hill-Burton Act, 119
and RS-70 weapons system, 117–18
signing statements, generally, 175 n.34
Agency for International Development, 99
Kmiec, Douglas W., 30, 132, 136, 138

La Follette Seamen's Act, 108
The Laura (1885), 190 n.4
Lebanon, 124
Lee, Richard Henry, 25
Legislative veto or approval provisions
bypassing, 121
defined, 84
noncompliance with, 123–25
as "report-and-wait" requirement, 84, 87
and signing statements, 76, 78–79, 83–90, 92, 95–96, 99–100, 193 n.60
validity of, 47, 84, 147
and War Powers Resolution, 68
See also names of specific presidents
Lessig, Lawrence, 29
Levinson, Sanford, 152
Libya, 124
Lincoln, Abraham
and Rush-Bagot Agreement, 117
and Secretary of War Stanton, 58–59
signing statements, generally, 73, 175 n.33
Second Confiscation Act, 86
suspending writ of habeas corpus, 16
Line Item Veto Act of 1996, xiv, 30, 45, 71–72, 136–37
"Literary theory" of the Constitution, 45–49
Love, John A., 85

Madison, James, 37, 163 n.124
and Bill of Rights, U.S., 25
constitutionally based vetoes, 40
and Council of Revision, 36
and presidential interpretation of Constitution, 26, 28, 33–34
and Senate resolution re nomination of minister to Sweden, 39
and significance of governmental practices, 48, 130–31
and Take Care Clause, 17
and veto power, 13, 14–15, 38
Magna Charta (1215), 19, 24, 34
Marbury v. Madison (1803), 24, 33, 35, 39
Marshall, John, 16, 24–25, 35, 45
Martin, Luther, 36
Maryland Ratifying Convention, 23
Mason, Col. George, 36
Massachusetts Ratifying Convention, 27
Maysville Road Bill, 84
McCray v. United States (1904), 180 n.97
McDonald, Forrest, 26
McKinley, William, 130
McReynolds, James C., 46, 151
Meese, Edwin, 75
Meigs, Montgomery C., 103–4, 127, 150
Melcher, John, 99
Merchant Marine Act, 107–9
Miller, Arthur S., 51, 147
Mining Enforcement and Safety Administration, 97
Monroe, James, 73, 116
Morgan, Edwin D., 172 n.64
Morrill, Justin S., 171 n.59
Morrill, Lot M., 172 n.64
Morrison v. Olson (1988), 142–43
Morton, Oliver P., 172 n.64
Myers v. United States (1926), 46, 58, 122, 123, 151, 168 n.26, 194 n.3

National Aeronautics and Space Administration (NASA), 109–10
National Labor Relations Act, 83

National Parks and Recreation Act, 99
National Rifle Association, 121
National Science Foundation (NSF), 83, 97
Nebraska
admission to Union, 57
Nelson, Thomas A.R., 59
New York Journal, 28, 29
New York v. United States (1992), 131
Nicholas, George, 24–25
Nixon, Richard M., 86, 124, 130, 153
signing statements, generally, 74, 75, 175 n.34
Cost Accounting Standards Board, 92
HEW regulations, 96
legislative veto or approval provisions, 83, 87, 92
Mining Enforcement and Safety Administration, 97
National Science Foundation, 97
Office of Energy Policy, 85
Senate Select Committee on Presidential Campaign Activities, 82
Voting Rights Act amendments, 41, 90
and War Powers Resolution, 68–69, 124, 151
Non Obstante, Case of (1487), 5–6, 7
Nonoriginalism, 9–10, 141
Norris-LaGuardia Act, 82
North Carolina Ratifying Convention, 23–24

Oath Clause, 17, 33
O'Connor, Sandra D., 143
Office of Energy Policy, 85
Office of Legal Counsel (OLC), 30, 98–99, 131, 134–35, 136, 138, 142, 143, 144, 145, 146, 147–48
Office of Management and Budget, 136, 148
Omnibus bills, 29–33, 136, 148, 152, 193 n.60
Originalism, 9–10, 143
Original understanding
and absolute veto, 11–15, 31
and duty to execute the laws, 16–18, 130
and early governmental practices, 48, 130
and executive review, 35–38, 45
and legislative riders, 31–32, 136
and nature of executive power, 18–21
and Oath Clause, 17, 33
and omnibus bills, 32, 136
and pardon power, 21–23
and presidential suspending power, xiv, 153–54
relevance of, 9–10
and suspension of habeas corpus, 15–16
and veto power, 11–15, 35–36, 38, 71, 143–44
See also Constitutional interpretation

Panama Canal Company, 95
Pardon power, 21–23, 37, 38, 111–12, 190 n.4
Paterson, William, 37–38, 39
Patterson, James W., 171 n.59, 172 n.64
Paulsen, Michael S., 33–35
Pennsylvania Ratifying Convention, 26–27, 35
Persian Gulf, 124
Petition of Right (1628), 19
Pierce, Franklin, 55, 69, 73, 130
Pinkney, Charles, 19
Pocket vetoes, 50, 53
Polk, James K., 73
Pomeroy, John Norton, 60
Powell, Sir John, 7–8
Prerogative powers
See Dispensing power; Pardon power; President; Royal prerogative; Suspending power
Prescriptive process, 48, 130–31, 190 n.4
President
and amendment or repeal of contested legislation, 40–41, 57, 68, 86–87, 91–92, 100, 110, 119, 147–48
appointment and removal powers, 39, 41, 57–59, 85, 88, 97–98, 104–6, 110–11, 115, 121–23, 133, 145, 150, 151

and bypassing contested legislation, 87–89, 100, 121; and Commander in Chief Clause, 40, 91, 94–95, 103, 116, 117, 150
compared to English Crown, 19–22, 28–29, 37
constitutional interpretation by, 33–37, 38–41, 137–38, 146–47, 196 n.41
dispensing power of, 11, 37–38, 141
duty to execute the laws, 16–18, 87–88, 143
and executive agencies, 98–99
executive power of, 18–21
and executive privilege, 39, 86–87, 97
and executive review, 33–37, 142–43
and foreign affairs, 39, 93–94, 107–10, 114–15, 132–33
and item veto, xiii–xiv, 30
and judicial review, 41, 89–91, 100, 123, 144–53
and justifications for noncompliance with laws, xiii, 59–60, 133–36, 144, 145, 146–47, 152–53
and limited right to defy the law, 64, 144–53
and national security, 133
noncompliance with laws, actual cases of, 57–64, 101–18, 121–30, 132–33
apocryphal cases of, 116–18
and Oath Clause, 17, 33
and objections to laws adopted by a prior administration, 50–51, 119–25, 148
pardon power of, 21–23, 38, 111–12, 190 n.4
protective power of, 18–19
recommending measures to Congress, 40, 97, 106–7, 150–51
and refusal to defend laws in court, 41, 89–90, 113, 119–21, 145
rhetoric, use of, xiii, 127–31, 133–36, 153
and shaping legislation, 39–40, 147
and suspending power, 11, 12, 15–16, 21, 34–35, 37–38, 64, 135–39, 142
and Take Care Clause, xiv, 16–18, 33, 38
veto power of, 11–15, 29–33, 35–37, 38, 49–50, 146, 147–48, 150
and war power, 47, 68–69, 114, 151
withholding signature from bills, 40
See also Signing statements; Vetoes; *and names of specific presidents*
Presidential practice
ascertaining, 49–51
and laws adopted by a prior administration, 119–26
significance of, 47–49, 130
and signing statements, 71–118
summarized, 127–39, 153–54
and vetoes, 53–69
Presidential review, 33–37, 142–43
Presumption of constitutionality, 146–47
Prosecutorial discretion, 142
Protective power of the president, 18–19
Public Broadcasting Act (1967), 113, 121
The Public Papers and Addresses of Franklin D. Roosevelt, 50
Public Papers of the Presidents of the United States, 50
Public Telecommunications Act (1978), 113, 121

Randolph, Edmund, 24–26
Read, George, 12, 26
Reagan, Ronald, xiv, 153
and Comprehensive Anti-Apartheid Act, 64, 132
and item veto, 135–36, 137
and justification for noncompliance with laws, xiii, 134, 146, 152
and Public Telecommunications Act, 113
signing statements, generally, xiii, 30, 31, 73, 74, 75, 132, 135, 136, 138
Competition in Contracting Act, xiii, 132, 134, 143, 145–46, 152
federal employee nondisclosure agreements, 133
and War Powers Resolution, 124, 133
Rehnquist, William H., 142
"Report-and-wait" requirements, 84, 87
Republican Party, 135
Residuum theory of executive power, 19–21
"Riders," legislative, 29–33, 136, 148, 152, 193 n.60
Roosevelt, Franklin D.

and dismissal of FTC commissioner, 122–23, 125, 150, 151, 194 n.3
papers of, 50
signing statements, generally, 50, 175 n.33
ban against government's employing certain individuals, 89–90, 142–43, 153
Elk Hills Oil Bill, 85, 96–97
Roosevelt, Theodore, 73, 130
Royal prerogative
and American presidency, 19–21
of lawmaking, 3–4
nature of, 3
and Parliament, 5–8, 31
of revocation, 4
See also Dispensing power; English crown; Pardon power; Suspending power; Veto, royal; Veto power
RS–70 weapons system, 117–18
Ruppert v. Caffey (1920), 174 n.133
Rush-Bagot Agreement (1817), 117

San Antonio Missions National Historical Park, 113–14, 153, 193 nn.60, 65
Scalia, Antonin, 20, 142–43
Schwartz, Bernard, 21
Second Confiscation Act, 86
Separation of Powers, 149–50
as basis for signing statements, 76–79, 83, 92–98, 110, 133
as basis for vetoes, 53, 68
encroachment on executive branch, 152
waiving violations of, 130–31
Seven Bishops, Trial of the (1688), 7–8
Seward, William H., 117
Sherman, John, 62, 171 n.59, 172 n.64
Signing statements
and amendment or repeal of offending law, 86–87, 91–92
and bypassing offending law, 87–89
and compelled acquiescence in offending law, 81–86
and compliance with contested law, 89–100
frequency of, xiii, 40, 73–76, 132, 135
and item veto, 71–72, 135–39
and judicial review, 89–91
locating, 50
nature of objections raised by, 76–80, 152
and noncompliance with contested laws, 101–18, 127–30, 132–33
and Office of Legal Counsel, 98, 136, 138
purposes of, 73–75
as reaction to omnibus bills and riders, 29–33, 136, 152
timing of, 50, 72
See also names of specific presidents
Solicitor general, 41, 147
Souter, David H., 143
South Africa, 64, 132
Spain, 93
Speed, James, 56–57
Sprague, William, 172 n.64
Stanbery, Henry, 56, 59, 63
Standing to sue, 101–2, 149
See also discussion of specific laws to whose validity presidents objected
Stanton, Edwin, 57–60, 62–63, 64, 148
Stimson, Frederic, 11
Stockman, David, 136
Story, Joseph, 16
Subversive Activities Control Act (1950), 67
Sumner, Charles, 62, 171 nn.56, 59, 172 n.64
Supremacy Clause, 17
Supreme Court
and Federal Election Campaign Act, 90
impact of governmental practices on, 48–49
and pardon power, 22
and presidential noncompliance with laws, 46, 141–43, 154
and president's removal power, 122, 123, 151
and Public Telecommunications Act, 113
and "unofficial Constitution," 47
and Voting Rights Act, 41, 90
and war power, 47, 49, 124
and War-Time Prohibition Act, 67
See also Judicial review; *and names of specific cases*
Suspending power
and Bill of Rights (1791), 23–26

and pardon power, 21–23
presidential, 11–13, 16, 21, 34–35, 37–38, 135–39, 142, 153–54
royal, 4–8, 18, 138–39, 142, 144, 153
and writ of habeas corpus, 15–16, 24
Sweden, 39, 114–15
Symmes, William, 27, 28

"Tacking," 29–33, 136, 148
Taft, William Howard, 122, 193 n.60
signing statements, generally, 73, 175 n.33
national budget, 106–7, 115, 150–51, 193 nn.60, 65
and Webb-Kenyon Act, 66
Take Care Clause, 16–18, 28, 37, 38
Taney, Roger B., 16
Telecommunications Act (1996), 133
Tennessee
restoration to Union, 82
Tennessee Valley Authority (TVA), 86
Tenure of Office Act (1867), 41, 53, 57–64, 119, 130, 131, 148, 149, 172 n.69
"Test-case defense," 59–64, 104, 143–49
Textualism, 9–10
Thomas, Lorenzo, 58, 63, 149
Thomas v. Sorrell (1674), 157 n.31
Tipton, Thomas W., 171 n.59
Translationism, 29–33
Truman, Harry S., 119, 130
and amendment of laws, 41
constitutionally based vetoes, 67–68
impoundment of Air Force funds, 117
papers of, 50
signing statements, generally, 73, 175 n.34
Bureau of Reclamation, 91–92
Government Printing Office, 92
loan to Spain, 93
Tucker, Henry St. George, 16
Tyler, John, 73, 82, 130, 175 n.3

United Nations Law of the Sea Conference, 94
U.S. Agency for International Development, 99
U.S. Air Force, 117
U.S. Air Force Reserve, 94
U.S. Air National Guard, 94
U.S. Consulates. *See* Consulates, U.S.
U.S. Department of Agriculture, 99–100, 123–24
U.S. Department of the Army, 88–89, 91, 96, 116, 121
U.S. Department of Commerce, 133
U.S. Department of Defense, 69, 94–95, 117, 137
U.S. Department of Education, 98, 124–25, 131, 133, 145, 193 n.60
U.S. Department of Health, Education and Welfare (HEW), 91, 96, 124–25, 142
U.S. Department of the Interior, 88, 94, 113–14
U.S. Department of the Navy, 97
U.S. Department of State, 86–87, 107–8, 110
U.S. Naval Academy (Annapolis), 95, 137–38, 147
U.S. Shipping Board, 108
United States Code Congressional and Administrative News, 50, 75
United States v. Lovett (1946), 142–43
United States v. Smith (1806), 37–38, 141
"Unofficial Constitution," 46–49

Vesting Clause of Article II, 18–19
Veterans Administration, 98
Veto, royal, 4, 161 n.77
Vetoes, constitutionally based, 40, 49–50, 53–69, 72, 127–30, 132
Veto power
alternatives to, 71–72
and Constitutional Convention, 11–15, 35–37, 38
and omnibus bills and riders, 29–33
and unconstitutional laws, 40, 49–50, 144, 146–50, 152, 197 n.56
See also Item veto; Pocket vetoes; Vetoes; *names of specific Presidents*
Vickers, George, 171 n.59
Vietnam War, 47, 68–69, 94, 98, 111–12, 153
Virginia Declaration of Rights (1776), 23, 25
Virginia Independent Chronicle, 29
Virginia Ratifying Convention, 23–25, 35
Voting Rights Act, 41, 90

Wade, Benjamin F., 62
War Department, 32, 58–59, 65–66, 116
War power, 47, 49, 68–69, 124, 151
War Powers Resolution (1973), 68–69, 124, 131, 150, 151
War-Time Prohibition Act, 66–67, 174 n.133
Washington, George, xiv, 37, 51, 75, 153
  and appointment power, 39
  constitutionally based vetoes, 40
  and House resolution re Jay's Treaty, 39
  and omnibus bills, 32
  and pardon power, 21
Washington Aqueduct, 103–4, 127, 150, 193 n.65
Water Resources Research Act (1964), 88, 175 n.32
Watershed Protection and Flood Prevention Act (1954), 123–24, 179 n.65
Webb-Kenyon Act (1913), 66, 174 n.133
Weekly Compilation of Presidential Documents, 50
Weinberger v. Salfi (1975), 142
Wiley, Waitman T., 172 n.64
Williams, George H., 171 n.59
Williams, Thomas, 171 n.47, 172 n.76
Willoughby, Westel W., 15
Wilson, Henry, 171 n.59
Wilson, James
  and English crown, 19–20
  and noncompliance with unconstitutional laws, 26–27, 28, 33–34, 35
  and veto power, 12, 13, 26
Wilson, Woodrow, 66, 116, 131, 146, 193 n.60
  and constitutionally-based vetoes, 40, 125
  and justification for noncompliance with laws, 146
  and "literary theory" of Constitution, 46–47
  and removal of postmaster, 122, 125, 150, 151, 194 n.3
  signing statements, generally, 175 n.33
    enforcement of antitrust laws, 87–88
    termination of treaties, 107–9, 131, 149–50
  and War-Time Prohibition Act, 66–67

Yates, Richard, 171 n.59

About the Author

CHRISTOPHER N. MAY is the James P. Bradley Professor of Constitutional Law at Loyola Law School, Los Angeles. Before entering law teaching he was a Legal Services attorney in San Francisco. He is the author of several books, including *In the Name of War: Judicial Review and the War Powers since 1918* (1989), which won the Alpha Sigma Nu National Jesuit Book Award.